AMERICAN HANNIBAL

The Extraordinary Account of Revolutionary Hero Daniel Morgan at the Battle of Cowpens

AMERICAN HANNIBAL

The Extraordinary Account of Revolutionary Hero
Daniel Morgan at the Battle of Cowpens

BY

JIM STEMPEL

ISBN-13: 978-1-946409-26-3(Paperback)
ISBN :-978-1-946409-27-0(e-book)

BISAC Subject Headings:
BIO008000 BIOGRAPHY / MILITARY
HIS031000 HISTORY / Revolutionary

Cover Illustration by Christine Horner

Address all correspondence to:

Penmore Press LLC
920 N Javelina Pl
Tucson AZ 85748

MAPS

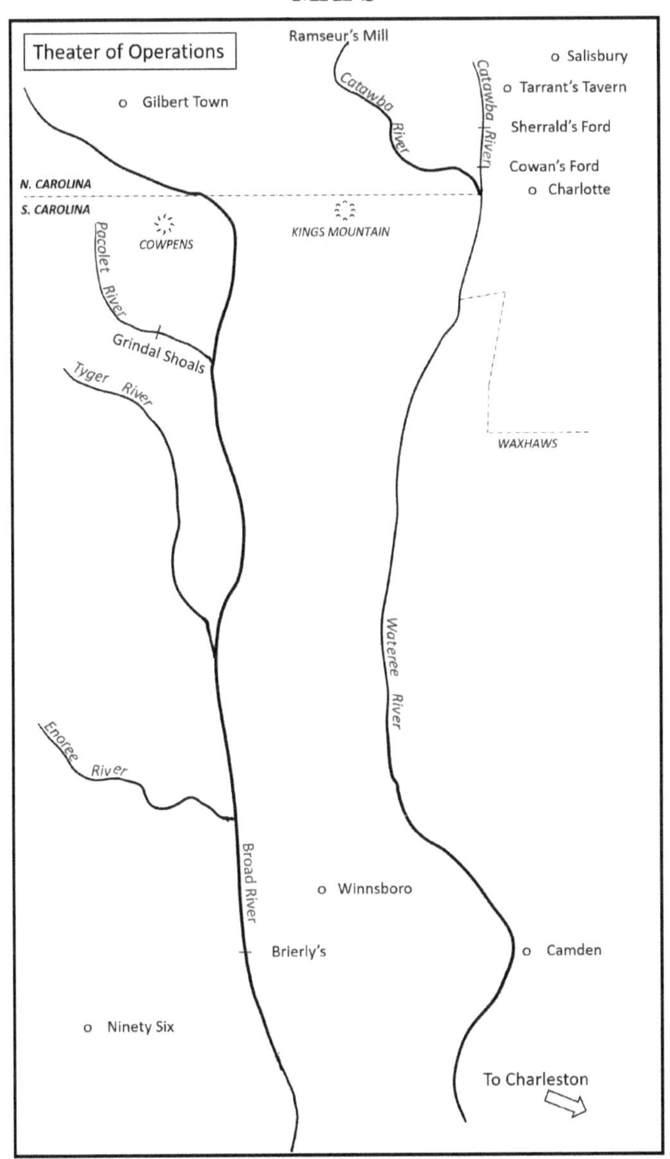

THEATER OF OPERATIONS

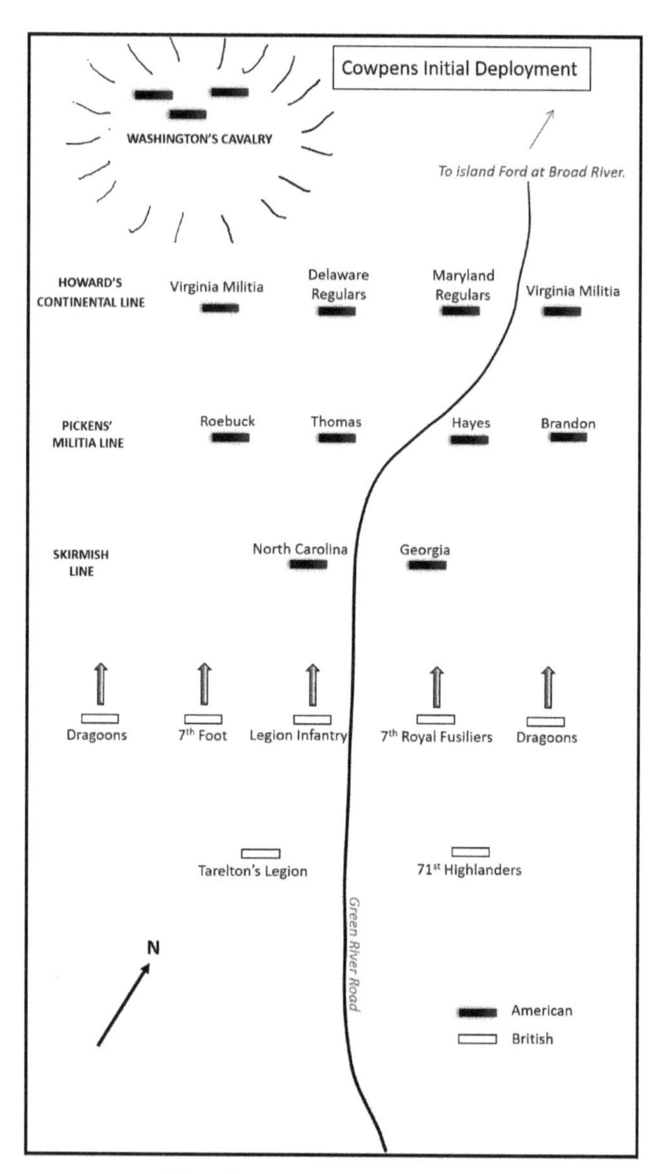

INITIAL DEPLOYMENT

PREFACE

The American Revolution was without question the seminal event in terms of the founding of the United States, but it also initiated the spread and acceptance of both democratic principles and civil liberties across the globe; a process that in many ways and in many places is still ongoing. Thus any grasp of the American nation, or of the world as it exists today, without a reasonable grasp of the Revolution remains fundamentally uninformed by definition and therefore flawed at best. For generations the American people took great pride in this heritage, worked to grasp and understand, if not all the details, at least the general flow of events and the personalities that comprised the revolutionary tale, but sadly today that dedication seems all but lost.

Indeed, the leaders, events, even the *reasons* the American Revolution was fought seem to be rapidly disappearing from the collective knowledge of the American public. In a recent survey conducted by the American Revolution Center of Philadelphia, Pennsylvania, for instance, a shocking 83% of American adults were found to be lacking even a basic understanding of the Revolution. How bad was it? Half of the respondents actually believed that the Civil War was fought *before* the Revolution; that is, the country was almost torn in half *before* it had even come into existence, and over 33% had no idea in which century the War for Independence even took place. The average score on the survey was a 44% and many taking the quiz could not answer more than four of the twenty-seven questions listed in the questionnaire. Knowledge of the Constitution, the Bill of Rights, and the Declaration of Independence were determined to be equally as dismal.

These are shocking facts, and facts that may well have far reaching consequences. As the English author George Orwell once pointed out, “The most effective way to destroy people is to deny and obliterate their own understanding of their history.” Is it reasonable to assume that citizens will handle their civic responsibilities sensibly (no matter what their political philosophy or orientation) when they have no grasp whatsoever of the history of their own nation, the structure of their government, and the laws by which they are called to govern themselves? I think not. “A country without a memory is a country of madmen,” wrote George Santayana. In this case our educational system (from elementary school through graduate school) has clearly failed the fundamental needs of our society, and it has much to answer for in that regard, but that failure remains an issue for another forum.

Importantly, while many respondents to the Revolutionary survey faired poorly, over ninety percent still firmly believed that a grasp of their American origins was vitally important for the health of the nation, and it was that remarkable sense of historical appreciation that inspired this book. To best accomplish this, I have chosen a presentation in narrative nonfiction, the nonfiction aspect providing the reader with an accurate and well documented look at history (often in the words of those who lived it), while the narrative formula embeds that history in a storyline that is at once strong and compelling.

The American Revolution was fought over a six year period (1775 – 1781), while the Treaty of Paris that officially ended the war and recognized the infant United States as a sovereign nation was not signed until 1783. During that six year period many men and women served the American cause, yet their names – beyond, perhaps, George Washington, the Marquis de Lafayette, or possibly a few members of congress like Benjamin Franklin or Thomas Jefferson – are today virtually lost and forgotten.

This book is about one of the more important and exciting engagements that took place during the course of the American Revolution, and it is populated by many of those same unknown characters who gave years of their lives over to hardship, danger, and constant toil to see the issue through to its final conclusion. The story is most principally about Daniel Morgan, a rough and tumble son of the American frontier who through hard work, intelligence, and strength of character rose through life to become a brigadier general, a man of wealth, and a United States Congressman, but many more lives than Daniel Morgan's shine through its pages.

By and large these were unremarkable people who did remarkable things simply because they were placed in situations where they were forced to rise to the occasion. They were far from perfect – some were coarse, many uneducated, others unfair, biased, or self-serving – but that tarnished humanity, I think, only serves to underscore what they accomplished all the more. Against almost incalculable odds they achieved something the world had never before witnessed – the founding of a new, democratic republic predicated upon the rule of law and civil rights of its citizenry.

In that sense, then, this is a book, not just about war or revolution, but rather about the emergence of a new way of life and a new way of conceiving ourselves as human beings. The American Revolution freed the human spirit in a way it had never before been freed, and while that accomplishment was at its inception surely limited by our standards of morality and inclusion today, from tiny acorns mighty oaks do grow. Ultimately that *freedom,* the capacity, not just to dream, but to *aspire* to be something far more than what we once were, was what the American Revolution was really about, and that sense of *aspiration* is hardly a uniquely American phenomena.

Thus the initial formation of the United States might best be viewed as an imperfect gift, secured through enormous blood and sacrifice, and bequeathed from one generation to all those that followed, yet a gift every citizen today enjoys, whether aware of it or not. But just as a flame slowly dies if unattended, that remarkable gift will surely wither and burn out in the hands of those who neither understand nor value what they have been gifted. The great Indian activist Jawaharlal Nehru once observed that "History is a record of human progress, a record of the struggle of the advancement of the human mind, of the human spirit, towards some known or unknown objective," and the Revolution was, I believe, a giant leap forward in the advancement of that human condition, repercussions of which still reverberate throughout our world to this day. In other words, the democratic revolution that began in the thirteen colonies is today far from over, its ultimate outcome still very much in question. As the young Frenchman Alexis De Tocqueville observed at the dawn of the 19th Century after visiting the infant United States, “The nations of our time cannot prevent the conditions of men from becoming equal; but it depends upon themselves whether the principle of equality is to lead them to servitude or freedom, to knowledge or barbarism, to prosperity or wretchedness.” On those important issues the jury remains out, and that is why a basic understanding of the American Revolution matters a great deal, indeed perhaps today more than ever.

J. S.

CONTENTS

A COMMENTARY

Almost everyone has heard of the soldiers of the Revolution being tracked by the blood of their feet on the frozen ground. This is literally true, and the thousandth part of their sufferings has not been told, nor ever will be told.

– Private Joseph Plumb Martin, *A Narrative of a Revolutionary Soldier: Some of the Adventures Dangers, and Sufferings of Joseph Plumb Martin*

America, then, exhibits in her social state an extraordinary phenomenon. Men are there seen on a greater equality in point of fortune and intellect, or, in other words, more equal in their strength, than in any other country of the world or in any age of which history has preserved the remembrance.

– Alexis De Tocqueville, *Democracy In America*

Daniel Morgan was the quintessential American, precisely the type Crévecoeur had in mind in "Letters from an American Farmer," a "new man" who had left behind in the Old World the designation and status of peasant... A commanding presence combined with valor, a high natural intelligence, and a stirring capacity to lead men would take him from the bottom of the heap to the very uppermost rank in the pantheon of heroes of the Revolution.

– John Buchanan, *The Road To Guilford Court House*

PROLOGUE

A summer dawn was rising along the mountain's slope as the lone rider picked his way across Virginia's sparkling Shenandoah River in the early morning hours of the 28th day of June, 1780.[1] The horse carried him easily, as if it recognized the route, and perhaps it did, for the rider had traveled the road from Winchester to Fredericksburg many times before. He was a big man, almost a giant by the measure of his day, over six-foot two inches in height and carrying over two hundred pounds of hard earned muscle. For most of his life he had been fast and fierce and tough as nails, but now it was June, 1780 and his body had begun to betray him. So today he rode gingerly in the saddle and nudged his horse around a few scattered rocks in the road, slowly making his way up the lower rise of the Blue Ridge toward the tavern that was his objective, now not so terribly far distant. Behind him the Shenandoah Valley stretched out in all its scenic splendor; towering mountains and undulating hills of green and stone, some of the most beautiful vistas in North America. Legend had it the Valley's name meant beautiful daughter of the stars, christened, many said, by the Native Americans who lived and hunted and fought there even hundreds of years before, but no one could say for sure.

Surrounding him as he rode, the rising hills were green with fresh growth, for the long, brutal winter – one of the coldest ever – had finally given way to a gentle spring which in turn had given birth to summer. He'd mounted early that morning for the ride up the Blue Ridge to Ashby's Gap, and as he neared Berry's Tavern it is hard to imagine that he was not feeling a great sense of joy, for this was a day of particular importance. Indeed, throughout a life of violence and tumult the rider had experienced many decisive and consequential days, but few if any held more importance or meaning than the one he now faced. It was as if he had been given a new lease on life and, despite weeks of illness, pain, and fatigue, on that June morning, he rode with newfound confidence and hope.

The horse ambled up to the tavern on the Ridge's western slope where he dismounted, perhaps handing the reins over to an eager youngster, for everyone there knew he was coming, and that soon he was expected inside. It is easy to imagine a crowd of respectful onlookers gathering to gawk as the rider dismounted, smiling and pointing, for in Virginia's Shenandoah Valley he was by 1780 a legend of some significance. Now forty-five years old – give or take a year or two – he was still tough and hard as granite, yet the truth of the matter was the war for American independence had taken its toll on his health which now seemed to rise and fall sporadically like waves on a fickle ocean. Today he felt strong enough to ride, but tomorrow he could easily be back suffering in his bed. The rider's name was Daniel Morgan.

In the fall of 1775 Morgan's regiment had spearheaded an expedition through Maine, the objective Quebec, Canada. It was hoped by the Continental Congress at the time that victories in that territory would reduce the British threat from the north, and hopefully even bring Canada into the war on the side of the Americans. Poorly provisioned and poorly planned, the expedition had struggled its way through hundreds of miles of frozen wilderness; across creeks, mountains, and rivers. Often in cold or even freezing water up to his neck, with little or nothing in the way of food or warmth or support, through the sheer force of his physical strength and uncompromising willpower, Daniel Morgan had driven the lead element forward until finally reaching Quebec in December of that year.

On December 31 an assault on the city was launched which soon, due to confusion, bad weather, and overconfidence, disintegrated. Leading one of the attacking columns directly into Quebec, Morgan was eventually trapped in a cross-fire on the city's streets and ultimately forced to surrender. Still in a fighting rage, he'd been surrounded by British soldiers, but he hated the British for the 500 lashes they had given him years before during the French and Indian War, and he refused to give up. Furious and stubborn and incapable of backing down, he probably would have been shot to pieces in a hail of bullets had not a local priest wandered by to whom he finally relinquished his sword.[2] Taken prisoner, Morgan spent months in confinement before finally being exchanged. While still strong and determined, the frigid expedition north had taken a severe toll on his health, leaving him often in distress with fevers, body aches, and weakness, all of which seemed to come and go with no more warning than the bad weather that tumbled over Massanutten Mountain from time-to-time near his valley home.

No, Daniel Moran was no longer the powerful presence who had marched a band of Virginia frontiersmen all the way to Boston five years earlier – every last one of them a crack shot with the long rifle, and an expert with the tomahawk – to the amazement of the locals en route. Morgan's Riflemen they were called back then and their mere presence in Upstate New York in 1777 had caused the Redcoats to hesitate, and their Iroquois allies – known as terrifying and fearless fighters themselves – to simply flee the field. Now a colonel in the Continental Line, perhaps its finest field officer, Daniel Morgan had ridden that morning up to Berry's Tavern hoping for a new opportunity to serve the cause of independence. Good with men and serene in combat, Morgan was by 1780 known on both sides of the Atlantic as a crafty tactician and fearless fighter. For weeks he had been down again with the condition he called sciatica – fevers, weakness, and extreme muscle aches – while ruminating unfavorably as to his future role in the revolution. Things had not been looking terribly good for him. Then the letter arrived.

That letter seemed to change everything in a single stroke. Penned by his old friend and military commander, General Horatio Gates, who was then at his country residence named Traveler's Rest on the Potomac River near Shepherdstown, Virginia (present day West Virginia), the letter could not have done more for Morgan had it been a magic potion. Once forlorn and out of the war, it seemed now that he would not only return to duty, but return in the manner he felt he deserved.

For on May 12 of that year, Charleston, South Carolina had fallen to the British, General Benjamin Lincoln surrendering some 5,500 men and mountains of ordnance and supplies to the Redcoats under the command of generals Sir Henry Clinton and Lord Charles Cornwallis.[3] That defeat proved a devastating blow to the cause of American Independence, indeed the most significant defeat of the entire war. Worse still, it left the entire South open to the potential of British control, as there was now no organized resistance of substance to oppose them. The British had simply to march north through the Carolinas clear to Virginia in order to subdue half of the United States and perhaps destroy the rebellion as a consequence. That could not happen if the infant nation was to survive. Something had to be done.

That something was contained in the letter Morgan received from Horatio Gates. Congress, frantic to respond to the situation at Charleston, had appointed Gates – the hero of the Battle of Saratoga, and one of the American luminaries of the war as a result – as new head of the Southern Army, and Gates wanted Morgan to handle a full corps of light infantry under this new command. It was precisely what Morgan excelled at, and the thought of returning to the war at the head of his own corps brought Morgan's blood to an immediate boil. "Would to god you'd a had it six months ago," Morgan wrote back immediately, referring to the debacle at Charleston, "our affairs would have wore a more pleasing aspect at this day than they do."[4] Morgan was convinced Gates was the right man for the job, and that he would breathe life back into the American war effort in the South. Gates wanted Morgan to come to Traveler's Rest in order to work out all of the details of the new command, but Morgan was still feeling far too feeble to make a trip of that distance. So they agreed to meet roughly halfway, at Berry's Tavern in Ashby's gap on the morning of June 28 as Gates began his trip south.

Flushed with fresh hope, Daniel Morgan made his way through the front door of Berry's Tavern. It was an establishment with which he was entirely familiar. For Morgan, unlike Gates – who was English born and had risen as an officer in the British Army, serving on the expedition to Halifax in 1749 and later in the French and Indian War prior to settling down at Traveler's Rest – had wandered into Virginia's Shenandoah Valley at the tender age of only eighteen, raw, uneducated, and virtually penniless. His place of birth was said to have been New Jersey or Eastern Pennsylvania, but of his past and origins Morgan rarely spoke. What he had done was *work*. Big, strong, and athletic, the Shenandoah was then the American frontier, and there was no shortage of good work for a youngster willing to toil. First taking a position as laborer, then as a wagon driver for a local farmer, he quickly saved enough to buy his own wagon, and before long had his own thriving business hauling goods over the Blue Ridge between Fredericksburg and Winchester. "The Old Wagoner" he still loved to call himself, as much a tribute to all he had overcome as it was a badge of genuine modesty. As well it made the troops under him aware of the fact that their leader was no different than them, a man who had worked and struggled his way to the top, no aristocrat's son, born to wealth and a life of ease. The two men – Gates and Morgan – were very different, but this was not Europe where one's station in life was virtually fixed at birth, but the newly minted United States of America where excellence and effort could set a man off on a course of his own creation.

Morgan instantly recognized his old friend, and Gates rose to greet him warmly. The two were about as physically different from one another as could be imagined. Horatio Gates was then fifty-four years of age, short in stature, "ruddy-faced, and bespectacled, with thin graying hair,"[5] while Morgan stood over six feet two, was broad at the shoulders, thickly muscled, with a jaw like an anvil. Morgan looked every bit the soldier he was, while Gates could easily have been mistaken for Morgan's tailor, but the two men liked and respected one another and had been friends in the Valley of Virginia for years. At Saratoga they had stopped the British Army dead in its tracks.

The credit for the victory at Saratoga – surely the most important American victory of the war thus far – had gone to Gates, but in the field it had been Morgan and Benedict Arnold who had fought the British to a standstill. In 1777 the British had initiated a plan to sever New England from the rest of the United States, and hopefully strangle the young rebellion as a result. In June of that year General John Burgoyne (Gentleman Johnny, as he was called) began the trek south from Montreal, Canada with some 9,500 British regulars, Hessians, and Indian allies. The goal was to march south along Lake Champlain, take Fort Ticonderoga at its southern end near Lake George, then continue down the Hudson and force the capitulation of Albany, New York, by siege if necessary. The plan was for General Howe to march north from New York City with his own British army and rendezvous with Burgoyne, the two armies meeting somewhere near Albany on the Hudson. With the Hudson River then under full British control, New England would be cut off from the rest of the colonies, the head of the rebellion, so to speak, severed from the body. Initially Burgoyne's march proved successful, but in early September, as he slowly made his way south along the river north of Albany, he ran headfirst into Gates, Morgan, and Arnold deployed and waiting for him at a place called Bemis Heights, New York.

Gates had been sent north by Congress specifically to confront Burgoyne, and he had selected his position with care. "It [Bemis Heights] was a high plateau, covered with broken elevations separated by deep ravines through which creeks turned and twisted. The region was densely wooded except for occasional farms and wagon trails stretching down to the Hudson."[6] While the position was highly defensible even against the formidable British Army, it would still be a difficult test for the waiting Continentals. "Marching directly into battle and fighting in tight linear formations required tremendous discipline and confidence in one's officers and comrades. England's army excelled in all these categories and was (and still is) universally recognized as the finest military machine of its age."[7] Yet Bemis Heights was the worst sort of terrain for the highly coordinated and disciplined British units to fight upon, while simultaneously a home away from home for Morgan's frontiersman.

By early September Gates had been able to cobble together an army of over 7,000 militia and Continentals to oppose Burgoyne, Morgan and his famed unit of riflemen having been transferred north reluctantly by General Washington from his army near New York City in late August. "Oh, for some Virginia riflemen,"[9] one New York resident had bemoaned, and once Morgan's unit arrived they were considered the very cream of Gate's entire army.

On September 19 Burgoyne advanced in three columns against the American position. The column on the far right headed for the highest and most critical position on the American line held, of course, by Morgan, who had wisely deployed his men behind trees, rocks, etc. to take advantage of the natural cover the Heights provided. Now heavily reinforced, it was Morgan's plan to fight from cover and let the British sacrifice themselves against his crack riflemen, who could kill a squirrel at two hundred yards. Indeed, one British officer later noted that he "never in my life saw better rifles (or men who shot better) than those made in America."[10] Known generally as the Kentucky long rifle, the weapon had been developed on the American frontier, where a lighter, more accurate piece with greater range was required for hunting. Spiraled grooves in an elongated barrel gave the weapon both its unparalleled accuracy and range, and in the hands of a skilled marksman it could be lethal at ranges unheard of by the musket carrying British, who often fought at distances inside of fifty yards. American riflemen could not stand up to a furious bayonet charge (the long rifle had a slow rate of fire and, individually crafted, could not be fitted with a bayonet), but used properly, skilled riflemen could make an enormous impression on any field of battle, and Daniel Morgan knew how to use them wisely. Morgan deployed in the woods overlooking the open fields of a farm owned by a man named Freeman and opened a severe fire on the British as they advanced, bringing the Redcoats to a sudden halt.

Again and again the British tried to advance into the fury of Morgan's rifles, only to be shot to pieces in the process. Meanwhile Benedict Arnold led his Continentals on counter thrusts across the open farm fields, only to be driven back time and again. Burgoyne then tried to force Morgan's withdrawal by having his artillery blast away at the woods where the riflemen were hidden, but Morgan responded by having his crack shots focus on the crews manning the guns, and by late afternoon Burgoyne's artillery had been silenced. Facing disaster, the British general was forced to withdraw.

Unable to move forward yet unwilling to retreat, Burgoyne had little choice but to dig-in and await Howe's arrival. Unfortunately, Burgoyne's supplies began to dwindle as the days wore on, and Morgan's men made life miserable for the British, peppering the Redcoats from a distance and constantly bushwhacking their patrols and foraging parties. Moreover, unknown to Burgoyne, Howe had unilaterally abandoned the Hudson plan, and had moved his command south instead toward Philadelphia without notifying Burgoyne of his change of plans. Burgoyne, watching his manpower wither away daily, finally made the fateful decision to try and force his way past the American position, again in the hopes of reaching Howe's phantom army that he still believed was marching to his relief. On October 7 he shifted his remaining force south of Freeman's Farm and took up a defensive line. Morgan immediately reconnoitered the new British position and suggested two flanking assaults to Gates, one led by his own corps which would pass quietly through the woods and take the British right by surprise, while another column simultaneously struck the British left. Gates immediately agreed.

The twin assaults were launched, and in only fifty minutes Morgan – assisted once again by Arnold – drove the British from their forward positions to a secondary line of redoubts back at Freeman's Farm. Morgan, sensing victory, attacked again and again, his men finally overrunning the key redoubt that exposed the British flank and rear to the surging Americans.

Burgoyne, his army now in tatters and in danger of being cut-off and destroyed by Morgan's efforts, pulled his battered force back from Freeman's Farm. Gates, at Morgan's urging, followed promptly and surrounded the beleaguered British. There was now no place for Burgoyne to go, north or south, and on October 17 he formally surrendered his entire command to Gates at the small country village of Saratoga, New York.

The victory at Saratoga proved monumental for the cause of independence. Not only had the British been thwarted in their plans to split the colonies in two, but they had lost a major army in the process, a debacle that provided profound and prophetic evidence that British arms were not invincible. Even more importantly, the victory at Saratoga convinced the skeptical French that the American cause now appeared viable, and brought that nation into the war on the side of the Americans – an enormous boost for morale, finance, and material for the fledgling Continentals. Horatio Gates received the glory for the victory at Saratoga, but it had been Morgan and Arnold who had conceived the strategy and executed the attacks that had brought the British to defeat.

But that had been 1777. It was now 1780, and since the impressive victory at Saratoga the cause of independence had vacillated between the opposite poles of hope and doom. The British had finally shifted their attention away from New York and New England toward the Southern colonies, and in May they had successfully taken Charleston. It was a stunning victory for the Redcoats that marked the beginning of a campaign also aimed at splitting the colonies asunder – but this time from the other end. After Charleston's fall Clinton departed again for New York, leaving General

Charles Cornwallis behind with a substantial force to lead the charge through the Carolinas. Cornwallis was a tough and able general. Who would stop him?

After Saratoga, Morgan and his riflemen returned to Washington's army about New York City where he handled the light infantry (Washington's rangers) with panache. But the rewards and promotion he thought due him had not been forthcoming, and in the spring of 1779 Morgan – suffering physically – quietly resigned his commission and returned to his home near Battletown (present day Berryville, Virginia). No man thought more of George Washington or cherished the cause of independence more than Daniel Morgan, and while he was a man of enormous spirit and talent, Morgan was also a man of pride, and that pride had been pricked one too many times.

But now things had changed. The British were once again on the march. Horatio Gates – the hero of Saratoga – had been summoned by Congress to confront them, and Gates, as before, desperately wanted Dan Morgan to handle a full light corps under his command. Though still ill and weary, Morgan could hardly resist such an offer.

So here now were the two old friends and compatriots meeting again at Berry's Tavern on the morning of June 28, the diminutive Gates and the imposing Morgan greeting one another warmly. Pleasantries aside, Gates quickly got down to business. Horatio Gates realized, of course, just how central Morgan's role had been to the American success at Saratoga. Not only did Morgan excel with light troops – in particular with backcountry riflemen – but he was also an instinctive warrior, quickly discerning the enemy's strength and intentions, always moving rapidly to employ counter measures. Moreover, unlike the fiery Arnold, who Gates had to order off the field at Bemis Heights for insubordination, Morgan took and received orders with professional calm. Although known to have a temper – Morgan had once cuffed a Congressional representative whom he considered disrespectful of Washington – Gates was confident he and Morgan could work together successfully due to their past relationship and mutual respect. "Whereas the previous year Morgan had felt neglected as a regimental commander with Washington's army, Gates was prepared to recognize Morgan's particular ability with light troops. He asked his former subordinate to head a special light unit similar to Morgan's old rifle corps."[11]

Morgan was elated by the proposal, but still had one serious concern. If he were to accept Gate's offer with his rank of colonel in the Continental Line, he might have to take orders from inferior militia officers who lacked his own training, experience, and skill, but still outranked him. That, Morgan knew, would eventually lead to fireworks. So he asked that Gates try and persuade Congress to promote him to the rank of brigadier general so that he would have the authority necessary to handle the job Gates wanted him to perform, and to this Gates readily agreed.

The meeting ended as cordially as it had begun. Morgan saw Gates and his party off as they headed east over the Blue Ridge, in all likelihood feeling more buoyant than he had in years. After all, he loved and respected George Washington, but it was Horatio Gates who seemed to best appreciate his talents, so it was Horatio Gates with whom he would now fight. If Congress would comply with his wishes, Dan Morgan was confident that he and Gates could stop

Cornwallis in his tracks, just as they had Burgoyne three years before.

Daniel Morgan remounted and began the slow ride back down the ridge toward his farm near Battletown, as sure of his decision as he was of his abilities. Morgan respected the British, but he did not fear them, and he was confident he knew how to fight them. Little did he know at the time, of course, that his decision to accept Gate's offer would have a dramatic effect on the course of American history. Indeed, the British would be checked in the South, but it would be Morgan, not Gates, who would devise and administer one of the most lopsided military victories in American history. In that contest Daniel Morgan, the uneducated backwoodsman, would meet and defeat the notorious Banastre Tarleton, the pride of Cornwallis' officer corps, by means of a psychological ploy and tactical scheme so masterfully conceived and executed that it is studied by military practitioners to this day. As historian John Buchanan observes: "The proper use of militia in formal battle awaited one of the rare generals of the war who can truly be called brilliant... This untutored son of the frontier was the only general in the American Revolution, on either side, to produce a significant original tactical thought."[12] That general was Daniel Morgan, and Morgan's victory would rekindle hope throughout the colonies, enrage General Charles Cornwallis, and initiate a chain of events that would eventually lead the British to defeat at Yorktown, thus catapulting the infant United States of America to its ultimate independence. It was a record of achievement that, by war's end, very few could match.

CHAPTER ONE

HOWARD

The hot, oppressive night was suddenly alive with gunfire and shouts, curses and confusion. On both the right and left the flash of nervous musketry could be seen just ahead in the thick pine forest that bordered the road; an impenetrable labyrinth of timber that seemed to stretch out infinitely into the darkness that surrounded the long marching column of American troops. Every head turned. From the sounds alone, the firing seemed to have erupted straight ahead on the roadway, a sudden, frightening explosion of small arms which then spread like a string of fireworks into the trees on both sides of the confused column of marching troops. It was obvious at once that the army had become engaged, but the enemy was not supposed to be ahead. Yet suddenly shots were crackling all across the front, and it was clear to even the dullest private that something had gone terribly wrong.

Then came the ominous pounding of hooves off in the distance, a thunder growing ever nearer, and then, as if from a nightmare, the dark, apparitional shapes of fleeing horsemen filled the road ahead, cursing, straining amongst the marching troops, knocking men to the ground as the riders, in apparent panic, attempted to escape the unseen foe ahead. It was the vanguard cavalry now in obvious flight, the sixty some odd troopers of what comprised Colonel Charles Armand's Legion, racing to the rear. But why? They were supposed to be screening the army's advance, not disrupting the entire column. What had they run into? Directly ahead the First Maryland infantry, leading the long, marching column through the dark night, had been hurled into utter confusion by the retreating horsemen. It was 2:00 AM, August 16, 1780. Fear, sharp, almost palpable, suddenly filled the air.

What is this? What's going on?

Lt. Colonel John Eager Howard, riding alongside his Second Maryland infantry, tried desperately to calm his men, knowing that confusion could quickly lead to panic in the maddening darkness, and that panic, unchecked, might soon sweep through the entire army. Armand's horsemen, having lost all sense of discipline, continued to stampede through the infantry, momentarily scattering the First Maryland that was marching just ahead.

Steady. Steady! Howard, turning on his horse to survey the column, tried to see what was happening, but in the darkness and swirling dust he could make sense of almost nothing.

The American Southern Army had been marching since ten o'clock that night on the Great Wagon Road, the colonial turnpike that ran from Philadelphia west to Lancaster, Pennsylvania, then turned south, passing through Frederick, Maryland and Virginia's Shenandoah Valley before finally grinding to a dusty halt at Camden, South Carolina. The army had departed Rugeley's Mill, just north of the South Carolina state line earlier that evening, marching straight toward Camden. They had been put in motion by the newly arrived commander of the Southern Department, General Horatio Gates.

Gates had arrived on July 25 and joined the army at Wilcox's Iron Works on the Deep River in North Carolina.[1] His intention from the moment of his arrival had been to march on Camden as soon as possible, and force the withdrawal of the British garrison that was stationed there. Gates considered the British force so inferior to his own that he was confident it would flee upon little more than word of his approach. The suggestion had been made by senior American officers that the army might take a different path, marching on a circuitous route through more friendly terrain where food and succor would be abundant, but Gates had ignored the suggestion, deciding instead to take the direct route across hostile, foraged-out land.

Thus the American Army, exhausted, half-starved, and very much undermanned, was expecting little more than a tiring night march in the hot, suffocating Carolina heat as it closed on Camden that night. Then suddenly shots rang out, the cavalry screen bolted, and who now could say what misfortune might lie ahead?

Howard watched as several men from the First Maryland tumbled backward into his own command then turned his horse gently to gather them up. These men were not cowards. Indeed, they were the finest Continental soldiers the army had, true veterans that could stand up to anything the British Army could throw at them. In fact, troops of the Maryland and Delaware Lines were considered the crack troops of the Continental Army. At Long Island in 1776 the Maryland Line had won fame immortal when they held the old defensive line along Gowanus Creek against overwhelming odds as the rest of the Continental army fled in rout and General Washington desperately tried to patch together a new defensive position behind them.[2] That stand helped save the revolution – at least for a day. But even these veterans could be spooked by a panic in front, so Howard did his best to simply corral them now, knowing their discipline would return once slowed. Then as Armand's dragoons continued their flight passed him Howard heard one, then another shout the infamous name that made the anger rise in his chest: "Tarleton!"

These breathless references were to Lt. Colonel Banastre Tarleton, "Bloody Ban" as he was known in the American South. Tarleton was the commander of Cornwallis' light division, and he was a hard, ruthless, and unforgiving adversary. At Waxhaws in May of that year it was said his division slaughtered defenseless Continentals under Colonel Abraham Buford as they tried to surrender, and ever since that engagement the term "Tarleton's Quarter" had been on the lips of the Southern Army, meaning that in revenge for Waxhaws no quarter was to be given to Tarleton's troops, no mercy shown at all. But Howard also realized that if the shouts were true, if Armand had in fact run headfirst into Tarleton, then there was a very good chance that the Southern Army had stumbled headfirst into the main body of Cornwallis' force there in the darkness of the Great Wagon Road, and that was a frightening thought. The army was not prepared for that!

Again, then again, Howard heard the guns crack, the flash of musketry sparkle in the trees ahead, then just as quickly the shots died away. Steady! Steady lads!

It appeared at that moment that the light infantry under Porterfield on the American right and Armstrong on the left, working out in the woods as flankers, had met and repulsed whatever force Armand's dragoons might have encountered, which then subsequently fled. But the damage to the marching column had already been done. As Colonel Otho Williams would later report: "Some of the cavalry of Armand's legion were wounded, retreated and threw the whole corps into disorder, which, recoiling suddenly on the front of the column of infantry, disordered the First Maryland Brigade and occasioned a general consternation through the whole line of the army."[3]

Otho Williams, then serving as Deputy Adjutant General to General Gates, as a general precaution ordered the marching troops to move from column into line of battle. Then he immediately made his way forward to Porterfield's command on the right to try and discern just what had taken place. Had the army stumbled upon a serious threat, an insignificant group of skirmishers or – no doubt he hoped – only a phantom enemy? Before the army could be started forward again, the facts had to be properly discerned. In warfare, Williams knew, disaster and ignorance often went hand-in-hand.

Quickly Williams located Porterfield at the head of the column, and there Colonel Williams noticed that several British prisoners had been captured in what appeared to have been a surprise encounter for both sides. The prisoners were wearing the green jacket of the British Legion,

Tarleton's Tory cavalry, and the knot in Otho William's stomach tightened a notch. How could it be that British cavalry had gotten so close to the column with no warning? Was Tarleton's entire command on their front, he wondered? The prisoners were quickly questioned, and the answers they provided proved even more troubling than Williams had at first feared. Williams questioned one of the dragoons himself, and was dismayed by what he learned. It wasn't just Tarleton's Legion the Continental column apparently had stumbled upon unknowingly in the darkness, but the entire British army. Said Williams, "He [the prisoner] informed that Lord Cornwallis commanded in person about three thousand regular British troops, which were in line of march about five or six hundred yards in front." What was intended as a simple night march had in an instant become an invitation to disaster. Williams quickly remounted, and raced toward the rear to report the uncomfortable facts to General Gates.

"Order was soon restored in the corps of infantry in the American army, and the officers were employed in forming a front line of battle,"[4] Williams reported, as he rode to the rear to find General Gates and communicate to him the grim situation he had discovered ahead. Meanwhile, directly across the field from the Americans, the British were also deploying in the darkness, taking up a position that could not be readily flanked for, "The British army displayed in one line, which completely occupied the ground, each flank resting on impervious swamps."[5] Williams, riding rapidly to the rear, located and explained the situation to a stunned

General Gates. Indeed, Williams later recalled that, "The general's astonishment could not be concealed."[6]

A council of American commanders was then hastily convened to determine what sensible course of action might be employed, but the fact of the matter was, events had already superseded all tactical deliberation – the enemy was too near to affect a successful withdrawal in the darkness. The unhappy facts were laid before the various commanders and at first no one spoke at all. The truth of it was, of course, there was precious little to say, for Gates had already marched them face first into potential disaster, and everyone knew it. A bewildered Gates asked finally: "Gentlemen, what is best to be done?"[7] Once more, all remained mute until General Stevens of the Virginia militia suggested nothing more than the obvious. "Gentlemen," he said, "is it not too late *now* to do anything but fight?"[8] Again, Gates was regaled with only a grim silence from his subordinate commanders, a jarring confirmation of the dire situation the army had somehow managed to stumble into, and the painful lack of options the situation entailed. The army could neither go forward nor backward; that left but one option. "Then we must fight," said Gates. "Gentlemen, please take your posts."[9]

That the American army should not have been led blindly into such a dilemma was obvious to all of Horatio Gates' subordinate commanders on the field that night, and for this misfortune Gates would eventually come under severe criticism. The dashing Light Horse Harry Lee, a young cavalry commander at the time, was typically critical of Gates' course of action. "The evacuation of Rudgley's mill and the falling back of Lord Rawdon from Lynch's Creek, seem to have inspired General Gates with the presumption that his approach would drive the enemy from Camden. No conclusion more erroneous could have been drawn from a fair view of the objects and situation of the respective armies... Unhappily for America, unhappily for himself, he acted under this influence, nor did he awake from his reverie until the proximity of the enemy was announced by his fire in the night, preceding the fatal morning."[10]

Horatio Gates had received enormous praise for the American victory over Burgoyne at Saratoga, and for that success he had been adjudged both a "competent and aggressive field commander."[11] His actions before, during, and after the coming fight along the Great Wagon Road near Camden, however, would offer only painful evidence of his incompetence. Horatio Gates had marched a beleaguered, exhausted, and hungry command through difficult terrain with no intelligence as to the enemy's activities or strength only then to literally stumble head-first into disaster, and he and his Southern Army were about to pay a very heavy price for his bungling.

On the American right John Eager Howard was busy moving his men through the dust and darkness to form a line of battle. That line deployed essentially as it had marched, the veteran Continentals taking up positions on the extreme right, while the untried North Carolina and Virginia militia moved off to the left of the road. Under a full moon, the vague shape of the field of battle that circumstance alone had dictated they occupy now began to crystallize before the tired troops. It was rolling woodlands, about three quarters of a mile from one side to the other, with heavy swamps and thick woods shielding both flanks. The Great Wagon Road ran essentially down the center of the field. "De Kalb, who commanded the American right... posted Lieutenant Colonel John Eager Howard and his 2nd Maryland Regiment on the far right abutting the swamp. The two generals trusted Howard, as acting commander of the regiment, to hold his ground."[12]

To Howard's left the crack Delaware troops under Captain Robert Kirkwood were placed, then on the far side of the road the North Carolina and Virginia militia deployed in order, the Virginians with their left flank anchored on the far swamp. The First Maryland regiment was held in reserve. Gates, with his staff, took up a position several hundred yards behind the line of battle, too far to the rear to be effective. The American line consisted of some 3,700 infantry of which approximately 2,500 were green militia. Facing them, the British posted over 2,300 veteran infantry and cavalry. Artillery for both sides unlimbered along the opposing lines and hastily pointed their angry tubes toward one another. As frequent skirmish fire erupted between the nervous, waiting armies, Gates awaited the rising sun. Daylight was not long in coming.

"At dawn of day (on the morning of the 16th of August) the enemy appeared in front," Otho Williams tells us, "advancing in column."[13] In the grey morning mist nothing was yet clear, but it appeared the British were moving forward toward the American left, about two hundred yards distant. "Cornwallis formed his men before dawn on either side of the Waxhaws Road [the Great Wagon Road]. His finest troops under Lt. Col. James Webster held the position of honor on the right wing... The left wing under Lord

Rawdon was composed of his own Irish Volunteers, infantry from the British Legion, the Royal North Carolina Regiment, and Morgan Bryan's North Carolina militia."[14] Banastre Tarleton's cavalry and light infantry comprised a general reserve in the center of the field held just behind the main line. While Gates was informed of the movement on his left, he gave no orders, but waited instead for events to unfold.

On the extreme right of the American line, John Howard prepared his command for the fight that now seemed imminent. Howard, a twenty-seven-year-old Marylander, had been born and raised on his family's estate in Garrison Forrest, some ten miles northwest of Baltimore. "When the war started in 1775, he had been a typical twenty-two-year-old son of an upper middle-class Maryland family, preparing for a life of planting, harvesting, and discharging the social and civic responsibilities of his class."[15] Quiet, steady and resolute, Howard had risen through the ranks of the Continental line as a result of his accomplishments on the field, and he was considered a dependable commander. Today at Camden he would be called upon to prove his mettle once more.

From his post out front Colonel Otho Williams noticed that the British seemed to be moving on the American left, shifting it appeared, at that very moment from a marching column into line of battle. Williams rode back and suggested to Gates that the British, if attacked quickly, might be surprised and caught in mid-maneuver. At Freeman's Farm, Gates had also remained well behind the action, but there he had relied upon the tactical suggestions of Benedict Arnold and Daniel Morgan, sage suggestions that, promptly executed, ultimately conferred upon Horatio Gates much success and notoriety. But the hot-headed Arnold had been given command of West Point, a fortress on the Hudson River, by General Washington, and the talented Morgan remained in Virginia, still ill and out of action. So today Horatio Gates would have to think for himself. Unfortunately Gates agreed with Williams that opportunity seemed to be smiling on the American left, and ordered the troops opposite the British in that sector to deliver an immediate blow.

Gates should have known better. For good reason, Williams should not have made the suggestion, and Gates should certainly not have compounded the mistake by agreeing. European armies such as the British facing the Continentals that day placed their finest troops on the right of their battle formations – the position of honor – and Horatio Gates, having served as an officer for years in the British army, should have been fully aware of this tactical propensity. Cornwallis no doubt had placed his strongest, most veteran regiments on his right, and Horatio Gates was about to attack them with his weakest militia units. His ill-considered order had debacle written all over it.

Williams rode forward and gave the order to General Stevens of the Virginia militia, who set his brigade in motion at once. The Virginia troops at first advanced with spirit, but the situation ahead turned out to be far less opportune than had originally been anticipated. Indeed, the British had already moved from column into line, and were at that moment entirely prepared for battle. Williams would later write: "The right wing of the enemy was soon discovered *in line* – it was too late to attack them displaying [in the act of deployment]. Nevertheless, the business of the day could no longer be deferred."[16] Gates could have cancelled the attack, but he was too far behind the lines to see for himself what had transpired, thus the attack went forward as ordered. It was to prove a tragic mistake.

The Virginia militia – many of whom had never before been tested in combat – was now moving against the finest troops under Cornwallis' command, all of them drawn-up and prepared for battle. A situation that only moments before had seemed to offer opportunity, now appeared a decidedly uneven contest. Williams, grasping the situation on the field, offered to take forward a small group of volunteers to draw off the enemy's fire prior to the main militia advance, and this was undertaken, but proved entirely ineffective. "They were led forward within forty or fifty yards of the enemy," wrote Williams, "and ordered to take trees and keep up as brisk a fire as possible. The desired effect of this expedient, to extort the enemy's fire at some distance in order to the rendering it less terrible to the militia, was not gained."[17]

British regulars knew precisely how to deal with American militia. Rather than standing and slugging it out with the musket at a distance, the British simply fired a single volley then lowered the bayonet and charged with a great, howling huzza! Militia, unable to reload and fire before being overwhelmed by the British advance, generally fled the field.

Cornwallis ordered his right wing to advance. "The veterans of the enemy, composing the right, were of course opposed to the Virginia militia; whereas they ought to have been faced by the Continental brigade," noted Light Horse Harry Lee. "Our left was instantly overpowered by the assault; and the brave Stevens had to endure the mortifying spectacle exhibited by his flying brigade."[18]

So sudden, so rapidly did the Virginia militia collapse after spotting the advancing British bayonets that hardly a shot was fired by the Americans before the entire brigade broke ranks and fled to the rear, hurling their muskets, flags, and accoutrements to the ground as they departed. Otho Williams, on the field as the debacle unfolded, recalled that "the impetuosity with which they [the British] advanced, *firing* and *huzzahing*, threw the whole body of the militia into such a panic that they generally threw down their *loaded* arms and fled in the utmost consternation."[19] Whether by design, default, or delusion General Gates had ordered the greenest troops under his command to assault Cornwallis' most veteran regiments, and the result was sadly predictable – disaster!

The sudden panic that had sent the Virginians flying rearward spread instantly to the North Carolina militia that occupied the next place in line, and they too fled the field, littering the woods with their abandoned muskets. In an instant, panic had turned the American attack into a fiasco of the most horrific dimensions. Colonel Williams, watching incredulously as the entire left wing of the American army simply ran and disappeared from view noted that "a great majority of the militia (at least two –thirds of the army) fled without firing a shot. The writer avers it of his own knowledge, having seen and observed every part of the army, from left to right during the action. He who has never seen the effect of a panic upon a multitude can have but an imperfect idea of such things... Armies have been routed by it, even where no enemy appeared to furnish an excuse."[20]

A militiaman in the North Carolina line recalled years later the stampede that ensued. "Amongst other things, I confess I was amongst the first that fled. The cause of that I cannot tell, except that everyone I saw was about to do the same. It was instantaneous. There was no effort to rally, no encouragement to fight. Officers and men joined in the flight. I threw away my gun, and, reflecting I might be punished for being found without arms, I picked up a drum, which gave forth such sounds when touched by the twigs I cast it away."[21]

In moments only the American situation devolved from one of strength and presumed opportunity, to one of utter horror. On the American right, John Eager Howard's Second Maryland was by now heavily engaged with the troops of the British left, who were vigorously advancing. Cornwallis, having noted the apparent success of his attack on the right, had ordered the troops on his left under Rawdon to advance at once in order to prevent the shifting of American units from one end of the line to the other as reinforcements. It was an expert move by an expert tactician, and it worked precisely as planned. But the Continentals on the American right were not about to flee like the militia had on the left, and they stood toe-to-toe with the British without budging an inch. Indeed, so stout was the American defense in this sector that as the British recoiled from the initial volleys, the Continentals thought to go over to the offense. "On the other flank, General de Kalb's Regulars held their own against a spirited advance by Lord Rawdon. General de Kalb, who was wounded early and often at Camden, launched a serious attack that forced Cornwallis himself to ride into the action and steady his men."[22]

Smoke obscured the field as volley after volley exploded between the lines. Artillery boomed, and men toppled to the ground on both sides before violent exchanges of musketry that shattered the morning air. It was as savage a fight as had taken place throughout the entire course of the war. John Eager Howard, riding behind his regulars, urged the men forward, and the Maryland line advanced with bayonets lowered, driving the British before them, eventually threatening even to turn the British left flank. Colonel Williams, in the center of the field, observed the Maryland troops sweep forward with unrestrained pride. "The regular troops," he wrote, "who had the keen edge of sensibility rubbed off by strict discipline and hard service, saw the confusion with but little emotion... The Second Maryland Brigade, including the battalion of Delawares, on the right, were engaged with the enemy's left, which they opposed with very great firmness. They even advanced upon them and had taken a number of prisoners when their companions of the First Brigade, being greatly outflanked and charged by superior numbers, were obliged to give ground."[23]

The First Maryland, which had originally been held back as a general reserve, moved up to what was now the exposed American left flank to try and stem the tide as the fugitives of the militia fled through their ranks or ran passed them in panic. For awhile they were able to slow the British advance, but greatly outnumbered, even the tough Maryland Continentals had eventually to give ground. Rapidly, very rapidly, what was left of the American line, from right to left, began to crumble.

Along the American center, Horatio Gates had ridden into the torrent of fleeing militia in the hopes of rallying his troops, but it was not to be. Rather than stopping the tidal wave of terrified foot soldiers, Gates and his staff had been swept away with them. "The torrent of unarmed militia bore away with it General Gates, Caswell and a number of others, who soon saw that all was lost."[24] The recently arrived commander of the Southern Army, sensing disaster, gathered his staff and rode for the safety of the rear never once turning back to help extract his embattled army from the death trap his tactics had served to create. It was a sad performance for which he would pay a heavy price, but not nearly as heavy as the ultimate price paid by many of the veterans he had abandoned.

Meanwhile on the American right the Continentals fought on. Smoke swirled, men shouted, cannon boomed. The Second Maryland under John Howard fought like demons, holding firm against everything Cornwallis could throw at them, his regulars loading and firing until the barrels of their muskets became almost too hot to handle. The Delaware regiment on their left also stood immovable as the fearless Kirkwood shouted orders to his embattled troops. General De Kalb, shot from his horse and having sustained more wounds than could be counted, dragged himself across the battlefield, and continued the fight on foot. The First Maryland, taking up a desperate, oblique line on the American left in order to try and prevent that flank from caving in completely, fought the advancing Redcoats furiously while slowly giving ground. The Continentals fought bravely, but despite their best efforts, the situation was rapidly deteriorating.

Cornwallis, watching from the center of his line, sensed the feeble, precarious nature of the American position. The Continentals, he saw, were putting up a terrific fight, but they were now outnumbered almost three to one, and their left flank was crumbling. They could not stand and fight that way much longer. One more hard push, he thought, and the Continental line would surely collapse in its entirety. So he would make that push – it was time to send in Tarleton.

CHAPTER TWO

TARLETON

Despite the blinding smoke that at times obscured the battle much like the swirling, angry clouds that presage a summer thunderstorm, Lt. Colonel Banastre Tarleton could readily observe most of the action from his position in the center of the field, directly behind the main British line. General Cornwallis had placed the Legion cavalry "in column, on account of the thickness of the woods, to the right of the main road, close to the first battalion of the 71st."[1] They were in reserve, a force that might be used to beat back a successful American attack if required, or deliver a decisive blow of their own. Tarleton's orders from the general were "to act offensively against the enemy, or in defense of the British troops, as opportunity offered, or necessity required."[2] Sitting his horse in front of the Legion cavalry, Tarleton waited patiently for that moment to arise; that precise instant when victory might be swept gamely from the jaws of defeat and glory fashioned from the beleaguered cries of the defeated. Then he would sweep into the action and cut the Americans to pieces once again, sabers flashing; the mere thunder of his dragoon's horse's hooves alone enough, often, to put the enemy to flight.

Banastre Tarleton had arrived in the New World in the summer of 1776, then a young coronet under the command of General Charles Cornwallis in a force that had sailed for Charleston, South Carolina from Britain in the spring of that year. Later removed to New York, he volunteered for a post with the 16th Light Dragoons, after which his star began to shine. Described by a fellow officer as "full of enterprise and spirit, and anxious of every opportunity of distinguishing himself,"[3] Banastre Tarleton had discovered in soldiering what had previously escaped him in civilian life.

Born on August 21, 1754, second son of John and Lady Jane Tarleton, a prosperous family of Liverpool merchants, while there is little record of his youth, it can be presumed that Banastre Tarleton had a normal if unremarkable childhood. Over the years his father had developed a far-flung commercial empire that provided the family a comfortable existence which was naturally coupled to considerable opportunity for their aspiring children. "At his death... John Tarleton possessed an estate named "Fairfield" in Derby, a house and store on both the islands of Curacao and Grenada, plus a home on Water Street in Liverpool. His estate's net worth was approximately eighty thousand pounds sterling, or close to eight million dollars by today's standards."[4]

Displaying no great interest or flair for his father's commercial affairs, in 1771 Tarleton enrolled at University College, Oxford, but proved an indifferent student. A stint as an aspiring lawyer also proved a dismal failure, and he soon "drank and gambled away most of his inheritance of five thousand pounds. He then withdrew from Middle Temple, a brooding, restless youth."[5] In April, 1775 a commission as a coronet – the lowest grade commissioned officer in the British army – was purchased presumably by his family for the youthful Tarleton, and it would be in the discipline, excitement, and opportunity of military command that Banastre Tarleton would discover his calling.

Glory and advancement appear to have been the twin god's of Tarleton's newfound inspiration, and while shallow and self-serving motives they were, the same incentives have clearly driven many of the world's top-flight commanders from Alexander to Custer, from Napoleon to Patton. In that sense, Tarleton was no different than many of the great captains of history, mirroring in action the standard military ethos of the 18th Century. In New York, New Jersey, and Pennsylvania Tarleton had taken part in any number of dashing cavalry raids and enterprises that more firmly established his reputation as an alert and energetic officer. In January, 1778 he was jumped to the rank of Captain, and in August of that same year, Sir Henry Clinton promoted Tarleton Lt. Colonel of the British Legion. "He had gone from coronet to lieutenant colonel in just four years, and he was not quite twenty-four years old."[6]

There was no Sandhurst or other military school or tradition in the day which offered a more "correct" military lineage for the families of the English elite, thus Tarleton's rise to stardom had followed the same pedigree as had the Howe's, Clinton's, or Cornwallis' own. His ascendance, for one so young, had been nothing short of meteoric, all of it based upon merit, and Banastre Tarleton had, by the year

1780, firmly established himself as a rising star in the British military firmament, and an officer to be taken seriously. "He was a very capable cavalry commander: brave, vigorous, bold, swift of movement, alert for opportunities, on the march a driver of men and horses, relentless in pursuit of his prey. That he had grave defects of character cannot take from him his brilliant exploits on behalf of King and Country—and Banastre Tarleton."[7]

Those defects of character would appear more prominently in the year 1780 in the South Carolina low country, and later as the British drove into the piedmont region of that state. After the fall of Charleston, the British moved to solidify control of South Carolina, and this was accomplished by establishing garrisons at key locations across the state. The movement into the interior was naturally led by the cavalry, and that meant Tarleton at the head of his legion cavalry, often accompanied by a company of sabers from the 17th Dragoons.

At Monck's Corner, Tarleton established the pattern of combat he would follow – and from which he would rarely vary – throughout the Southern Campaign, and for which he would become acclaimed throughout his native land: "swift approach, sudden appearance, immediate assault with British officer's weapons of choice – sabers and bayonets. He used it time after time, and it is not unreasonable to suggest that American commanders, learning of his tactics firsthand or from embarrassed comrades, also would have learned early in the campaign to be ever alert when there was the slightest suspicion that Tarleton was afield."[8]

Monck's Corner was little more than a village crossroads some thirty miles north of Charleston on the Cooper River, but before Charleston had fallen into British hands it represented a key route through which supplies might be filtered into the city as well as an avenue of potential escape for the beleaguered Continental garrison. On April 12 Tarleton therefore departed Charleston, tasked with cooperating on a mission to take and hold Monck's Corner where a force of some 500 Americans guarded the crossroad. En route Tarleton was joined by a large force of infantry under Lt. Col. Webster, but it would be Tarleton's job to rush and subdue the Americans while Webster later moved up with his infantry in support.

Tarleton's recollections of the contest, which were published in Britain in 1787 to much acclaim, provide clear insight as to his thoughts and methods. "An attack in the night was judged most advisable," he wrote, "as it would render the superiority of the enemy's cavalry useless, and would, perhaps, present a favorable opportunity of getting possession of Biggin bridge, on Cooper river, without much loss to the assailants. Profound silence was observed on the march."[9] Gaining precise information as to the American's defensive arrangements while on the move toward Monck's Corner by means of a captured courier, Tarleton was ready to spring his trap at the appointed hour with complete confidence in his plans. "The order was executed with the greatest promptitude and success. The Americans were completely surprised: Major Vernier, of Pulaski's legion, and some other officers and men attempted to defend themselves, were killed or wounded; General Huger, Colonels Washington and Jamieson, with many officers and men, fled on foot to the swamps, close to their encampment, where, being concealed by the darkness, they effected their escape."[10]

The nighttime raid on Monck's Corner proved a complete success for the British assailants. It was not the hard marching, good planning, or the execution of the assault, however, for which Tarleton would forever after become known as "Bloody Ban," but rather the raid's aftermath; and an aftermath that unfortunately became common whenever and wherever Tarleton's Legion struck: The abuse and butchery of the vanquished along with the abuse of civilians, particularly unprotected women.[11] Monck's Corner would mark the beginning of a violent and savage campaign across the South during the American Revolution, and while Banastre Tarleton cannot be singled out as being responsible for the escalating violence, the actions and deportment of the troops under his command far more than once set the tone for the barbarism that would follow. As historian John Buchanan points out, "Monck's Corner revealed Tarleton's darker side, which was never distant... There were few complaints on that score about the record of Patrick Ferguson, who led both Tory regulars and militia. Of Banastre Tarleton, however, it is not unfair to state that in time and with reason he became the most hated man in the South."[12]

If Monck's Corner marked the beginning of Tarleton's "bloody" reputation, the fight at Waxhaws set it firmly in stone. In late May, after the fall of Charleston on May 12Colonel Abraham Buford was ordered to march his few remaining American troops north to Hillsborough, North Carolina in order to remove them from potential British incursions. Marching with Buford was John Rutledge, then governor of South Carolina, hoping to maintain his office, albeit at arm's length.[13] Buford got quickly on the road, and it would be days later before Cornwallis discovered the movement and decided to try and intercept the marching column. But Buford had by then a ten day head start, and was thus far too removed to be caught by marching British infantry. Cornwallis wondered: Could Tarleton and his hard-riding cavalry accomplish the task?

Tarleton headed off on May 27, driving a force of approximately 270 men on horseback through the scorching Carolina heat, utterly determined to ride down the fleeing Americans, no matter how many days they had been spotted. Given another opportunity to shine, Tarleton had no intention of disappointing Cornwallis. The sweltering heat was appalling. Men fell behind, fell out, or simply fell off their horses, but nothing could make Tarleton slacken his pace. "By this time many of the British cavalry and mounted infantry were totally worn out," wrote Tarleton, "and dropped successively into the rear, the horses of the three pounder [the artillery piece] were likewise unable to proceed."[14] Nevertheless, Tarleton pressed on, finally making contact with Buford's rearguard just south of the North Carolina state line in a remote region of South Carolina known as the Waxhaws around three o'clock on the afternoon of the 29th. "At that point, with a column strung out for miles, many commanders would have stopped. Not Tarleton. When in hot pursuit he was like a man possessed."[15]

Keeping to the tactics that that would mark his career in the South, Tarleton attacked at once and with virtually no reconnaissance. The fact that his men were exhausted and considerably outnumbered by the Americans did not faze him at all. "At three o'clock in the afternoon, on the confines of South Carolina, " Tarleton recalled, "the advanced guard of the British charged a sergeant and four men of the American light dragoons, and made them prisoners in the rear of their infantry. This event happening under the eyes of the two commanders, they respectively prepared their troops for action."[16] Buford, refusing Tarleton's demand to surrender, deployed his Virginia Continentals in a line fronting a small wood. He had about 350 infantry and a small detachment of cavalry at his disposal. While he also had two artillery pieces that could have played havoc with charging cavalry, he chose not to unlimber them, but rather sent them along with his fleeing baggage train. Tarleton immediately deployed on a hill opposite and led the charge forward himself. "The disposition being completed without any fire from the enemy," the British commander wrote, "though within three hundred yards of their front, the cavalry advanced to the charge."[17]

Down one hill then up the other, straight into a wall of Continental muskets the British rode, Tarleton leading the way, but rather than opening fire at a distance by sections and unhorsing the lead British elements, Buford foolishly had his troops hold their fire until the charging cavalry was almost on top of his line. While holding fire until seeing the "whites of their eyes" was at the time a sound tactic against advancing infantry (long-range musketry was often hopelessly inaccurate against distant infantry for a number of reasons), against charging cavalry it had little if any effect at close range. At ten paces the Continentals finally opened fire, but Tarleton's troopers were by then so close that they simply rode right over the stationary Continentals. Tarleton's horse went down in the American volley, but he was uninjured, soon remounted, and the American line was promptly overwhelmed. "Thus in a few minutes ended an affair which might have had a very different termination," Tarleton later speculated, had the Americans opened an enfilading fire at a distance and not foolishly held their fire until the last instant.

Once again Tarleton's highly aggressive tactics proved successful, but once again it was not his tactics or boldness that was later questioned, but rather the contests aftermath. As at Monck's Corner, Tarleton either would not or could not rein in his command and a slaughter of the wounded and surrendered Continentals commenced, not ending for at least fifteen minutes. Buford apparently attempted to surrender early after his line had been breeched, but his white flag was not honored, the officer bearing it was butchered, and no cry for quarter observed by the members of Tarleton's British Legion. Buford's surgeon, who witnessed the aftermath, would later write that "the demand for quarters, seldom refused a vanquished foe, was at once found to be in vain; not a man was spared, and it was the concurrent testimony of all the survivors that for fifteen minutes after every man was prostrate they went over the ground plunging their bayonets into every one that exhibited any signs of life, and in some instances, where several had fallen over the other, these monsters were seen to throw off on the point of the bayonet the uppermost, to come at those beneath."[18] Unfortunately for Banastre Tarleton, it was not

Buford's surgeon alone who recalled the ugly aftermath at the Waxhaws. The events were recounted by other British witnesses, and even Tarleton himself, in his *A history of the campaigns of 1780 and 1781, in the southern provinces of North America,* admitted that, the thought that he had been unhorsed and either dead or seriously wounded, "... stimulated the soldiers [of the British Legion] to a vindictive asperity not easily restrained."[19]

Writing after the war, Light Horse Harry Lee would have none of Tarleton's rationalization. "The unrelenting conqueror shut his ears to the voice of supplication," Lee insisted, "as he had steeled his heart against the claims of mercy. By the official report, one hundred and thirteen were killed, one hundred and fifty so badly wounded as to be paroled on the ground, most of whom died; ... Lieutenant Colonel Tarleton excused this butchery by asserting that, after their submission, some of the Americans re-seized their arms and fired upon his troops....In the annals of our Indian war nothing is to be found more shocking; and this bloody day only wanted the war dance, and the roasting fire, to have placed it first in the records of torture and death in the West.

"This tragic expedition," Lee went on, "sunk deep in the American breast, and produced the unanimous decision among the troops to revenge their murdered comrades whenever the blood stained corps should give the opportunity."[20] In that manner the term Tarleton's Quarter had come into existence, the verbal equivalent of the black flag, and a violent and merciless demand for retribution that Tarleton's own actions had provoked.

Thus had Lt. Colonel Banastre Tarleton risen to become Cornwallis' figurative stroke of lightning on any field of battle, and it was for that reason he'd been summoned that fateful August 16 to supply the coup de grace against the American line at Camden, just as the raging battle lurched toward its most critical moment. For months Tarleton would continue his freewheeling ways across South Carolina: hard marching, relentless pursuit, instantaneous assault, bloody aftermath, until a wily American officer arrived to turn the tables on him, crushing the British cavalryman by means of his own rash formula for success. But on August 16, that day was still months in the future.

The Continental line at Camden was at that critical moment wavering, assaulted on the left and front by veteran British infantry. Otho Williams, then fighting with the First Maryland on the left flank as it fought in the retrograde, recalled that as the British advanced, the First Maryland "were obliged to give way, and were again rallied. The Second Brigade were still warmly engaged. The distance between the two brigades did not exceed two hundred yards, their opposite flanks being nearly upon a line perpendicular to their front."[21] Bowed backwards, the Continentals were in serious danger of being cut off, pinned against the swamp, and surrounded.

In the center of the action, Cornwallis spotted the opportunity to complete the encirclement by sending Tarleton's cavalry across the field to attack the American rear. Pinned against the swamp, the Continentals would be virtually surrounded, forced to fight front, flank, and rear, and destroyed. Tarleton received the order and responded at once. "The contest was yet supported by the Maryland brigades and Delaware regiment," he later recalled, "when a part of the British cavalry, under Major Hanger, was ordered to charge their flank, whilst Lieutenant colonel Tarleton, with the remainder of his regiment, completed their confusion."[22]

Tarleton gave the order to charge, and the British Legion swept forward into the center of the field of battle, skirted the American left and, with sabers flashing, in moments only struck the American rear.

Fighting simultaneously now on three fronts, the situation along the battered American front devolved into one of bedlam, bordering rapidly upon implosion.

CHAPTER THREE

KIRKWOOD

For almost a half hour the stout Continental line had stood against everything the British managed to hurl at them. Captain Robert Kirkwood, in command of the Delaware "Blues," had deployed his regiment that morning, some 250 strong, on the immediate left of the Second Maryland. Like Howard's Marylanders, they not only fought the British to a standstill, but had advanced on Howard's left into the teeth of the enemy's bayonets, driving them back and threatening to sweep the field. Lead flew by the peck that morning and men toppled into the bloody grass all along both lines, and no doubt the Second Brigade could have held the field had not the militia across the road flown at the first sight of British bayonets. But fly they did, and in their absence the situation rapidly devolved from one of desperation into one of utter despair.

Days later Kirkwood recorded the events of that somber day in his journal, and he recalled vividly the entire line of Continentals laying on their arms in the dark morning air until the British advanced, "and attacked our Left Flank where the Militia Lay, who gave way which gave the enemy's horse an opportunity to gain our Rear, their Infantry at the same time gaining our Flank, and their Line advancing in our front which Caused the Action to become very Desperate;"[1] Tarleton's advance had virtually completed the encirclement. The British were now on the Continental's front, left and rear, and the final American collapse came quickly. As Light Horse Harry Lee later summed up the situation, "Meantime De Kalb, with our right, preserved a conspicuous superiority. Lord Cornwallis, sensible of the advantages gained, and aware of the difficulty to which we were subjected by the shameful flight of our left, concentrated his force, and made a decisive charge."[2] As the American position crumbled all around him, there was little for Kirkwood to do but to try and save what remained of his shattered command.

In December, 1775, at the age of only nineteen, Robert Kirkwood had been named a first lieutenant in the Delaware Battalion, and he received that commission in January of the following year. He then participated in virtually every battle fought by George Washington in New York in 1776, and later in defense of Philadelphia in 1777, and he'd already seen more action than most men do in a lifetime of soldiering.[3] Kirkwood had been there that awful day on Long Island when the American line had collapsed on the left – just as at Camden – and the Delaware and Maryland troops had been called upon to somehow hold the British advance at bay when everything else around them was collapsing in utter confusion, a stand that had since become virtually legendary in the Continental Army. "Colonel John Haslet would describe how his 'Delawares' stood with 'determined countenance,' in close array, their colors flying, the enemy's artillery 'playing' on them all the while, and the enemy, 'though six times their number,' not daring to attack."[4] Then again at Brandywine and Germantown, the Delawares had stood up to the British, only again to be flanked or fooled, and forced to abandon the field yet again. Sadly, for the proud Delaware troops, Camden would be no different.

Kirkwood had marched South in April of 1780 when General Washington had determined it imperative to oppose British efforts in South Carolina near Charleston with some of his finest fighting units. It would be a long and desperate march on terrible roads through an impoverished land. In April Kirkwood wrote, "I left Morristown [New Jersey] four days before the Maryland and Delaware Line, and arrived at Newark, in the Delaware State."[5] From Delaware he went to Head of Elk in Maryland, arriving on May 8. The trip to South Carolina would be both long and fatiguing. "Set sail from Head of Elk," wrote Kirkwood, "in Compy with 30 sail of vessels, being the Second brigade In the Maryland Line, Destin'd for Petersburgh [Virginia], and marched to Rockaway Court House."[6]

The small army sent south by Washington consisted of two infantry brigades only, these comprised of seven regiments of Maryland troops and Kirkwood's Delaware contingent. Counting every last infantryman, officer, artilleryman, cook, teamster, even stragglers, the marching column numbered approximately 2,100 men; hardly a formidable force by any standard, and all under the command of General Baron Johann De Kalb.[7] The army may have been small, but it was comprised of tough, veteran troops, and as such a force far different than the American regiments that had taken the field in the early days of the war, when it was thought that the spirit of liberty and the correctness of their cause alone would somehow confer victory on the rebelling united colonies. The imprint of Baron von Steuben was now on the marching column, the tough training of the Prussian drillmaster who at Valley Forge had trained the undisciplined Americans to march and fight as well as any troops might march and fight anywhere in the world. "The infantry of the Maryland Line and the Delaware Line," historian John Buchanan suggests, "were as good as any British army could offer, which made them very good indeed."[8]

It was as they marched through Virginia in early June that news arrived of Charleston's capitulation to the British, news that beleaguered the small command, for everyone knew that Charleston – an important port city – had been the rebellion's stronghold in the South, but that dispiriting intelligence failed to dull their determination. They resolved to press on. Otho Williams, then hard on the march along with Kirkwood, De Kalb, and John Eager Howard wrote, "Here [in Virginia] the unwelcome news of the surrender of Charleston (on the 12th of May) was first communicated to the detachment, the principal object of whose destination was lost; but the country was not yet conquered; and it was presumed that the countenance of a body of regular troops, however small, would constitute more than any thing else to sustain the fortitude of the militia."[9] So they would march on and do what they could to protect the Southern states from further British incursions, while hopefully rallying the state militias to their cause. That, at least, was the consensus of thought, truthfully, more hope than it was strategy.

The British did not interfere with their immediate progress but hunger soon did. Their supply train was supposed to follow along, but never appeared, and the government of North Carolina had made no provision for their arrival. Foot sore and half-starved, the column ground to a halt at Hillsborough, North Carolina on June 22, where it rested for a week, some 150 miles of hard marching from Petersburg.[10] Finding the surrounding region sadly short of provisions, the column pushed on again, but finally had to call it quits at Wilcox's Iron Works on the Deep River in North Carolina where Kirkwood's *Journal* notes simply that the army ended its march.[11] There the brigades encamped, having no capacity to move farther due to a shortage of rations for the hungry men or sufficient forage for their weary animals. Food had to be procured, and De Kalb was forced to try and collect as much as possible from the local citizens. He therefore sent out "small detachments, under discreet officers to collect provisions from the inhabitants, who, at that season of the year, had but little to spare; many of them were subsisting themselves upon the last of the preceding crop of grain, and the new, although it promised plenty, was not yet mature."[12]

Despite the lack of food, the difficult circumstances, oppressive heat, and the distance from home, the army, due to its discipline, somehow managed to remain upbeat. The Continental officers, used to sharing the privations of the men they commanded, did their best to see to it that what meager provisions they had were at least distributed fairly, the officers at times refusing to eat until all the men had been fed. There is little doubt, however, that it was the sheer devotion of both officers and men to the cause for which they were fighting that kept their spirits up. Many had already marched, fought, starved, and suffered for almost five years of war; a sudden lack of provisions was not, therefore, going to send them off into the woods as deserters. Indeed, Kirkwood himself would confide in his journal his deep feelings toward the struggle he had embarked upon: "When I Consider the Cause, for which we have Drawn our Swords," he wrote, "and the Necessity of Striking an effectual Blow, before we Sheath them again, I feel Joifull hopes arising In my mind, that in one day an opening Shall be made for the Restoration of American Liberty, and for shaking off the Infamous Yoke of British Slavery.

"America is yet free, the all grasping power of Briton has not yet been Able to seize our Liberty, but it is only by Valor. As it is by Arms, that the brave Acquire Immortal fame, so it is by arms, that the sordid must defend their lives & Properties, or lose them. We are the very men, my friends, who have hitherto set bounds to the Unmeasurable Ambition of the Britons."[13] And in May, 1780 that "unmeasurable ambition" of the Britons was then casting a covetous eye across the states of South and North Carolina.

De Kalb pleaded with Congress as well as the governor of North Carolina for supplies, all to no avail. Indeed, the army was promised ample supplies and reinforcements from the North Carolina militia, which "about that time took the field, under the command of Mr. Caswell, who was appointed a major general."[14] But no provisions were forthcoming. Otho Williams recalled bitterly that "The supplies, however, did not arrive, and the commandant of the militia, ambitions of signalizing himself, employed his men in detachments against small parties of disaffected inhabitants, who, to avoid being drafted onto the service of their country, retired among the swamps and other cover, with which that country abounds."[15]

Such, then, was the small army's condition – ill-fed, ill-clothed, and ill-quartered – on July 25 when General Horatio Gates made his first appearance at the entrance of the encampment. Kirkwood, in his typical Spartan style, noted in his journal only that: "This Day the Honorable Majr. Genl. Gates arrived and took Command of all the Southern Troops."[16] Despite the difficult conditions in camp, Gates was received with pomp and ceremony by De Kalb who "ordered a Continental salute from the little park of artillery, which was performed on the entrance into camp of his successor."[17] Gates entered the camp grandly, thanked De Kalb for his politeness then, without inspecting his troops, camp, or supplies, immediately ordered that all the men in the command "hold themselves in readiness *to march at a moment's warning*."[18] It would prove an almost incomprehensible mistake.

Given the pathetic condition of both man and beast, not to mention the lack of proper supplies and provisions for any extended field operations, Gate's pronouncement stunned his officer corps. But Horatio Gates had not arrived to ask advice, but rather to seize the initiative. Promising that both ample supplies of rum and food were on their way, on the morning of the 27th he imprudently put the hungry army in motion toward Buffalo Ford on the road to Camden, South Carolina; food or no food.

Indeed, so confident was Gates of his plans that he did not bother even to inquire as to the confirmed strength of his own forces – better yet the enemy's – before putting them in motion, presuming for some unknown reason that his force was vastly larger than a simple head count would have revealed. Somewhat remarkably, it would not be until August 15, one day before he stumbled directly into the British vanguard on the Old Wagon Road north of Camden, that Gates would become aware of his army's true strength, and this almost by accident. It was on that date, after issuing the order of march, that Gates finally turned to Otho Williams and showed him a rough estimate of the force he believed he had currently fit for duty; some 7,000 officers and men. Williams, knowing this number to be vastly inflated, called for an actual return (a count) by each unit commander, and later that day the true number was presented to Gates – 3,052 officers and men, or less than half the force the delusional Gates believed he had under arms.[19] But for Horatio Gates the disparity in numbers did not matter. Looking over the actual returns, a confident Gates simply shrugged them off and advised Williams that "these are enough for our purpose."[20]

It would appear that Horatio Gates had by August, 1780 become a victim of self-infatuation. Internalizing the accolades that had come his way due to his victory over Burgoyne at Bemis Heights, New York, the "Hero of Saratoga" appears to have developed a rather overinflated opinion of his own martial abilities, and as a consequence had placed both fact and reality at arm's length; in everyday life a prescription for failure, while in warfare a formula for disaster. His handling of the situation upon arrival seems to have contradicted virtually every rule of warfare, not to mention simple common sense, and soon the innocent – men like De Kalb, Howard, and Kirkwood – would pay a heavy price for his incompetence. Gate's orders for the march that August 15 revealed the degree of his irrational overconfidence at the time: "In case of attack by the enemy's cavalry in front," he insisted, "the light infantry upon each flank will instantly move up and give, and continue, the most galling fire upon the enemy's horse. This will enable Colonel Armand, not only to support the shock of the enemy's charge, but finally to rout them; the colonel will therefore consider the order to stand the attack of the enemy's cavalry, be their numbers what they may, as positive."[21]

That Colonel Armand's cavalry did not "stand to the attack of the enemy's cavalry" as ordered, but flew upon mere contact, should provide some reference as to Gates' complete misunderstanding of the forces under his command, their numbers, state of mind and body, and true capabilities.

Yet Robert Kirkwood would stand and fight no matter how irrational his orders or foolish the deployment. Born in 1756 on a farm outside of Newark, Delaware to Robert and Sarah Kirkwood, the only son in a family of eight daughters, at an early age young Robert displayed a keen interest in reading and study. His father enrolled him therefore in the Newark Academy (later to become the University of Delaware), where he studied the classics and graduated in good standing. But 1775 was in the American colonies a time of great political upheaval and, imbued with the spirit of liberty, the young scholar quit his studies and was named a lieutenant in the 1st Delaware Regiment at the age of only nineteen. A quick study and a tough fighter, Kirkwood fought in virtually every battle the Continentals faced in the early years of the war, and over time developed into an excellent field officer.[22] A true revolutionary and patriot in every sense of the word, Kirkwood would declare: "On our side, an Army united in the Cause of their Country, their Wives their Childres, their Aged Parents, their Liberties, their lives, at the head of this army I hope I do not offend against Modesty in Saying, there is a general [George Washington] Ready to exert all his Abilities, to Hazard his life in Leading us to Victory, and to freedom."[23]

In the early hours of August 16, 1780 on the field at Camden, young Captain Robert Kirkwood would face a grueling test. The Delaware Regiment deployed in line that morning west of the Great Wagon Road some 250 strong. John Eager Howard's Second Maryland was on Kirkwood's right, while the North Carolina militia filed into position on his immediate left. At first light the British advanced across a wide front. For about an hour Kirkwood's Delaware Continentals stood firm against these relentless British advances, but the collapse and rout of the American militia on his left placed his unit in a dicey situation indeed. The First Maryland had leaped into the fray to try and hold the left flank once the militia had fled the field, but it too was being pushed back by overwhelming numbers, and what remained of the American line was beginning to bow backward dramatically.

Then Lord Cornwallis, seizing the moment, launched his cavalry reserves under Tarleton in a sweeping assault that struck the American rear. Suddenly the outmanned

Continentals were almost surrounded and the situation collapsed in the blink of the eye. "Our brave troops were broken," wrote Light Horse Harry Lee, "and his lordship, following up the blow, compelled the intrepid Marylanders [and Delaware troops] to abandon the unequal contest. To the woods and swamps, after performing their duty valiantly, these gallant soldiers were compelled to fly."[24] With the British now closing on three sides – the British regular's bayonets gleaming in their faces, while Tarleton's dragoons were slashing at their backs – there was really only one place to go, and that was into the swamp that had previously anchored their right flank. Describing the American implosion succinctly, Otho Williams wrote simply that: "Lord Cornwallis, perceiving there was no cavalry opposed to him, pushed forward his dragoons, and his infantry charging at the same moment with fixed bayonets put an end to the contest. His victory was complete."[25]

All now was chaos. Kirkwood gathered what few troops he could manage and headed for the swamp, his men firing occasionally as best they could to cover the desperate withdrawal. The Delaware regiment would suffer tremendously as a result of the fighting at Camden. Of the 250 men who took to the line that morning, 125 were reported as either killed, wounded, or captured, a 50 percent casualty rate.[26] The two Maryland regiments would not fare much better. "Our loss was very heavy," Henry Lee readily admitted. "More than a third of the Continental troops were killed and wounded; and of the wounded one hundred and seventy were made prisoners. The regiment of Delaware was nearly annihilated."[27] In the ungoverned retreat, the army's wagons, supplies, and artillery were all abandoned to the British. Many of the Continentals ran for the thick woods and swamp lands, where the British infantry did not follow, and Tarleton's dragoons could not pursue. For those who made the unfortunate choice of retreating back up the Great Wagon Road toward Charlotte, death or capture awaited. As Tarleton would later admit, "After this last effort of the continentals, rout and slaughter ensued in every quarter.... The continentals, the state troops, and the militia, abandoned their arms, their colours, and their cannon, to seek protection in flight, or to obtain it from the clemency of the conquerors. As soon as the rout of the Americans became general, the legion dragoons advanced with great rapidity toward Rugeley's mills."[28] Behind Tarleton's slashing dragoons, the Great Wagon Road lay littered with American dead, wounded, and the abandoned accouterments of war.

For the infant United States, the calamity at Camden would prove a national horror. As Light Horse Harry Lee later lamented, "In the dreadful gloom which now overspread the United States, the reflecting mind drew consolation from the undismayed gallantry displayed by a portion of the army, throughout the desperate conflict; and from the zeal, courage, and intelligence exhibited by many of our officers."[29] But those meager truths in the end proved small consolation. The horrible fact of the matter was the American Southern army had not only been defeated at the Battle of Camden; it had literally ceased to exist.

But the American Revolutionary War effort had proved time and again that it was nothing if not resilient. Even as the shattered remnants of the Southern Army fled in utter rout and confusion into the swamps north of Camden, a heartbeat, small, almost undetectable, still beat on. As Otho Williams noted after the horrible defeat, "Colonel Gunby, Lieutenant Colonel Howard, Captain Kirkwood, and Captain Dobson, with a few other officers, and fifty or sixty men, formed a junction on the rout, and proceeded together."[30] From that small, desperate junction new life would eventually arise, indeed a new life that would one day utterly reverse the fortunes of Camden.

CHAPTER FOUR

HOWARD

Dodging tree-to-tree, hauling themselves at times through knee deep water, the Continental soldiers scrambled into the woods that bordered the field of battle. Smoke still swirled, muskets still cracked, and along the abandoned Continental line the plaintive wail of the wounded was still painfully audible. But the Continentals were running for dear life now, only a few stopping occasionally to fire back at the advancing British or help a wounded comrade to safety, most simply seeking some form of shelter from the storm in the dark and forbidding depths of the swamp. Hungry, exhausted, and surely beaten, it was a demoralized mob that now staggered into the mud and muck of the South Carolina wilderness in hopes of escape; an army now in name only.

Like a rocket that had exploded high overhead, the American army had not simply been dispersed, or defeated, or even destroyed for that matter, but rather it had been atomized, hurled in a hundred different directions and into a thousand different parts. Having no central command upon which to congeal, the fleeing remnants coalesced around what meager authority that here and there could be discerned, from junior to senior officers, more often around no officers at all. Individually, in two's and three's, and in small globules of exhausted men, what remained of the army began first to run deep into the woods to escape the vengeful British, and then at last to rest and begin the long trek north toward Charlotte.

Far ahead of them, now well north on the Great Wagon Road, General Horatio Gates was riding hard with the intention of putting as much distance between himself and the field at Camden as horse and time would allow. He would later claim that he had tried valiantly to rally the routed militia, but as night closed on that awful August 16, Gates had already hailed Charlotte, North Carolina, a good sixty miles from the morning's debacle, and at that distance his claim of fortitude in the face of disaster takes on a decidedly hollow ring.[1] Riding a racehorse well known for its speed, Gates flew by reinforcements headed on their way toward Camden without even stopping to confer, and not even Charlotte could hold him for a day. On August 19 Horatio Gates rode into Hillsborough, North Carolina, over 180 miles from the field at Camden, a remarkable equestrian feat for a man pushing sixty years of age.

Indeed the almost breathtaking speed with which Gates had managed to gain Hillsborough in the wake of the unmitigated disaster Camden was then known to be, hardly passed unnoticed, and naturally proved ripe for critical commentary. Alexander Hamilton, for instance, offered this sardonic observation: "Was there ever an instance of a general running away as Gates had done from his whole army? And was there ever so precipitous a flight? One hundred and eighty miles in three days and a half! It does admirable credit to the activity of a man at his time of life. But it disgraces the general and the soldier."[2] Over time Gates would have his defenders, of course, but the glaring and uncomfortable fact remained that Horatio Gates had fled the field at Camden and deserted his embattled army, leaving the Continentals to fight and die on their own hook, the sound of their valiant effort ringing in his ears as he sped his way north to safety; as ugly a picture as might be painted for any leader of men.

Meanwhile back in the swamps, what remained of the Continental line struggled to find cover and safety. John Eager Howard, later joined by Robert Kirkwood, led an initial group of some sixty men and officers into the tangled woods; a group that slowly grew to about ninety as time wore on. Howard realized the British would be looking for stragglers emerging from the woods on the road north of Camden, so he initially led his group south for about five or six miles before finally turning west.[3] It would be a long journey back to Charlotte, but he aimed to avoid Tarleton's dragoons that were, he accurately surmised, rampaging up and down the road that led to Hugeley's Mill and from there north to Charlotte.

That morning Howard had stood his ground as well as any man might, and even in defeat the Continentals had at least garnered significant respect. Light Horse Harry Lee would later insist that "Lieutenant-Colonel Howard demonstrated a solidity of character which, on every future occasion, he displayed honorably to himself and advantageously to his country,"[4] and in this Howard was far from alone. Maryland's General Mordecai Gist had once again performed admirably, and De Kalb, having suffered numerous wounds during the course of battle – from bayonet, to musket ball, to saber cut – was found prostrate on the field by the British long after the fight. Cornwallis, to his credit, had the fallen general removed to a field hospital, and there De Kalb would linger for thee painful days before finally succumbing to his wounds.

Around one o'clock in the afternoon the small group of Continental refugees led by Howard had put enough distance between themselves and the British that Howard finally deemed it safe enough to stop for a short rest. Most of the men collapsed under the trees, and some were asleep almost before their heads hit the ground. "A Straggler joined them and reported that a badly wounded officer remained on the battlefield, so Howard permitted a few men to return and carry him back. The officer survived, but one of his arms had to be amputated later."[5] After resting, Howard had the men up and moving again, and they journeyed in a wide sweep in order to avoid British and Tory patrols that were out scouring the countryside in search of American stragglers. If captured by the British, prison was a certainty; death more likely if cornered by the Tories. Thus it would be three days of hard marching before the small detachment finally reached Charlotte, moving all the while through barren territory, the men eating watermelons, green apples, peaches or any other edible commodity they could get their hands on just to keep putting one foot in front of the other.[6] It proved a long and difficult march. Kirkwood, exhausted from the effort, would later write only that "I can give no account of our Marches on the Retreat until we came to Salisbury which we arrived at on the 21st."[7]

On the road leading north between Camden and Hugeley's Mill, the scene proved both bloody and chaotic, the slash and slaughter tactics of Tarleton's dragoons and the pandemonium produced by the pure panic of the American fugitives being everywhere in evidence. Lt. Colonel Tarleton would later describe the situation: "As soon as the rout of the Americans became general, the legion dragoons advanced with great rapidity towards Rugeley's mills: On the road, General Rutherford, with many other officers and men, were made prisoners. The charge and pursuit having greatly dispersed the British, a halt was ordered on the south side of the creek, in order to collect a sufficient body to dislodge Colonel Armand and his corps, who, together with several officers, were employed in rallying the militia at that pass, and in fending off the American baggage... In a pursuit of twenty-two miles, many prisoners of all ranks, twenty ammunition wagons, one hundred and fifty carriages, containing the baggage, stores, and camp equipage of the American army, fell into the hands of the victors."[8]

American Tory Charles Steadman, traveling with the British van at the time, also described the carnage. "The road for some miles was strewed with the wounded and killed who had been overtaken by the legion in their pursuit. The numbers of dead horses, broken wagons, and baggage scattered on the road formed a perfect scene of horror and confusion: Arms, knapsacks, and accoutrements found were innumberable; such was the terror and dismay of the Americans."[9]

For those Americans who had somehow managed to elude the British pursuit, it would be a long, arduous, and exhausting trip north toward the tiny village of Charlotte, North Carolina. Otho Williams, having retreated into the swamps along with the remaining Continentals, only later to emerge on the road heading north, described the devastating scene he discovered: "The general order for moving off the heavy baggage , &c., to Waxaws was not put in execution, as directed to be done on the preceding evening. The whole of it, consequently, fell into the hands of the enemy.... Other wagons also had got out of danger from the enemy; but the cries of the women and the wounded in the rear and the consternation of the flying troops so alarmed some of the wagoners that they cut out their teams and, taking each a horse, left the rest for the next that should come. Others were obliged to give up their horses to assist in carrying off the wounded, and the whole road, for many miles, was strewed with signals of distress, confusion and dismay."[10]

According to Williams, Armand's cavalry not only failed to properly perform its duty as rearguard, but actually fell to ransacking the American wagons. "The tent covers were thrown off the wagons," he observed, "generally, and the baggage exposed, so that one might take what suited him to carry off."[11] Some militia reinforcements, on their way to join the Americans at Camden, quickly turned coat when word of the American defeat reached them, and in conjunction with the Armand's dragoons, the British Legion, and other lawless fugitives, began looting and abusing those fleeing American troops who unhappily wandered into their midst. All in all, it proved a miserable, dangerous, and depressing retreat – if such a mass, chaotic flight could even be called a retreat – toward the North Carolina line. Otho Williams was later to admit that he stopped by General Caswell's mess wagon where he found "a pipe of good Madeira, broached, and surrounded by a number of soldiers." Williams was happy to take a long draught of the wine, which "was the only refreshment he had received that day,"[12] before resuming the march north.

And conditions did not improve terribly much at Charlotte, "an open village with but few inhabitants, and the remains of a temporary hospital, containing a few maimed soldiers of Colonel Buford's unfortunate corps, which had been cut to pieces on the retreat, after the surrender of Charleston."[13] Still, a small open village was far better than no village at all, and here at least the defeated troops could rest and gather themselves for the time being. "Fortunately," noted Williams, "there was small supply of provision in the town – the inhabitants did all they could to refresh both men and officers – and, by the provident care of Colonel Hall, of Maryland, a quantity of flour was sent back on the route of the retreating troops,"[14] to be cooked and consumed by the weary men on the road as they marched as time and circumstance might allow.

Slowly, very slowly, over several days the pitiful remnants of the American Army began once again to congeal. For while that army had been more or less "atomized" at Camden as previously noted, random atoms do still possess some small measure of mass, and according to the rules of basic physics, mass attracts mass, and so the army began slowly to consolidate on Charlotte, drawn to that location, perhaps, by little more than the attractive force of gravity alone. For days troops continued slowly to trickle into the small, North Carolina village. "On the two days succeeding the fatal action," Williams recalled, "Brigadier General Gist, who commanded the second brigade of Maryland troops, previous to its misfortune at Charlotte, arrived with only two or three attendants, who had fallen into his route. Several field officers, and many officers of the line also arrived similarly circumstanced; and, although not more than about a dozen men of different corps arrived in irregular squads, from time to time, not less than one hundred infantry were collected in the village within that time."[15] Many of those men collapsed upon arrival, footsore and exhausted, more than a few still suffering from serious wounds. "They gave indeed," Williams recalled, "proofs of the uttermost pain and fatigue that the human constitution can bear – others sunk under their accumulated distresses."[16]

John Eager Howard, Robert Kirkwood and the ninety or so men who had traveled with them, finally dragged themselves into Charlotte on the 19th of August, hungry, exhausted, but at least in one piece. They were but a few of the fortunate survivors who had slowly managed their way north. The weary officers were all gathered about the village square that morning, a clear and comfortable day it was, encouraging one another with positive affirmations. They were sure, they all agreed, that things would soon be better; that food and adequate provisions would arrive; that ample support would flock to their cause, and that they would all live to see the British defeated again – at some imprecise time, of course, in the future. It had already been determined that Charlotte was a poor place to try and mount an adequate defense, and that, rather than attempting a questionable stand at that location, it would be more practical for what remained of the army to push further north and seek a more desirable location where it could resupply and sensibly regroup. This course seemed both logical and practical, and that decision provided yet another spark of energy and optimism for the demoralized men.

But that sense of newfound optimism proved short-lived indeed, for terrible reports arrived that morning, news that was as shocking as it was disquieting. The American partisan Thomas Sumter, in command of one of the few remaining forces still then intact in the South, had been surprised at a place called Fishing Creek and his entire force "killed, captured, or dispersed."[17] These reports for the demoralized Continentals proved nothing less than catastrophic. First Camden, now *this*? How could such a thing have happened? How could Sumter have allowed himself to be surprised and routed so completely? Then the answer came – the hated Banastre Tarleton had struck yet again.

CHAPTER FIVE

TARLETON

Just when it seemed that things could not possibly look worse for the Americans, they managed to do just that – and this in spades. For in the early morning hours of August 17, the day following the American defeat at Camden, Banastre Tarleton had his British Legion on the road once again, this time in search of fresh prey in the form of Thomas Sumter and his band of partisan raiders. While the Americans had been whipped terribly at Camden, there still remained some mopping up to attend to, and after a decent night's rest, Lt. Colonel Tarleton was more than up to the task. In Tarleton's own words: "Though the late victory was complete, and the principal army of the Americans was defeated, there yet remained in South Carolina some troops under Colonel Sumpter, well furnished with arms, and provided with cannon."[1]

Sumter— who had been recently and foolishly reinforced by Horatio Gates – was moving north with a column of approximately 800 militia and Continentals.[2] Prior to the battle of the 16th, Sumter had convinced Gates to send him troops in order to surprise a British supply column that was on its way to Camden. Gates responded favorably with North Carolina militia, artillery, and about 100 Continentals, all of which he should have maintained on hand to confront the British at Camden, but Gates' loss would prove Sumter's gain. Sumter's surprise attack worked superbly, and he was able to make off with a raft of British prisoners, wagons loaded with supplies, and the partisan commander. He then promptly headed north to put distance between his small force and Cornwallis, whom he knew was bound to mount a spirited pursuit.

General Charles Earl Cornwallis was not at all amused by any of this, of course, and late on the 16th ordered "Lieutenant-colonel Turnbull, to move instantly with the New – York volunteers, Major Ferguson's detachment, and the loyal militia, in pursuit of Colonel Sumpter."[3] Tarleton's command, along with the light infantry, exhausted from the battle and the pursuit at Camden, were allowed to rest overnight before joining the hunt the following morning. Typically, Tarleton had his men on the road early the next day, driving through the oppressive Carolina heat, hard on Sumter's trail. As Tarleton put it, he "desired to harass or strike at Colonel Sumpter, as he should find it most advisable when he approached him: For this purpose he directed his course next morning through the woods, with three hundred and fifty men and one piece of cannon, and marched up the east side of the Wateree [River], intending to pass it at or near Rocky mount."[4] Tarleton's aim, as stated, was to attack Sumter immediately. But, of course, to accomplish that, he first had to find him.

Informed of Turnbull's movement, Sumter was able to avoid that approaching column by means of a quick march north, but Sumter was initially unaware of Tarleton's involvement in the pursuit, and foolishly stopped for a night of rest near Rocky Mount. "Sumter seems to have indulged a belief that he was safe," notes Light Horse Harry, "and accordingly encamped on the night of the 17th at Rocky Mount, about thirty miles from Camden, and much nearer Cornwallis. To halt for the night within striking distance of the British army was evidently improvident."[5] With Banastre Tarleton pounding through the woods on the east bank of the river like a bloodhound, Sumter's evening delay would prove not only improvident, but fatal.

By the late afternoon hours of the 17th Tarleton had rounded-up some twenty Continental fugitives, and as a result had gained clear intelligence that Sumter was on the march up the opposite bank of the river. Tarleton continued his hurried pursuit on the east side, always scouting ahead for signs of the American column, which he finally located upon his arrival at the ferry crossing near Rocky Mount early on the evening of the 17th. "On his arrival at dusk," Tarleton tells us, "he perceived the enemy's fires about a mile distant from the opposite shore: Immediate care was taken to secure the boats, and instant orders were given to the light troops to pass the night without fires."[6] Tarleton had made up much ground, for as Harry Lee describes, "Lieutenant-Colonel Tarleton moved with his accustomed velocity; and after a rapid march on the 17th, approached Sumter's line of retreat."[7] Across the river from Sumter at Rocky Mount, Tarleton was prepared to assault the Americans if they crossed over the river in front of him, or cross the river himself on boats he had secured for that purpose and continue the hunt for Sumter up the opposite side. But one way or another, it was clear that Tarleton now had Sumter in his sights.

Morning came, August 18, warm and humid, and even in the early morning light it was clear to Tarleton that the Americans had broken camp, but where exactly they were, or where they were headed, remained unclear. So he sent a small party across to the opposite bank with instructions to climb the mount and display a white handkerchief if Sumter's column was spotted moving north along the river. In short order the signal was observed and then, "The boats, with the three-pounder and the infantry, immediately pushed off, and the cavalry crossed the part which was not fordable by swimming."[8] Wasting not a moment, Tarleton was on the move again, closing in for the kill.

By now Sumter had received information that Tarleton had joined the chase, tracking him now along the opposite bank, but for some reason that intelligence failed to light a fire under his movements. Indeed, Sumter departed that morning without even dispatching scouts to locate and observe Tarleton's movements and report back to him; a failure of the most rudimentary of military protocols, and a failure in the art of war that would not be his last.

The sun rose, the heat increased, and the Carolina day proved tedious for man and beast alike. It was a grueling march, and Thomas Sumter did not get far. Moving only eight miles in the morning, Sumter then called it quits at Fishing Creek on the Catawba River, and allowed his column to fall out and rest as his men saw fit. The decision remains to this day incomprehensible. Sumter was moving with captured British prisoners and booty from his successful ambush near Camden, and Light Horse Harry describes the fundamental steps Sumter should have taken after such a success: "the captured with a portion of the victorious corps, ought to be immediately dispatched, with orders to move night and day until out of reach; while the commander, with the least fatigued troops, should hold himself some hours in the rear, sweeping with the best of his cavalry all the country between him and his enemy, thus procuring correct information, which will always secure a retiring corps."[9] Not only did Sumter not have the "correct information" regarding Tarleton's approach, he had no information at all because he had taken no steps to procure it.

Thomas Sumter was then known in South Carolina for his fighting spirit, and he seems certainly to have had a powerful affect on the loyalties of men in the region. But he was also vain, egotistical, and at times utterly heedless of sensible military fundamentals. Says historian John Buchanan: "Thomas Sumter (1734-1832) is not a sympathetic character. Wearing his ego on his shoulder, he had few peers as a prima donna and could spot a slight, intended or not, around a corner. He was careless with security and lives.[10] Known as the "Gamecock," Sumter was certainly brave and combative, at times an effective partisan leader, but his ignorance of, and failure to employ, even the most basic of military practices more than once got him and his followers into serious trouble. Fishing Creek would soon be added to the long list of those instances.

At approximately noon Thomas Sumter called for a halt, stripped off his shirt, and lay down in the grass to sleep. His men followed suit. Cooking fires were lit. Some went down to the river, others slept in what shade they could find, still others headed off to nearby plantations in search of food and drink. A picket was placed on the main road not far from the rear of the column, but no vedettes were established far behind on the road to give good warning of any approaching trouble, and while Sumter did apparently send out a small patrol to scour the road, they did not go very far, and returned somehow without having spotted Tarleton's advance.

Meanwhile, as Sumter's column was resting comfortably at Fishing Creek, Banastre Tarleton was driving his men in ferocious pursuit through the murderous August heat. He had developed solid information that Sumter still had in his possession the British prisoners and wagons he had taken near Camden. "He [Sumter] had taken above one hundred British soldiers," wrote Tarleton, "he had secured one hundred and fifty loyal American militia, and he had captured near fifty wagons loaded with arms, stores, and ammunition. Information was obtained at Rocky mount, that these trophies of success were in Sumpter's possession, and under the escort of his advanced guard."[11] Tarleton had every intention of reclaiming those troops and wagons, but knowing that they were moving at the head of the American column forced him to follow carefully in the rear. He was still convinced that Sumter was unaware of his pursuit, thus he took every precaution to insure that his presence went undetected, while ever watchful of an opportunity to strike.

But the British proved just as affected by the unmerciful heat and oppressive humidity as were Sumter's troops, and Tarleton soon discovered that a great number of his men were so fatigued from the heat and the pace of the march that they simply could not press on. Rather than allow his men to fall out en masse, as had Sumter, however, Tarleton – as usual, utterly remorseless on the chase – vowed to press on. "He therefore determined to separate the cavalry and infantry most able to bear farther hardship, to follow the enemy, whilst the remainder, with the three pounder, took post on an advantageous piece of ground, in order to refresh themselves, and cover retreat in case of accident."[12] Tarleton culled out about one hundred dragoons and sixty light infantry from his exhausted command, the infantry doubling up with the cavalry on horseback in order to press the pursuit, and in short order he was back on the road, across the river and headed north from Rocky Mount.

The British column moved with great care and stealth, following the tracks left along the road by the departing Americans for about five miles, until finally stumbling upon the American picket post near Fishing Creek. The Americans, hidden behind some bushes, were entirely startled by the Redcoats' sudden appearance. Shots rang out, and a dragoon was unhorsed. Exhausted, and now enraged, the dragoons immediately charged the shocked pickets and hacked them to death with their sabers. While understanding their reaction, Tarleton was upset by the loss of a potential source of valuable intelligence so near his prey. "Two of the enemy's vedettes, who were concealed behind some bushes, fired upon the advanced guard as it entered a valley and killed a dragoon of the legion: A circumstance which irritated the foremost of his comrades to such a degree, that they dispatched the two Americans with their sabres before Lieutenant-colonel Tarleton could interpose, or any information be obtained respecting Colonel Sumpter."[13] Tarleton always understood the value of fresh intelligence, even if his dragoons did not.

The column had little choice but to press on, still unmindful of the American's location and movements. Not long thereafter, however, five men of the British van climbed a small hill, spotted the American bivouac just ahead, and signaled to Tarleton below. The British commander rode promptly to the top of the hill, crouched low, and "discovered over the crest of the hill the front of the American camp, perfectly quiet, and not the least alarmed by the fire of the vedettes." It was later discerned that the Americans had heard the shots fired by their own pickets, but had written them off as a few of their own men off on a nearby hunting expedition. So convinced, they had not even bothered to investigate the origin or nature of the shots; a startling indication of the false sense of security the American column, for some reason, was then under. Tarleton, through hard riding and brutal persistence, had stumbled upon the most inviting of targets – a sleeping, unwary, enemy camp. "The decision, and the preparation for the attack," Tarleton later wrote with understatement, "were momentary."[14]

Momentary indeed. One can only imagine the haste with which Lt. Colonel Tarleton prepared to strike such an attractive objective, and there was nothing fancy about the way he went about it. He would attack perhaps 800 Americans with 160 of his own without thinking twice about the odds. The cavalry and infantry were quickly formed into a single line, then advanced with a shout. Before Sumter could even grasp what was happening, British dragoons were charging through his camp, cutting down what few men managed to get to their guns, and sabering or shooting those who tried in vain to escape. Surprise was complete, and the clash at Fishing Creek was over in moments only. Those Americans who managed in frantic haste to dash into the woods and escape were the lucky ones. Tarleton describes the outcome: "The arms and artillery of the continentals were secured before the men could be assembled: Universal consternation immediately ensued throughout the camp; some opposition was, however, made from behind the wagons, in front of the militia. The numbers, and extensive encampment of the enemy, occasioned several conflicts before the action was decided."[15]

Fishing Creek was for the American cause an unmitigated disaster. Light Horse Harry Lee tallies the grim results: "some were killed, others wounded, and the rest dispersed. Sumter himself fortunately escaped, as did about three hundred and fifty of his men; leaving two brass pieces of artillery, arms, and baggage, in possession of the enemy, who recovered their wagons, stores, and prisoners."[16] Just as at Camden, the American defeat was simultaneously complete and catastrophic. "It was another superb coup for Tarleton, overwhelming and quite incredible. Outnumbered five to one, up against seasoned partisans and 100 first-rate Continentals, his audacity and aggressiveness, his refusal to bow to adversity, had once again humiliated the Rebels. For the price of a mere sixteen men killed and wounded the

British killed and wounded 150 Rebels and captured about 310, including all the Continentals."[17]

After the debacle at Camden, the defeated Americans had looked to Sumter's partisans as at least a small command upon which they could rally and perhaps reinforce in the hopes of reestablishing a vital presence in the South. That hope – even if it had been little more than fanciful – had now been utterly dashed. All seemed lost. This, then, was the disquieting news Howard, Kirkwood, Williams and others received as they gathered in the small square at Charlotte, North Carolina on the fair morning of August 19, three days after their bitter defeat at Camden. With the Southern Army dispersed and Sumter routed, where, now, were they to turn?

Unknown to these exhausted, beleaguered officers at the time, however, the winds of fortune were about to shift in their favor. For in late August Daniel Morgan, at long last healthy enough to travel again, would with a small party of trusted, seasoned men, mount his horse in Virginia's Shenandoah Valley, and finally begin the long journey south. [18]

CHAPTER SIX

WILLIAMS

While the news from Fishing Creek proved demoralizing for the men and officers of the Continental Line, there was little time to brood over the loss, even less to dally. For any number of reasons it was clear that those remnants of the Southern Army that had managed to find their way back to Charlotte could not for long remain dormant. Yet the army had been so shattered at Camden that no formal chain of command even existed at Charlotte through which order might be fashioned out of chaos, or direction given for any additional movement, thus inertia reigned. Now more than ever the army required a strong leader, but Horatio Gates had ridden off to Hillsborough where he remained entirely out of touch. Otho Williams, deputy adjutant under Gates when the army had taken the field at Camden, tried his best, but despaired of the results. "No organization, nor order, had yet been attempted to be restored among the few troops that had arrived in Charlotte,"[1] he recalled. Individual men, officers, and scattered units simply made the best of the situation they could manage. "The care of the wounded – the collection of provisions – and the transportation of the heavy baggage (preserved by Major Dean's small guard) and other matters," wrote Williams, "which might, in any way, alleviate the general distress, engaged the attention of those who had no division of the men."

While there were more ranking officers than the remnants of the army required, no one, it seemed, cared to take command, thus the army floundered in a state of structural impotence. "There was no council, nor regular opinion taken, respecting this irksome situation," Williams lamented. "The general idea was, that Charlotte, an open wooded village, without magazines of any sort – without a second cartridge per man – and without a second ration, was not tenable for an hour, against superior numbers, which might enter at every quarter – moreover, it was estimated by those who knew the geography of the country, that even then the victorious enemy might be in the vicinity of the place. It was admitted, by every one, that no place could be more *defenseless*."[2] In short, with no food, ammunition, or organization, the army could not possibly sustain a defense.

Yet fight it might very well have to do, should the British aggressively follow up their victory at Camden, as was soon expected by almost everyone. And why not? One more hard push and all American resistance in the South might well collapse for good, and few thought Cornwallis ignorant of that most critical fact. So, for the Americans, the situation was dire. If attacked again the Southern Army would be routed again – there seemed little question as to the outcome. Who then could say where – or even if – the fleeing remnants might again be consolidated? With no one in command opinions abounded, but opinions achieved nothing, while action remained negligible. What was to be done with the wounded at Charlotte? What was to be done with the many American fugitives still on the run, or those who had escaped Tarleton's attack at Fishing Creek? How was the army to secure food and transportation? Where was the army to go? For these questions, and many more, there were many opinions, but no firm answers.

Otho Williams recalls the pitiful situation: "Difficulties, almost innumerable, presented themselves to obstruct a march – several officers, with small parties, were known to be on the route from Camden – some refugees might possibly escape from Sumter's detachment – many of the wounded were obliged to be left in the old hospital, dependent, probably, on the enemy, or on a few of the inhabitants who were unable to retire – and even some who might have got off on horseback, were deprived of the means by the alarming incident of the preceding night. Were all to be abandoned?

"Time was never more important to a parcel of wretches than now; but, how to take it, whether '*by the forelock*,' as the adage is, or wait its more propitious moments, none of us could decisively resolve."[3]

General Smallwood of Maryland, then the ranking officer, finally made his appearance at Charlotte and, issuing no orders, directives or, for that matter, even appearing to have much concern for those "innumerable difficulties" detailed by Otho Williams, simply put his horse on the road toward Salisbury, his staff following forlornly behind, and headed north. Slowly, one man at a time then, a vast human river of the dispossessed, dragging themselves up the road, the

Continentals, their Indian allies, and many of the locals, began to follow in Smallwood's tracks. Luckless, leaderless, the hungry, wounded, and dispirited began one of the most sad and pathetic marches in American military history; from Charlotte to Salisbury, then eventually on to Hillsborough, N.C.

Dreams of a united, American nation must surely have seemed in tatters. Otho Holland Williams captures the pathetic scene: "By noon a very lengthy line of march, occupied the road from Charlotte to Salisbury. It consisted of the wretched remnant of the late southern army; a great number of distressed whig families, and the whole tribe of Catawba Indians; ..among the rest were six soldiers, who left the hospital with other convalescents; they had all suffered in Buford's unfortunate affair, and had but two sound arms among them, indeed, four of them had *not* one arm among them; and two only an arm a piece; each of them had one linen garment. Those officers and men, who were recently wounded, and had resolution to undertake the fatigue, were differently transported; some in wagons, some in litters, and some on horseback – their sufferings were indescribable. The distresses of the women and children, who fled Charlotte and its neighborhood. The nakedness of the Indians, and the number of their infants and aged persons, and the disorder of the whole line of march, conspired to render it as [a] scene too picturesque and complicated [for] description."[4]

The Catawba Indians, who in prior generations had a reputation as fierce warriors much like the Northern Iroquois, had from the very inception of the Revolutionary War, been firmly on the side of the Americans. They would pay a heavy price for that loyalty. "In 1780 the Catawba reservation became a focal point of rebel resistance, with General Thomas Sumter commanding 500 troops—mostly white, some Native American. Catawba men fought side-by-side with other patriots at Rocky Mount, Hanging Rock, and Fishing Creek, but they had to retreat after the British victory at nearby Camden. Men, women, and children abandoned the reservation and fled north to Virginia. Upon their return several months later, they found their towns had been destroyed and 'all was gone; cattle, hogs, fowls, &c., all gone.'"[5] Their retreat proved a dismal scene, thus was Otho Williams literally at a loss to describe the magnitude of the human suffering he experienced first hand.

Otho Williams, like Howard, Gist, and Smallwood, was one of those Continental officers who had emerged to prominence through the Maryland Line. Born in 1748 in Prince George County, Maryland, his family moved to Frederick County in the Western part of that state while Otho was still young, and not long thereafter both his mother and father passed away. Raised then by a man named Rosa who had married one of his sisters, Otho was in time provided a position in the clerk's office of that county, where he thrived. Just prior to the outbreak of hostilities between Britain and its colonies, Williams took a position in the clerk's office in Baltimore, and after the fireworks at Concord and Lexington he offered his services to a rifle company being raised in Frederick, where he was promptly appointed a lieutenant.

Williams saw action during the siege of Boston, and his rifle company acquitted itself well during Washington's ill-conceived defense of New York in 1776. There Williams, along with many of his company, was taken prisoner during the defense of Fort Washington. Seriously wounded in that engagement, Williams was removed to a brutal prison called the Provost in New York City, "a three-and-a-half story stone building that stood on the east side of the municipal Common, facing Chatham Street, now Park Row. Originally designed to serve as the municipal jail, it had six cells on each of its top two floors and three large vaults in the cellar, which functioned as dungeons." Historian Edwin G. Burrows tells us that "the Provost's most conspicuous occupants after the occupation [of New York] began were high-ranking American officers and 'state prisoners'—civilians accused of supporting the rebellion." Burrows reminds us that the treatment of rebel prisoners while in British hands was virtually barbaric, and that a large percentage of those incarcerated never returned; an almost forgotten aspect of the war. "I think," writes Burrows, "the number of captives may actually have exceeded 30,000 and that 18,000 (60 percent) or more of them did not survive—well over *twice* the number of American soldiers and seamen who fell in battle, now believed to have been around 6,800."[6] Later exchanged, Otho Williams would suffer for the remainder of his life from illness contracted during the poor treatment he endured while in captivity at the Provost; a fate in which he was hardly alone.

Williams stood some five feet, ten inches in height, and was "erect and elegant in form, made for activity rather than strength." Light Horse Harry Lee, who knew Williams well, describes him with personal insight: "His countenance was expressive, and the faithful index of his warm and honest heart. Pleasing in his address, he never failed to render himself acceptable, in whatever circle he moved, notwithstanding a sternness of character, which was sometimes manifested with too much asperity. He was cordial to his friends, but cold to all whose correctness in moral principle became questionable in his mind. ... He possessed that range of mind, although self-educated, which entitled him to the highest military station, and was actuated by true courage which can refuse as well as give battle."

Williams, according to Lee, was adverse to the intrigue and hypocrisy that often characterized the activities of officers like General William Smallwood, for instance, and he never belittled the accomplishments of others in order to advance his own reputation or career. "In the field of battle he was self-possessed, intelligent, and ardent; in camp circumspect, attentive, and systematic; in counsel sincere, deep, and perspicacious."[7] Through competence, courage, and the normal attrition of an army at war, Williams had risen to the rank of Deputy Adjutant General of the Southern Army, and as he watched in despair the human debris of that army stumble up the road from Charlotte, he later recalled the scene as a complex drama that seemed to run the full range of human suffering: "A just representation would exhibit an image of compound wretchedness – care, anxiety, pain, poverty, hurry, confusion, humiliation and dejection, would be characteristic traits in the mortifying picture."[8]

This, then, was what remained of the officers and men of the American Southern Army. At Charlotte those meager remnants could accomplish nothing, thus northward the movement continued, northward until a suitable location could be found where reinforcements, provisions, and time to heal might be discovered. Smallwood, a political intriguer by nature, stopped at Salisbury and there set up a headquarters and began an attempt at restructuring of the army. "At Salisbury, Smallwood resumed the machinations that had characterized his career in the northern theater. Expecting that Gates would be removed, Smallwood began angling for command. First he reorganized the remaining Continentals, whom 'he officered according to his pleasure.' Those officers without a place in the reconstituted units received permission to go to Hillsborough; Howard and Williams, neither of them desiring a confrontation with their argumentative superior, did so without complaint."[9] Robert Kirkwood, as well, continued the northern march, his journal noting that he arrived at Salisbury on the 21st, and then on the 24th: "Marched and crossed the Yadkin river. From thence we marched to Guilford Courthouse. And from thence to Hillsborough."[10]

At Hillsborough, North Carolina the grueling march at long last ground to a merciful halt. And if that area hardly represented a land of milk and honey, it was at least distant enough from Camden to dispel fear of British assault, thus much needed rest and refitting were in order. Williams recalled that, "Hillsborough had been a place of rendezvous for all the militia raised in the interior for North Carolina; and a stage of refreshment for all the troops which had marched from the northward to succor Charleston, or re-enforce the southern army; consequently, the resources of the country had been generally collected and applied."[11]

In that sense, then, there was scarcely enough food to feed this newest collection of refugees or roofs to shelter them, and the physical needs of the men quickly overwhelmed the capabilities of the small community. Men were quartered in homes with local residents, others put up in tents that had been pitched on the green near the courthouse. At the time the North Carolina Assembly was in session nearby, and the lawmakers, noting the primitive conditions and lack of food, took immediate steps to try and provide at least some meager relief. "A comfortable supply of fresh meat, cornmeal, and wheal flour, was procured," Williams noted, "for the hospital; and the rest of the men were subsisted by provisions furnished by the state commissaries, in part, and partly by the old expedient of collecting by detachments – an expedient which gave great umbrage to the country."[12]

The disaster at Camden, Sumter's defeat, and the seemingly endless requirements forced upon the citizens of North Carolina, began to have a very negative effect upon the American cause. Suddenly it was the Continentals, not the British, who were seen as predatory interlopers, and the citizens began to arm themselves in retaliation. It was a problem that constantly plagued the Continental Army, North or South. George Washington had previously complained, for instance: "How disgraceful to the army is it that the peaceable inhabitants, our countrymen and fellow citizens, dread our halting among them, even for a night and are happy when they get rid of us?"[13] But in North Carolina it had gone far beyond dread, for now the citizens in the area surrounding Hillsborough had taken up arms. "Even in Chatham county," notes Otho Williams, "a considerable body took arms and threatened to disperse the assembly of the state from Hillsborough; indeed so serious was the alarm upon this occasion, that to guard against a surprise of the town, on a night when the insurgents were confidently expected, all the troops were kept under arms the whole night. ... The inhabitants were ordered to arm, and even the members of the assembly thought it incumbent on them, to arm themselves also;"[14] a situation which soon led to one of the more humorous episodes of the Southern campaign.

It seemed appropriate at the time to have a regular officer of the Continental Line handle the local militia, who were often willing in spirit but bereft of military know-how, thus prone to strange and unfortunate miscues. It was assumed that this officer would call the militia to assembly, arrange them properly in squads then place those squads in a sensible defensive perimeter around the town, all of this administered within the strictures of a rigid military protocol. The Continental officer arrived at the prescribed hour and found a passel of civilians armed, or in the process of arming themselves, near the courthouse whom the officer naturally assumed to be the militia he had been ordered to take in hand. With stiff military bearing this Continental officer, no doubt desirous of making a sharp and immediate impression on the undisciplined militiamen, brought the assembly to attention and began ordering the militia about in a gruff but disciplined manner that perfectly suited the occasion. What the officer did not realize, however, was that the men he was addressing in such a brusque manner were not the militia at all, but rather the body of North Carolina legislators who had come to arm themselves in the event of a partisan assault. Rather than voicing outrage, however, the assembly of legislators quickly fell in and followed orders without complaint or protest, and the picture of this junior officer ordering the North Carolina legislature about in the strictest military terms was only later appreciated for its obvious comical elements. "No exception, however, was taken to the conduct of the officer," Williams later recalled. "The circumstance was mentioned afterwards, only as one of these ludicrous incidents (and there were many) which occurred during the night of the alarm."[15]

Meanwhile back at Camden, South Carolina, General Cornwallis had decided not to pursue the ragtag remains of what was left of the American Army, and from the British perspective this may well have been one of the great miscalculations of the war. A hard and energetic pursuit by his cavalry alone may well have scattered American resistance to the point that it might never again have consolidated south of Virginia, but that possibility, of course, must remain forever in the realm of speculation. Indeed, Cornwallis had many good reasons of his own not to push the Americans. First and foremost, his army, while clearly winning an overwhelming victory at Camden, had still been roughly handled by the Continentals during their stand on the American right, and the casualty list – sixty-eight dead and two hundred fifty-six wounded[16] – confirmed the fact. These wounded required care and provisions, and the British Army's supply line was, at Camden, already stretched extremely thin, reaching all the way back to Charleston harbor. To stretch that line even further on a march to Salisbury, North Carolina or beyond might well have broken it entirely, and left the British stranded for want of food and material in a barren country that could not well support them.

Tarleton readily admits that, "The immediate advance of the King's troops into North Carolina would undoubtedly, at this critical period, have been productive of various and important advantages." But that advance was not to be because "many material requisites and necessary arrangements were not in convenient state or sufficient forwardness to warrant the undertaking. The number of sick in the hospital, the late addition of the wounded, the want of troops, and the deficiency of stores upon the frontier, operated with the present heat of the climate, and the scarcity of provision in North Carolina." Cornwallis still intended to push into North Carolina, but with Sumter now out of the picture, and the American Army beaten and scattered, he decided that haste was not of necessity. So the British Army retired upon Camden to await resupply, recovery, and reinforcements, but still with a strategic eye upon North Carolina. "Major Ferguson's corps of rangers," Tarleton tells us, "and about one thousand loyal militia, were advanced to the western borders, to hold communications with the inhabitants of Tryon county till the King's troops under Earl Cornwallis were in condition to advance."[17]

Major Patrick Ferguson was a capable officer, and his force was hardly insufficient in terms of its strength, makeup, or determination. From Cornwallis' perspective, Ferguson's advance on the western side of the mountains was meant to screen the main body's anticipated march north, shielding it from partisan raiders or the Over Mountain Men, those settlers and frontiersmen who occupied the uncharted regions on the western slopes of the Blue Ridge. Many of these families had settled upon Cherokee lands that were out of bounds by British law, and the Over Mountain Men were always fearful of British retaliation. While disorganized and generally undisciplined, the Over Mountain Men were nevertheless known to be tough and wily fighters, and Cornwallis realized that keeping them from bushwhacking the British Army's long line of supply was of paramount importance to any major movement north. That job would fall to Major Patrick Ferguson.

Ferguson got his orders in late August, just as Daniel Morgan was saddling-up to begin his long ride south to join Horatio Gates, but rather than initiating a campaign of pacification, Ferguson tossed down the gauntlet and threatened the Over Mountain Men with death and destruction if they remained in opposition to the king, and this was interpreted by the settlers as a threat to their lands, indeed their very existence west of the Blue Ridge. Ferguson's verbal threat was sent by means of a paroled rebel rider: "If they did not desist from their opposition to the British arms, he would march over the mountains, hang their leaders, and lay their country waste with fire and sword."[18] Clumsy and foolishly inflammatory, Ferguson's attempt at intimidation would in the end have the exact opposite effect, and he would pay with his life for his mistake; a story that will soon be told.

Feeling now that the rebellious forces in South Carolina had been thoroughly subdued, at Camden Cornwallis began again administering the provisions of a harsh proclamation previously issued by General Clinton which called for all prior rebels to swear an oath of allegiance to the king. Those who were discovered to have violated their oath were dealt with harshly. "Death was again denounced against all persons," fumed Light Horse Harry Lee, "who, having received protections, should be found in arms against the king's troops. Some of the militia, taken in the late defeat, being charged with that offence, were actually hung."[19] This was, like Ferguson's provocative threat to the Over Mountain Men, a move occasioned more by hubris than any social or military necessity, and it would soon backfire on the British cause.

As to his next move, Cornwallis' thinking at the time was made clear in a dispatch dated August 21 written to Lord George Germain in London. In part it reads, "On the morning of the 17th I dispatched proper people into North Carolina [Ferguson], with directions to our friends there to take arms and assemble immediately and to seize the most violent people, and all military stores and magazines belonging to the rebels, and to intercept all stragglers from the routed army; and I have promised to march without loss of time to their support. Some necessary supplies from the army are now on their way from Charles town, and I hope that their arrival will enable me to move in a few days."[20] But Cornwallis would not move in a few days. Indeed, he would not begin the movement north until September 8, and then it would take over two weeks for the British Army simply to gain Charlotte, thus giving the beaten Continentals a much needed breather in order to gather themselves and regroup at Hillsborough.

In North Carolina, Smallwood's attempts to wrest command of the remnants of the Southern Army from Gates got him nowhere, and in time he followed orders from Gates to march with his troops from Salisbury to Hillsborough in order to consolidate what was left of the army. There "Gates, Smallwood, and Gist consolidated the surviving Continentals into a single regiment that numbered between 700 and 800 men. The Delaware Regiment was reduced to two companies and the Maryland regiments were similarly restructured."[21] Otho Williams was placed in command of this single Continental regiment with John Eager Howard as his second. It was a small, but tough, veteran unit, and with rest and time the spirit of the Continental soldiers began to improve dramatically. Otho Williams, for one, was amazed at the transformation. "Absolutely without pay; almost destitute of clothing; often with only a half ration, and never with a whole one (without substituting one article for another) not a soldier was heard to murmur, after the third or fourth day of being encamped. Instead of meeting and conferring in small sullen squads, as they had formerly done, they filled up the intervals from duty, with manly exercises and field sports; in short the officers had very soon, the entire confidence of the men, who divested themselves of all unnecessary care, and devoted themselves to duty and past-time, within the limits assigned them."[22]

As the van of the British Army slowly lumbered toward Charlotte in late September, the Americans gradually regained their strength and confidence, and so it was until one day late that month when the men and officers of the army looked up as several unexpected riders appeared in camp. One of those riders, a large, powerful man was immediately recognized by Otho Williams who had campaigned with him at Boston, and while many did not recognize him personally, almost all were perfectly aware of his reputation. No doubt a silent but palpable thrill swept through the ranks of tattered Continentals as the man dismounted in front of the courthouse in Hillsborough where Horatio Gates now made his headquarters. For as Otho Williams aptly describes the moment, "Colonel Morgan of Virginia, whose heroic conduct under General Montgomery at Quebec, General Gates at Saratoga, and other meritorious actions, ... had arrived in camp."[23]

CHAPTER SEVEN

MORGAN

While Daniel Morgan had become aware of the American defeat at Camden long before he rode into the camp at Hillsborough, he probably did not understand just how much that defeat had impacted his future role with what little remained of the Southern Army. Not until he reviewed the troops in person, and saw with his own eyes the dire state of the army, would that picture truly crystallize. And a pretty picture it was not.

It can be recalled that in June Horatio Gates had offered Morgan command of a corps of light infantry, but the fact of the matter was, by late September the entire Southern Army had scarcely the manpower to comprise a single legitimate "corps," better yet any number of them that might take the field as a collective army. The manpower that had comprised the army at Camden was now dead, wounded, taken prisoner, or scattered to the seven winds, and what remained was barely a shadow of its previous numbers. Immediately prior to Morgan's arrival, for instance, Horatio Gates had convened a board of officers that "determined that all the effective men should be formed into two battalions, constituting one regiment, to be completely officered, and provided for in the best possible manner that circumstances would admit – sick and convalescent were to remain – but, all the invalids were to be sent home – and the supernumerary officers were to repair to their respective states to assist in the recruiting service."[1] This reorganization accomplished, returns from all these newly formed units were called for, and upon receipt the number of active officers and men firmly accounted for. The results proved far less than encouraging.

Of the Maryland Line, only 1,052 officers and men remained, and this number included 62 musicians. The Delaware troops had suffered even more grievously. Only 189 officers and men now answered the role call for the Delaware Line, and of this number fourteen were officers, eleven musicians, and the remainder either non-commissioned officers or rank and file. Thus the total effective strength of the two Continental Lines – the very backbone of the Southern Army – in late September tallied a mere 1,241 officers and men, and of these only 926 were rank and file infantry.[2] It was no doubt apparent to Daniel Morgan upon his arrival at Hillsborough that the Southern Army existed in a figurative sense only, and that any "corps" he therefore assumed command of would likewise be a corps in name alone.

Yet just as something is always better than nothing at all, Horatio Gates slowly began to pull together what little remained of his command, his equipment, and his shattered reputation. Over the intervening weeks some new militia units – rough, ill-clothed, and untested in combat – marched into camp to augment the count of effective troops, if not in terms of real fighting capacity, at least in terms of the muster roles. Old, forgotten guns and equipment were dragged back into camp. Otho Williams tells us that "Two brass field-pieces, which General Gates had left under a small guard at Buffalo Ford, for want of horses, the first day of his march after taking the command[in August], were brought to camp with a few iron pieces picked up at Hillsborough, and formed a little [artillery] park in the center of the ragged regiment of Maryland and Delaware troops, which constituted *the southern army*, until the 16th of September, when Colonel Buford arrived from Virginia with the mangled remains of his unfortunate regiment, re-enforced by about two hundred raw recruits, all of them in a ragged condition, uniforms and clothing were to be sent after them, but never arrived."[3] Soon thereafter another group of Virginia militia marched into camp destitute even of weapons with which they might at least defend themselves, and still more small bodies of militia gradually trickled into camp like driblets from a faulty faucet. While these new arrivals were hardly the veteran fighting stock required to truly reinvigorate the army, they at least had a positive affect upon morale, and soon, we are told, "The officers and men began to recover their usual spirits."[4]

Yet if spirits rose merely as a result of the sputtering arrival of this motley collection of militia, it manifestly demonstrates just how low morale had deteriorated at the time, and unfortunately that sense of deteriorating morale now extended well beyond the Southern Theater. For these were trying, virtually heartbreaking times for the American

Revolution. While we have already catalogued the pathetic conditions at Hillsborough that September, in the fall of 1780 the situation in the Northern Theater had also taken a drastic turn for the worse. Indeed, in that theater Washington's army had not fought a major engagement since the battle at Monmouth Court House in the spring of 1778. Essentially fought to a draw at Monmouth, Clinton was able to escape with his army intact across New Jersey and eventually settle comfortably into a defensive posture in New York City. Stalemate ensued. Clinton had no desire to sally forth and risk his army – which had been reduced in size due to troop redeployments to the Caribbean in order to face a potential French incursion in that theater – while Washington could not chance a bloody repulse against the strong defensive position the British had assumed.

Years passed as both armies essentially did little more than eye one another pensively across the marshes and rolling hills of the New Jersey landscape. That would change, however, in September 1780 for – just as Cornwallis was marching his army into Charlotte, North Carolina, and as Daniel Morgan was about to arrive in Hillsborough to offer his services to Horatio Gates – on September 23 "Major John André, Clinton's aide, was apprehended by three militia men near Tarrytown, New York. He carried identification as John Anderson, a military inventory of West Point, and a pass signed by General Benedict Arnold, the commanding officer of West Point. Arnold had been cooperating with the British for over a year and had worked hard to achieve command of West Point as part of his deal. Now his infamous treason was discovered. Through a series of lucky circumstances, Arnold was able to flee, but André was to pay with his life."[5] Arnold's treachery proved a painful shock to the cause of liberty and rocked George Washington to the core. Arnold would escape and eventually take up arms against his country, while André was hung as a spy on October 2. That news, devastating as it was, would not reach Gates, Cornwallis, or Morgan for weeks, and by then they would have far more pressing matters on their hands to deal with.

We are told that Daniel Morgan was greeted upon arrival by Horatio Gates with great warmth and enthusiasm, and why not, for now at least Gates had a senior officer at his side whom he was confident could be trusted both on and off the field of battle.[6] Gates promptly introduced Colonel Morgan to the North Carolina legislators, with whom he shared the courthouse, and Morgan's reputation as a fighter went a long way to restore at least some confidence in the army's senior leadership. Gates then, it can be presumed, took Morgan on a short tour of the camp, and if Morgan was either shocked or disappointed by what he discovered, the record does not reflect it. He had ridden for the better part of a month to join the Southern command, and he would fight with that army, no matter its condition.

Yet shortly after Morgan's arrival apprehension was clearly in the air. Riders had for several days been arriving with disquieting news – the British were once again on the move. Major Patrick Ferguson, it can be recalled, had been dispatched by Cornwallis into the western part of North Carolina, and a few weeks thereafter Cornwallis himself put the main body in motion. While that invasion force moved at an almost a glacial pace, it moved nevertheless, and by late September the British had taken Charlotte, and Cornwallis immediately deployed units further north on the road toward Salisbury. Where would the British stop? Were they bound for Hillsborough? The North Carolina legislature was abuzz with worry.

In response to this threat the North Carolina Board of War took immediate action. It requested that Gates send General Smallwood west, along with those Continentals fit for campaigning, to join with the North Carolina militia in order to confront Cornwallis. "The board also requested that Colonel Morgan, 'the famous Partisan' accompany Smallwood. As the board wrote regarding Morgan, that his well-known 'Character as a Soldier' would infuse new morale into the militia."[7] It was agreed by all that the few troops that might be scraped together could not possibly take on the British Army nose-to-nose, so to speak, in open battle, thus a campaign of hit-and-run tactics was suggested, and everyone knew that Morgan was a master of this style of warfare. Gates believed this to be the only method by which Cornwallis' advance might be delayed, and he, of course, realized just how effective Morgan might be in command of such a deployment. But that same situation also suggested a potential problem. Morgan had not yet received his commission as brigadier general, and that small problem, Gates knew, might easily escalate into an even larger one. "Morgan was already on edge because he had received no word from Congress about his promotion; he correctly considered himself a superior soldier to the North Carolinians. That Morgan's explosive nature might collide with the imperious attitude of certain Southern militia leaders who saw their own locales as private preserves was alarmingly clear to Gates."[8]

To remove this potential problem Gates again wrote to Congress, reminding them of the need for Morgan's advancement, and the North Carolina Board of War followed suit, urging Morgan's immediate promotion. Secondly, Gates shrewdly reminded Smallwood of Morgan's volatile propensities, perhaps recalling the incident while the Northern Army had been encamped in New Jersey. That incident had by then become legend within the service, recounted earlier herein, when Morgan had openly and violently confronted a Congressional representative whom he considered disrespectful of George Washington, thus Gates sagely suggested that Smallwood might be wise to maintain his distance.[9]

For Daniel Morgan was not of the aristocratic stock from which many Continental officers had sprung. Morgan, rather, was a son of the frontier, an inveterate drinker, gambler, and brawler during his wagon hauling days. Indeed, Morgan was as well known for his fearsome fists as he was for his command of light infantry, and a single insolent word spoken at the wrong time or in the wrong manner, might well have placed William Smallwood on the wrong end of a large pair of knuckles; an event that might have haunted both men to their graves. While Morgan had grown enormously as a leader of men in his mature years, his past seemed often to hover just below his present, and it was a past as much filled with drunken, rowdy spats as it was with wise and commendable achievements. "The Daniel Morgan of those days was well known to sheriffs and magistrates," John Buchanan tells us, "being charged among other things with horse stealing, arson, assault and battery, and arming himself and refusing the lawful order of a deputy sheriff. Had he not possessed driving ambition and a strong character he might well have ended just another frontier ruffian one step ahead of the hangman's noose."[10] But time, hard work, uncompromising desire, and a dose of good fortune had turned Daniel Morgan from an unruly brawler into a respected husband, farmer, and military leader par excellence. Yet his pride remained typically razor-thin for a man who had risen from such common threads, and his temper as a result remained potentially volcanic. In the simplest terms, Daniel Morgan was not a man to be toyed with while William Smallwood had an uncomfortable record of toying with his military inferiors.

Finally, and most significantly, Gates formed a small "corps" of light infantry for Morgan to handle as an independent command apart from Smallwood, just as he had promised to do at their meeting earlier that June. Though much leaner than originally contemplated by either man, the new corps did consist of some of Gate's finest men and officers: "three companies of Continental infantry, sixty Virginia riflemen, and seventy cavalrymen."[11] John Eager Howard was given command of the infantry; Robert Kirkwood the Delaware regiment under Howard, and William Washington, a cousin of George Washington's, commanded the small detachment of dragoons. Washington, like many of the Continental officers in the South, had suffered more than once at the hands of Banastre Tarleton, and had a score to settle with the British cavalryman. He would prove an excellent officer of cavalry in the coming days. "At the same time," Otho Williams recounts, "it was contemplated to send forward as many of the regular troops, as could be tolerably equipped for service; and it fortunately happened that, at that time, the state agents had forwarded to Hillsborough, a small supply of coarse clothing and other articles convenient for the purpose."[12] Not only would Morgan have his own corps, but they would march from Hillsborough newly fitted in fresh uniforms to boot.

Morgan's spirits may have been rekindled by all of this, but his mission remained fuzzy. He was to take his corps south and either feel for or harass the British in the vicinity of Charlotte. His was, in the modern parlance, a reconnaissance in force. No doubt Horatio Gates thought Morgan far better suited to outline his own mission than Gates might do for him, and trusted that Morgan would handle any unexpected trouble with his accustomed skill. Rain delayed the march for several days, but the weather finally cleared, and "The little corps, minus Washington's cavalry, left Hillsborough on October 7" reaching Salisbury after a leisurely eight-day march, yet having discovered no sign of the British van.[13] So there Morgan encamped for three days while sending out scouts in all directions to locate the nearest enemy postings. None were found; which seemed odd, to say the least. After three days rest Morgan had his corps back on the road again. "Yet he showed his customary vigor by inquiring of the roads to the west, of the ability of the militiamen, and of the number of men who owned rifles. Though interested in adding experienced fighters to his corps, Morgan's immediate attention was directed to his shortage of food; he found nothing to purchase except meat and flour."[14] Robert Kirkwood tells us that on the 22nd the infantry "Marched to Six mile run there joined No. Carolina

Militia under Command of Genl. Davidson." Then on the 25th the corps "Moved our Encampment in Front of the Militia" in a hamlet known as New Providence, only fourteen miles from Charlotte. Importantly, while resting there, Kirkwood noted in his journal, "Col. Morgan Received his Commission of Brigadier Genl. From Congress."[15]

Great news this was! The long awaited promotion to brigadier must have sent Morgan's spirits soaring, yet there was something afoot that must also have seemed rather odd, if not downright troubling, especially to a veteran commander like Morgan. All the scouts sent south and west had returned with the same news: the British could not be located anywhere near Charlotte. Why? Cornwallis had marched into North Carolina clearly intent on subduing that state, his arrival sending the state leaders into a near panic, yet now no sign of his army could be discovered. The British, once firmly entrenched near Charlotte, were *gone*! It seemed to make no sense. "Lord Cornwallis, without any known adequate cause," wrote Otho Williams, "thought proper to retire through Charlotte, cross the Wateree River, and encamp at Winnsborough [South Carolina]."[16]

The fearful British invasion seemed to have faded like a phantom into the mist. What could have made Cornwallis suddenly abandon his plans? The answer to this troubling question seemed a complete mystery to the Americans at the time, and the explanation will be presently revealed.

CHAPTER EIGHT

CORNWALLIS

The fundamental problem with Cornwallis' much-feared invasion of North Carolina was not the count of effective troops under his command – although they would ultimately prove inadequate – the routes chosen, or even the daunting logistical problems inherent in such a distant movement. Rather, the most essential problem with the plan was the set of gross miscalculations and false assumptions upon which the entire campaign was founded. General Cornwallis firmly believed, for instance, that with the twin American disasters at Camden and Fishing Creek, all serious, organized rebel resistance in the Carolinas had been subdued. With American resistance thus demolished, the British should only then have to march north and show the flag, so to speak, such that the vast numbers of loyal subjects who had been previously cowed into submission by the rebellious Americans, would rise to the king's cause and flock to his standard. The British march north would therefore be augmented each step of the way by fresh regiments of loyal troops, recently and happily mustered to the cause, while provisioned by the ample plantations and ready hearts of the king's loyal subjects. Whatever rebel sentiment that might still be perking between the Atlantic and the Blue Ridge would simply evaporate under the sheer weight of this joint British/American juggernaut. The South would then happily rejoin Britain and the American Revolution would collapse for want of support.

This was in essence Lord Cornwallis' view of the situation at the time in the American South, and in this he was not alone, so much so, in fact, that we might call this conception of things the British Model. Indeed, this was the view that dominated the hierarchy of British thinking – from Camden to Charleston, from Charleston to New York, from New York to London – and the fact that this strategy was based upon a profound misreading of American values, attitudes, and abilities, all firmly conditioned by British aristocratic hubris, would require six years of war to demonstrate, and even then some few would refuse to face the truth.

Typical of this mindset, was a letter sent by Sir Henry Clinton, shortly after he had forced the surrender of Charleston in July. Writing to Secretary of State George Germain in London, in part it reads, "With grateful pleasure I farther report to your lordship, that the inhabitants from every quarter repair to the detachments of the army, and to this garrison, to declare their allegiance to the King, and to offer their services, in arms, in support of his government. In many instances they have brought prisoners their former oppressors or leaders; and I may venture to assert, that there are few men in South Carolina who are not either our prisoners, or in arms with us."[1]

Likewise Cornwallis wrote to Lord Germain in August, shortly after the twin British victories at Camden and Fishing Creek, his confidence in the supremacy of British arms throughout the Carolinas now set firmly in stone. "The rebel forces being at present dispersed, the internal commotions and insurrections in the province will now subside. But I shall give directions to inflict exemplary punishment on some of the most guilty, in hopes to deter others in future from sporting with allegiance and oaths, and with the lenity and generosity of the British government."[2] So confident were the British of success in North Carolina, that Clinton issued orders to General Alexander Leslie in New York, ordering him to the Chesapeake Bay with a contingent of troops to "pursue such measures as you shall judge most likely to answer the purpose of this expedition; the principal object of which is to make a diversion in favor of Lieutenant-general Earl Cornwallis, who, by the time you arrive there, will probably be acting in the back parts of North Carolina."[3] The idea was that Leslie, acting as a diversion, would draw off any potential militia units in Virginia while Cornwallis had free reign throughout North Carolina, the two then to rendezvous somewhere in Southern Virginia after Cornwallis had successfully subdued the North state.

These dispatches suggest far more than mere overconfidence. The prospect of opposition, better yet failure, at the moment seemed to the British military and political hierarchy utterly implausible, yet those possibilities – always very real in any enterprise as unpredictable as war – were not entertained at the time because the worldview of officers like Cornwallis, Clinton, Leslie, and the brothers

Howe before them, were simply bereft of such notions. And they were not included because they did not correspond to the structural elements of the British Model; again, the notion that the rebels were at all times no more than inferior and undisciplined warriors; that the vast majority of colonial citizens remained firmly loyal to the king and would, not only rise to his standard, but happily offer generous support to the king's army; that the British army could somehow occupy and enforce martial law over a vast and untamed land, a land in many areas unmapped, often wanting even of roads, and divided by a staggering number of wild, unbridged rivers, indeed, a land utterly unlike *anything* they had ever encountered in Europe. This British Model, this autocratic world view, proved in the end a stupendous miscalculation, a self-imposed fiction so overreaching that it came very close to delusion, and in war delusion generally begets disaster. Enter General Charles Earl Cornwallis.

That Charles Cornwallis of all people should have fallen prey to the British Model only proves how beguiling, how captivating and controlling was its hold on the British, aristocratic psyche. For while Charles Cornwallis had been born to English royalty – his father was the First Earl Cornwallis, and upon his father's passing in 1762 he assumed the title of earl – while a member of the House of Lords prior to the revolution, Cornwallis consistently opposed the King's American policies, voting against many of the punitive acts and taxes that the king insisted upon, and which the American colonists despised. Thus it can be rightfully asserted that Cornwallis may have been born to royalty, but he was his own man when it came to policy, no matter whose feathers he ruffled.

Born in 1738 in London, by the outbreak of hostilities in the New World, Cornwallis had been in the British military service since his eighteenth year, and had seen considerable action on the Continent during the Seven Years War (known as the French and Indian War in North America). He returned to England after his father's death and assumed his father's seat in the House of Lords. In 1768 Cornwallis met and wed the lovely Jemima Jones, and from all evidence their life together seems to have been both pleasant and loving. They enjoyed a son and daughter, and for a few years Cornwallis put both politics and military service aside, and doted on his wife and young family.

But country soon called, and Cornwallis answered, returning to both political and military duty. His star steadily ascended. "He was made aide-de-camp to the King in 1765, a member of the Privy Council in 1770, and Constable of the Tower of London in 1771,"[4] all positions of power and approval within the king's government. After the hostilities at Lexington and Concord, Cornwallis volunteered his service, and was promptly promoted to the rank of Lieutenant General. He served as a deputy officer to Henry Clinton, and saw considerable action in the campaigns in New York, New Jersey, and in the region surrounding Philadelphia.

In the late fall of 1778, Cornwallis returned to England on leave from the colonies, and there he found his young wife wasting away, deathly ill. For weeks he attended to her needs, but she continued to lose ground, and she finally died in late January, 1779. Cornwallis was shattered by her loss. For him, whose marriage had been far more than a stepping stone to power, the loss of his life's love proved almost overwhelming. Desperate, he soon returned to the service in North America, where he threw himself into the war as only someone bereaved can do. The army became his new love and victory his only goal. While hardly innovative – few if any generals on either side of the conflict could be considered innovative – Cornwallis ultimately came to be known as a solid field general with a willingness to march hard and fight even harder. It was this man, then, wounded, grieving, yet loyal and driven, who in the summer of 1780 had taken command of the British Army in the South.

Cornwallis was certainly no fool, yet every expectation he had concerning his army's movement into North Carolina during the fall of 1780, every thread of the British Model, so to speak, soon unraveled right before his eyes, and most unraveled almost instantaneously. Tarleton explains, for instance, with obvious understatement that "Notwithstanding the commotions had been violent, and almost general, in South Carolina, it was imagined and hoped that these internal troubles would subside, when the inhabitants gained information of the late distinguished superiority which had attended his Majesty's arms: But accident now discovered how much the enemy's exceeded the King's friends in artifice."[5] Not only did the "commotions" not subside, but they increased radically, and they increased despite the demonstrated superiority of his majesty's arms. This was not a planned uprising or coordinated partisan assault, by the way, but rather a general rebellious response whenever and wherever the opportunity presented itself to oppose the king's forces – precisely the *opposite* of what had been predicted by the British Model.

The main players in this rebellious drama on the American side were initially William Richardson Davie, William Lee Davidson, Francis Marion, and Thomas Sumter, the latter who had by the strength of his personality alone managed to raise another partisan band, despite his humiliating defeat at Fishing Creek. Indeed, Davie, as intrepid a hit-and-run operative as any the American side ever produced, was waiting for Cornwallis' van the day it rode into Charlotte with a small contingent of North Carolina militia just to give the British a taste of what they could expect if they pushed their campaign deeper into the state. It was hardly the greeting Cornwallis had anticipated.

The van that day was Tarleton's British Legion, minus Tarleton himself who was ill with a terrible fever. We will let Light Horse Harry Lee describe the action: "Colonel Davie, being informed of the approach of the enemy, and relying on the firmness of his troops, determined to give them an earnest of the spirit of the country into which they had entered. Dismounting his cavalry, who, in addition to the sword and pistol, were armed with muskets, he posted them in front of the court-house, under cover of a strong stone wall, breast high. His infantry, also dismounted, with Graham's volunteers, were advanced eighty yards in front, on each side of the street, covered by the inclosures of the village."

Spotting what appeared to be an ambush ahead, the dragoons of the British Legion, now under Major Hanger due to Tarleton's absence, formed on the village square, and with bugles blaring, went pounding down the street directly toward the Americans. Again, Light Horse Harry narrates the action: "The moment these parties engaged, Hanger rushed along the street to the court-house, where Davie poured in his fire, and compelled him to recede. The dragoons fell back hastily, and were rallied on the common." British infantry deployed rapidly on each flank, and began to sweep forward, forcing Davie, who was now substantially outnumbered, to fall back. "The British light infantry continued to advance, and the action was vigorously renewed on our flanks. The centre reserved its fire for the cavalry, who, now returning to the charge, met with a repetition of their first reception, and retired in confusion to their former ground."

The British infantry kept up the advance, however, and Davie gave ground while reforming east of town. Cornwallis – furious that his famed British Legion had been twice repulsed by the unruly Americans – flew into a rage, lambasted the dragoons, insisting upon yet another effort. This was promptly attempted and again violently repulsed. Charging forward, Harry Lee tells us, the British dragoons, "meeting with our brave corps, now mounted, they received as usual a well-aimed fire, and were again repulsed... The enemy lost twelve non-commissioned officers and privates killed; Major Hanger, Captains Campbell and McDonald, and many privates were wounded."[6]

This affair at Charlotte was a minor action to be sure, but it provided jarring evidence that the "commotions" and "insurrections" previously thought pacified by the British high command were in fact still alive and well. In war as in life, reality seems often to have a way of embarrassing our most cherished convictions. Marching into North Carolina was going to be no picnic after all.

Davie, of course, never intended to stand and fight the entire British Army, only to give the lead element a taste of what might be expected in the future, and in this his little stand proved entirely successful. Davie, Davidson, Sumter, and Francis Marion, would harass Cornwallis' army at every opportunity, and rapidly turn this first British occupation of North Carolina into a nightmare. With small garrisons strung across South Carolina from Ninety Six in the west to Georgetown in the east, the British Army was utterly susceptible to guerrilla warfare, and guerrilla warfare is exactly what it got. Tarleton: "The foraging parties were every day harassed by the inhabitants, who did not remain at home, to receive payment for the produce of their plantations, but generally fired from covert places, to annoy the British detachments. Ineffectual attempts were made upon convoys coming from Camden, and the intermediate post at Blair's mill; but individuals with expresses were frequently murdered. An attack was directed against the picket at Polk's mills, two miles from the town."[7] Put simply, the British army could not move without violent harassment, and single riders or dispatch carriers were routinely shot from their horses.

Every assumption central to the British Model soon unraveled under the grinding weight of reality. The land and people were supposed to support the invasion, but the exact opposite proved the case. "The town and environs abounded with inveterate enemies," Tarleton admitted; "the plantations in the neighbourhood were small and uncultivated; the roads narrow, and crossed in every direction; and the whole face of the country covered with close and thick woods. In addition to these disadvantages, no estimation could be made of the sentiments of half of the inhabitants of North Carolina, whist the royal army remained at Charlotte town... The vigilance and animosity of these surrounding districts checked the exertions of the well affected, and totally destroyed all communication between the King's troops and the loyalists in the other parts of the province."[8] At Charlotte the British Army could not forage for food, maintain open communication with its far-flung posts, move without violence or remain for long without supplies. Quickly, very quickly, the invasion went from hopeful to hopeless, these multiple miscalculations rendering the powerful British Army almost as impotent as a beached whale on a sandy spit. As daunting and debilitating as these problems proved to be, the final miscalculation that ultimately forced Cornwallis' hand involved the column previously sent over the Blue Ridge to control the Over Mountain Men under Major Patrick Ferguson.

One of the numerous and unexpected "commotions" that ensued during this period was an assault upon the British post at Augusta, Georgia. This assault was gallantly resisted by the British garrison, and ultimately repulsed. The American assaulting column then withdrew and began a winding retreat back toward the mountains. Getting wind of this movement, the British commander at Ninety Six, Lieutenant Colonel John Cruger, conceived a joint attack upon the American retreat by a contingent of British from Ninety Six and Ferguson's command. The idea was to catch and crush the fleeing Americans between the two, and initially it seemed a sound proposition.

Ferguson readily agreed with Cruger's suggestion and began a movement toward Gilbert Town, the direction by which he hoped to waylay the retreating American column. Unfortunately for Ferguson, Cruger called off his part of the attack once he had drifted too far from Ninety Six to adequately defend his principal post, but Ferguson pressed on, now also aware of the fact that another strong column of rebels was fast approaching from another direction. It can be recalled that Ferguson had sent a declaration to the Over Mountain Men that they had better lay down their arms and desist from any further rebellious activity, lest he hang their leaders and burn their villages to the ground, and that threat, Ferguson was soon to learn, had been taken very seriously by the settlers on the western slopes of the Blue Ridge. But rather than lay down their arms as Ferguson had either hoped or presumed they would, they actually took them up, and the Over Mountain Men were now, virtually en masse, on the hunt for Ferguson and his Tory column. Ferguson's clumsy threat had backfired completely.

Moving rapidly on horseback, the American frontiersmen, numbering about 1,000, tracked Ferguson's column as they would game in the wild, and on Saturday, the 7th of October, they finally had the Tory column in their sights. Now, Ferguson had gotten wind of the size and nature of the partisan column that was approaching, and according to Tarleton he "dispatched information to Earl Cornwallis of the superior numbers to which he was opposed, and directly commenced his march to the Catawba [River],"[9] hoping to be reinforced by Cornwallis somewhere enroute . It can be presumed that Ferguson intended to either march to the

British lines or turn back, once reinforced, and confront his tormenters with superior numbers somewhere along the way. But then Ferguson did something odd. Rather than press the march back toward the safety of the British lines, he hesitated, then hesitated yet again, sending off dispatches to Cornwallis to quick send reinforcements while Ferguson wasted precious time encamped. Those dispatches finally got through to the British general, but for Ferguson and his men they would unfortunately arrive too late.

For some reason Major Patrick Ferguson had made the decision to stand and fight rather than retreat to safety. Whether this had been the product of valor, foolishness, ambition, or the sheer arrogance of the British Model will never be known. But fight he would and he picked the summit of a heavily wooded eminence nearby upon which to make his stand. It was named King's Mountain, and this, too, was an odd decision. For as we have seen, the British – in this case an American Tory force – were particularly well trained and adept at dispersing American militia in the classic style of European combat, with the bayonet, that is, on the open field of battle. Just as at Camden, militia could not get off enough rounds to stop a bayonet charge, and generally ran for the hills whenever the British offered a loud hurrah and lowered the cold steel. But Ferguson rejected this option, and instead took up a position entirely unfavorable to his own force while simultaneously favoring his foe. The Over Mountain Men were perfectly adept at fighting in the trees and undergrowth of the Carolina backcountry, where they might move from tree-to-tree, rock-to-rock, reloading as they moved, backtracking when and if necessary, be they tracking Native Americans, hunting bear, or fighting British infantry. The British, on the other hand, were at a distinct disadvantage in the woods, firing downhill at little more than blurs and phantoms in the underbrush and shadows. It was a curious deployment for the British, to say the least, and one unfortunately, that Major Ferguson would not survive to explain.

It was mid-afternoon when the Over Mountain Men spotted Ferguson's deployment, about 3:00 PM when they all dismounted and encircled King's Mountain, moving slowly and carefully through the thick underbrush toward the summit. There was little if any military planning, organization, or discipline to the attack. In three separate groups the frontiersmen simply circled the base of the mountain and attacked when the first shots rang out. It was all over in about an hour. Above on the summit Ferguson had perhaps 1,100 men, slightly more than his attackers, but they were ill-trained and ill-equipped for the sort of combat that now confronted them. "The shrill, drawn-out war cries of the Over Mountain Men resounded clearly on the crest,"[10] a horrible sound that terrorized all who heard it, the same battle cry that some eighty years later would surely come to be known as the rebel yell. The sound alone of the approaching frontiersmen demoralized the waiting Tories.

Yet it is said that the Tory militia fought hard and that Ferguson died valiantly. They stood their ground, even charged with the bayonet on more than one occasion, but the Over Mountain Men avoided the British steel by simply disappearing amongst the trees, then regrouping and renewing their own assault once the British attacks had run out of steam. Patrick Ferguson and his loyal militia were shot to pieces by able riflemen who, hiding behind rocks and trees, had them surrounded. In the end it was little more than a turkey shoot. It was as simple as that.

Had the end of the affair at King's Mountain been as decisive as was its beginning, the engagement might have been recorded as yet another valiant American victory over a worthy British opponent, and the chapter closed. Sadly, it was not. Ferguson dead, the shaken Tory militia retreated and fought valiantly until overwhelmed by sheer numbers. Then they tried to surrender, but surrendering to an unorganized and undisciplined force of angry mountain-men proved nearly impossible, and the killing unfortunately continued after men had surrendered and, in some instances, had even been granted quarter. It is here that the cry of "Tarleton's Quarter!" was supposedly shouted, perhaps long and hard. Just how badly the Over Mountain Men acted at this point has been a subject of debate since the last shots at King's Mountain died out, but there seems little doubt that many helpless Tories were shot down after surrendering. What is not subject to debate, however, is the fact that by the end of the day Patrick Ferguson was dead and his entire command killed, wounded, or captured. Cornwallis' flanking column had simply ceased to exist, and for the British it was a debacle of the first order; the loss of Ferguson's entire Tory column represented the loss of one quarter of Cornwallis' effective strength, and a loss – it was apparent now – that could not soon be made good.

On the 10th of October, still having no idea what had become of Ferguson, Cornwallis dispatched Tarleton to try and locate the Tory militia and reinforce Ferguson if practicable. However, news of Ferguson's death and the annihilation of his entire command reached General Cornwallis at Charlotte before Tarleton's return, and on October 14th Cornwallis, his flanking column destroyed and mischief and mayhem seemingly attending his every movement, decided upon a retreat back to Camden. The British had fully expected the "commotions" to have ceased and the loyal citizens to flock to their standard. Instead they had been greeted by Davie's militia on the 26th of September, and a rash of guerrilla violence ever since. Davie's stand marked only the beginning of a very rude, uncomfortable, and unforeseen welcome. A mere three weeks after their arrival, those same columns were in full retreat. For the British, the air was out of the balloon.

Cornwallis quickly recalled Tarleton and surveyed the map for a proper location for winter's quarters. For the time being, at least, he'd had enough of North Carolina and its swarming partisans. The British began a march toward the Catawba River but that movement almost immediately ran aground due to a deluge of rain. "Soon after his lordship left Charlotte," Light Horse Harry explains, "the rainy season set in, which rendered his march very inconvenient and harassing. The ground being saturated with incessant rain, the troops were exposed to its chill exhalations, and became sickly. The general himself was seized with a bilious fever, and was so much indisposed as to resign the army to the direction of Lord Rawdon."[11] In a few days Cornwallis recovered and was well enough to travel once more, and the army was once again able to resume its march. In time a suitable location for winter's quarters was located, central to the other British posts where communications could be maintained. Tarleton tell us that "After minute inquiry and examination, Wynnesborough presented the most numerous advantages: Its spacious plantations yielded a tolerable post; its centrical situation between the Broad river and the Wateree afforded protection to Ninety Six and Camden; and its vicinity to the Dutch forks, and a rich country in the rear, promised abundant supplies of flour, forage and cattle. As soon as the army arrived on this ground, the sick were conveyed to the hospital at Camden; rum and other stores were required from that place, and communication was opened with Ninety Six."[12] The British settled in for the winter.

This, then, was the reason Daniel Morgan's scouts had been unable to locate any sign of the British Army near Charlotte on or about the 25th of October, though they had ranged far and wide. By then Cornwallis' army was long gone, and Morgan, on the road since October 7 and naturally unaware of Ferguson's defeat, had been initially at a loss to make any sense of the absence of Redcoats. Now with the British Army suddenly discovered far removed at Winnsboro, Morgan was ordered to remain at New Providence with his command as a sort of tip to the Continental defenses in North Carolina. Morgan, Gates knew, could be trusted to keep a vigilant eye on all the roads, rivers, and fords that might convey British forces northward again, for no one expected Cornwallis to remain dormant for long.

While constant vigilance was a military necessity, for Morgan it proved a boring and tedious task, ill-suited to his warrior's temperament. For Daniel Morgan the coming winter months therefore appeared to suggest little more than all quiet at New Providence, a situation hardly relished by a man who had ridden for the better part of a month through pain and discomfort to fight the British.

But what Morgan did not know as he rested his command near New Providence was that substantial changes were just then in the offing, indeed changes that would far better suit his martial instincts. As a result of those changes two distinct columns would soon emerge, one under Morgan, the other under Banastre Tarleton, two forces that would be sent hurtling toward one another on a collision course that would soon change the destiny of the infant, struggling United States.

CHAPTER NINE

MORGAN

Once it had been positively determined that the British had gone into winter's quarters at Winnsboro, South Carolina, the situation for the Continental Line went from one of nervous apprehension to thankful relief. While constant vigilance remained the order of the day, at least now the prospect of imminent battle for the beleaguered army no longer seemed a realistic possibility, thus forces and provisions could be gathered over time and made ready for the coming campaign. For the time being General Horatio Gates remained in charge of the Southern Department – although rumors swirled that he was soon to be replaced – and he did his best to try and ready his hobbled command for the combat that surely was coming. Light Horse Harry Lee tells us that "In the mean while Gates was laboring with unceasing zeal and diligence to prepare a force capable of meeting his successful adversary... The deliverance of North Carolina from the late invasion, the fortunate victory of King's Mountain, afforded time for the government of the State to understand its real condition, and to prepare for the impending danger. A division of its militia had been called into the field under the command of the Generals Sumner, and Davidson, to which was united a volunteer corps under colonel Davie."[1]

Daniel Morgan and his small "corps" of light infantry and cavalry remained on the Wateree River, not far from New Providence, screening the American forces to his north while patrolling the area for any British activity, little of which was discovered. For the time being, it appeared, Cornwallis was content to simply lick his wounds and rest his army until the coming spring weather dried the roads and made swift movement more practical. One thing Cornwallis did do, however, was to send a fresh set of orders to General Leslie who, it can be recalled, had been dispatched by General Clinton to the area of the Chesapeake Bay to serve as a diversion for Cornwallis as he campaigned throughout North Carolina. In that the initial British advance into that state had ended in failure, and the timetable for the union of these two British commands fractured as a consequence, Cornwallis, rethinking the situation, ordered Leslie to embark his force by water to Charleston as soon as was possible in order to serve as a ready reserve in that theater. This movement of troops, while seemingly of small significance at the time would later have important consequences for the looming showdown between Morgan and Tarleton.

October soon gave way to November, and while Morgan itched for action, the lack of activity that fall actually proved an unexpected boon. "Despite his disappointments that autumn of 1780," one of Morgan's biographers tells us,

"Morgan could point to some pleasant developments. He had no real problem with the North Carolina brigadiers, and he got along exceptionally well with General Davidson, an enterprising backwoodsman and former Continental whom he had known at Valley Forge. Morgan's health appeared to be completely restored by mid-November; he felt as strong and energetic as ever."[2] Gates, meanwhile, determined it best to move his small army to a more central location for the winter, and according to Otho Williams, "The brigade marched on the second day of November, immediately after the light dragoons, with two brass field-pieces, some ammunition-wagons, and a small train of baggage. They followed the rout(sic) of the light infantry to Charlotte, where they encamped."[3]

In just that manner, then, the army took up a blocking position, the three elements under Gates, Smallwood, and Morgan all within easy supporting distance of one another, yet all firmly on the path Gates presumed the British would follow once again into North Carolina. While the area surrounding Charlotte had been picked almost clean of provisions by both the Continentals and British as they made their various passes through the village, Charlotte remained a sensible position from a strictly defensive perspective. Otho Williams noted that Gates considered Charlotte "the most eligible place to encamp for the winter, with the principal part of his army. The light troops [under Morgan] were to keep the field, and to act as an advance-guard. With this view, he ordered preparations to be made for building huts, and directed General Morgan to make a foraging excursion toward Camden."[4]

Light Horse Harry Lee, who was severely critical of Gate's strategy, tactics, and personal deportment at Camden, later wrote approvingly of Gate's Charlotte deployment: "The position now taken by Gates," he said, "and the arrangement of his force, presented a strong contrast to his former conduct, and afforded a consoling presumption that he had discovered his past error, and had profited by the correction of adversity."[5] Whether Gates had in fact learned a critical lesson due to the debacle at Camden was a question being debated in chambers far removed from Charlotte at the time, and by men far less inclined to grant Horatio Gates the better of the argument. Indeed, the question would never truly be answered, for Horatio Gate's replacement had already been picked, and he was making his way south even as the Southern Army initiated its new deployment at Charlotte.

Yet Daniel Morgan now had at least some marching orders, even if they were to do little more than search for corn and forage for his horses, and in short order he had his command on the road toward the Waxhaws. Sadly, he found virtually nothing of substance in the area north of Camden, but the expedition did at least provide some entertainment for the bored Morgan, and in the end produced a humorous, if minimal, military triumph of sorts.

North of Camden at Rugeley's Mill, Mr. Rugeley, an ardent supporter of the king, had been appointed lieutenant colonel in the British Army (apparently with the hint that he might soon be promoted brigadier if all went well) and had also managed to somehow secure the rank of major for his son-in-law. As Morgan's column wound its way back north from the Waxhaws, it passed near Mr. Rugeley's farm where he and his son-in-law and some 100 British troops were encamped. Otho Williams explains that "The post was on the left of Morgan's route, as he returned from foraging – but too near Camden for him to risk any thing like a siege or blockade. It was suggested that the cavalry might go and reconnoiter it – Washington, pleased with the idea, approached so near, as to discover that the enemy had discovered him and were intimidated."[6]

With the British troops lurking just behind him at Camden, Morgan could not afford much in the way of either time or manpower simply to harass Lt. Colonel Rugeley, and Washington was well aware of these limitations. So the cavalry commander decided to play a little trick. Now, the British had retired to a large log barn that had been reinforced outside with a meager trench and some abatis (sharpened branches pointed outward) and, relatively sure that their position could not be carried by horseman armed with saber and pistol only, confidently waited the American attack.

But Washington had no intention of wasting his men and ammunition in a profitless assault, so he turned instead to a little ruse, and a deception that was not uncommon during the period. Robert Kirkwood, marching with the Continentals under Morgan, heard later of the mischief played by Washington, and recorded the facts in his journal: "This day had orders to hold our selves in readiness in a moments warning to March. Accordingly left our tents standing with all our sick behind and marched to twelve mile Creek, which at this place Divides No & So Carolina; & from thence to Hanging Rock, the Infantry remained at this place until Col. Washington went down to Col. Rugeley's, and with the Deception of a pine knot took the garrisons Consisting of one Col. One Majr. and 107privates."[7]

The "pine knot" deception that so baffled the British into immediate surrender is explained in detail by Otho Williams: It seems that Col. Washington "humorously ordered his men to plant the trunk of an old pine tree, in the manner of a field-piece, pointing towards the garrison – at the same time, dismounting some of his men to appear as infantry, and displaying his cavalry to the best advantage, he sent a corporal of dragoons to summon the commanding officer to an *Immediate* surrender," no doubt insisting that once the American "artillery" opened, Mr. Rugeley's wood fort would be reduced in short order to little more than splinters and the garrison flattened. "The order was executed with so firm a manner, that Colonel Rugeley did not hesitate to comply *instantly,* and the whole garrison marched out prisoners of war.

"The corporal was made a sergeant of dragoons – the old fort was set on fire; and Washington retired with his prisoners without exchanging a shot."[8]

We can only imagine that Morgan roared with delight when apprised of the surrender by Colonel Washington, for he later remarked, somewhat sarcastically, it can be assumed, that Rugeley's immediate surrender due to a pine log artillery piece did not suggest, he thought, the mark of a "great military character."[9] While the incident gave the Americans a small victory and some much needed comic relief, Lord Cornwallis was far from amused by Rugeley's toothless capitulation. "Rugeley will not be made a brigadier," the Earl fumed to Tarleton on December 4. "He surrendered without firing a shot, himself and one hundred and three rank and file, to the cavalry only."[10]

The fact that Daniel Morgan was now in the field maneuvering near Camden, Sumter again threatening Ninety Six, and Francis Marion causing havoc in the eastern portion of South Carolina, aroused much concern in the British camp. Cornwallis, who only weeks before had been confident that all organized opposition in South Carolina had been suppressed, now suspected an imminent attack upon Camden. Tarleton later recalled of these days that "Earl Cornwallis was impressed with an idea that the Americans had a design upon Camden: The report of the advance of General Morgan towards the head of Lynche's creek, with Colonel Washington's cavalry, and a body of continental infantry, together with the exaggerated accounts of Marion's force, gave plausibility to the supposition."[11]

Tarleton was subsequently ordered to Camden to reconnoiter the situation and serve as a potential reinforcement for that post. But as we already know, Morgan was on a foraging mission only, not on the offensive, and by then Morgan had found little if any in the way of corn for his men or forage for his horses. Thus by the time of Tarleton's arrival Morgan had already retired north toward Lt. Col Rugeley's fort. Tarleton was unable to locate anything in terms of a threat, but Cornwallis remained on edge nevertheless, entirely in the dark, unable to make any sense of the American movements, and his agitation only continued to mushroom. "I wish you to try all you can about intelligence,"[12] he wrote Tarleton on December 4, and followed-up with yet another directive on the 15th of the month: "I have no material intelligence, and I am sorry to say, none that I can depend on from the enemy on our front. If you can meet with any persons more enterprising than those I can find, I beg you will employ them."[13]

So while Cornwallis scrambled for intelligence at Winnsboro, Morgan marched back to Charlotte at the head of his small corps, only then to realize that the long anticipated change in high command of the Southern Army had already taken place during his absence. General Nathanael Greene had arrived at the Charlotte camp on the 2nd of December[14] and Morgan rode in to report to him on the 3rd.[15] Greene had served well under George Washington, and Morgan and Greene were well acquainted with one another, having campaigned together at Boston, New York, and in New Jersey. "Rarely have two men of such uncommon martial gifts had the opportunity to complement one another."[16]

Greene had served in the field under Washington then accepted the position as Quarter Master General for the American cause. Nathanael Greene was highly regarded by Washington, who had made it clear that, should Washington himself fall or become disabled, he hoped that Nathanael Greene would be appointed as his replacement in overall command of the Continental Army. By the time of Greene's arrival, of course, Daniel Morgan had already established a reputation for martial excellence, and Nathanael Greene was well aware of Morgan's fighting capabilities. "Renowned from Quebec to the Carolinas," writes historian John Buchanan of Morgan, "celebrated in one army and feared by another,"[17]Daniel Morgan teamed with Nathanael Greene suggested a powerful, driving combination for the future success of the Southern Army.

Nathanael Greene, like Daniel Morgan, provides the modern reader with an interesting American story, a tale not of royal birth or aristocracy, but of talent, hard work, and determination. Born into a Quaker family residing in Potowomut, Rhode Island in the year 1742, Greene early on enjoyed the work, wealth, and rigors of a successful New England family. His father had become a prosperous businessman, and the young Nathanael spent much of his time working on the family farm and in his father's ironworks, learning the trades that one day he would be expected to embrace. But Nathanael Greene had a great, natural thirst for learning that went far beyond the foundry, a thirst that over time radically conflicted with the Quakers distaste for formal learning and higher education. On his own he educated himself, reading books on a wide variety of topics, expanding his knowledge and broadening his mind. Slowly, as his learning developed, so did his distance from the religion of his youth, which eventually he would voluntarily depart during the course of the Revolutionary War. In particular he chafed at the Quaker's pacifism, and as he grew he began to consume literary works regarding warfare and tactics, topics that one day he would put to practical use.

In 1774 Nathanael Greene married the lovely Caty Littlefield, the love of his life, and about the same time became involved in the formation of a militia unit named the Kentish Guards. Greene, one of its founding forces, naturally expected to be appointed an officer in the unit, but was voted down by his fellow organizers when the time came. That vote came as a severe jolt and harsh rebuke. Greene, who walked with a limp, had difficulty with asthma, and was not as physically imposing as a Daniel Morgan, had been left out in the cold, dismissed by men he thought his equals. Light Horse Harry Lee – who in December of 1780 was about to arrive with his own detachment of dragoons to reinforce Greene's army – described Nathanael Greene as follows: "In person he was rather corpulent, and above the common size. His complexion was fair and florid; his countenance serene and mild, indicating a goodness which seemed to shade and soften the fire and greatness of its expression. His health was delicate, but preserved by temperance and exercise."[18]

The disturbing vote of his peers cut Nathanael Greene deeply, but rather than march off in a huff and nurse a grudge, Greene remained in the unit, serving as a simple private. Yet as a private his intelligence and grasp of military affairs were consistently on display and often consulted, and when the unit finally marched from Rhode Island to Boston in 1775, it was the private Nathanael Greene who was appointed brigadier general of all Rhode Island troops – a remarkable, if not astonishing, leap in rank. Fortunately, Nathanael Greene would not disappoint.

At Boston, Greene soon came under the approving eye of General George Washington, who almost immediately found in the Rhode Island brigadier a man of intelligence, candor, and competence. George Washington has had his own military critics, of course, but the commanding general had unquestionably a keen eye for solid, intelligent, and dependable subordinates, and rarely misfired when it came to selecting them. Indeed, George Washington had the thankful capacity to surround himself with intelligent men – unlike many officers, politicians, and businessmen to this day who often surround themselves with little more than a gaggle of sycophants – and had as well the rare quality of character to take their ideas and suggestions seriously. Nathanael Greene would over time become George Washington's most trusted subordinate, and that as much as anything speaks to Greene's intelligence, character, and devotion to country. Greene, while never a great field commander, nevertheless developed a deep, strategic grasp of geography and logistics which, in the Southern Theater, would serve him well.

While traveling south to assume his new command, General Greene made stops in Delaware, Maryland, and Virginia trying his best to procure material and provisions of all description, but he was stymied at every turn. The logistical apparatus of the fledgling United States – if it ever existed to begin with – was by then sadly crippled and incapable of rendering much, if anything, in terms of support. So in Virginia he left behind the competent Baron von Steuben with orders to try and round up as many men and as much material as could possibly be secured for shipment south. He also ordered a survey of the fords and safe passage points on the Roanoke and Dan Rivers in North Carolina. Then, upon his arrival in Hillsborough, he sent two additional officers off on similar assignments; to survey and mark all the reasonable fords on the Yadkin and Catawba Rivers, and it can be deduced from these activities the strategic drift his mind had already taken. Greene had been with Washington during the Continental Army's dismal trek across New Jersey after the catastrophic campaign in New

York in 1776. He had seen first hand how Washington's advanced scouts had secured every boat along the Delaware River for miles around, thus allowing Washington to cross over in safety, while denying passage to his pursuer. That bit of good thinking saved the revolution in 1776, and with North Carolina crossed by a host of rivers, using them to advantage, Greene surely realized, might just save it again. Nathanael Greene might not have been as experienced as Cornwallis in the art of war, nor was his army as well supplied, trained, or manned, but it appears he had no intention of being either out-thought or out-prepared by his adversary.

While Greene and Gates were by no means fond of one another, the transfer of command at Hillsborough went off as smoothly as might be imagined for such a touchy situation. Otho Williams, who was present at the time, later wrote that, "A manly resignation marked the conduct of General Gates on the arrived [arrival] of his successor, whom he received at head quarters with that liberal and gentlemanly air which was habitual to him." Gates may not have been an exceptional field captain, but he was certainly a man of breeding and accomplishment and besides, a show of pique after the debacle at Camden might well have doomed any hope he had at the time of resurrecting his career. "General Greene observed a plain, candid, respectful manner," noted Williams, "neither betraying compassion nor the want of it... In short, the officers who were present, had an elegant lesson of propriety exhibited on a most delicate and interesting occasion."[19] While Congress had determined that a court of inquiry was to be established in order to look into Horatio Gates' performance at Camden, the fact of the matter was, there were too few officers of appropriate rank at or near Hillsborough to convene such a hearing, thus within a few days General Gates had packed his bags, mounted his horse, and begun the long trip back to Philadelphia.

Nathanael Greene got straight to work, and in short order had a firm feel for the situation he'd inherited – and that feeling was not good. The army he now commanded appeared to him "rather a shadow than a substance, having only an imaginary existence."[20] The physical returns totaled 2,307, but less than 1,500 of those troops were actually present, and of that number only 949 were Continentals.[21] Moreover the army was poorly fed, shabbily clothed, ill-equipped, and the prospect for a quick improvement in any of those necessities appeared at the time out of the question. Realizing that he had to have energetic, competent men on his staff if he was to be at all effective, he quickly appointed Lt. Colonel Edward Carrington as Inspector General, and Major William Richardson Davie, the famous North Carolina partisan, as Commissary General. Davie did not want the post and had to be talked into it, but finally accepted, and both appointments would prove their worth over the coming months.

Greene also quickly grasped the fact that the region encompassing Charlotte had been picked clean of provisions, thus the army would starve if it remained put for any length of time. His new command, Greene wrote, consisted of "a few ragged, half-starving troops in the wilderness, destitute of everything necessary for either the comfort or convenience of soldiers... the country is almost laid waste and the inhabitants plunder one another with little less than savage fury. We live from hand to mouth."[22] In short, Nathanael Greene realized in a few days only what had eluded Horatio Gates for months: the army was destitute of supplies and could not remain at Charlotte for long. What to do?

The Southern Army had to move, but the question was where? Greene called a council of war attended by Morgan and Smallwood, and laid out a plan for a quick strike upon Cornwallis at Winnsboro. His hope was to surprise the British in their winter quarters – attack quickly then move off rapidly. If successful, Greene believed he might deal a serious blow to any plans Cornwallis had for reentering North Carolina in the near future. Both Morgan and Smallwood objected, however, recalling the debacle at Camden when the army had moved much too hurriedly while in essentially the same pathetic condition, and Greene, to his credit, accepted their advice – the army was not yet ready to fight. That decision eliminated one option, but it did not solve the problem. What to do? If they could not fight then at least they might move. So Greene dispatched Colonel Thaddeus Kosciuszko, an excellent staff volunteer from Poland, in search of a more inviting place to establish a winter camp, and in short order Kosciuszko returned after having conducted a thorough search. The spot he selected was Cheraw on the Pee Dee River, some 75 miles distant from Charlotte.

Hearing Kosciuszko out, Greene concluded to make the move to Cheraw, but he decided as well on something of far more importance. In one of the most striking decisions of the war, Nathanael Greene decided to divide his small army while in the presence of a larger foe, a violation of one of the most basic rules of warfare. It was obviously a decision he had been toying with for some time, and like any radical expedient, it combined high risk with high reward. The risks were obvious. Cornwallis might, by means of a well-concealed, swift strike, fall upon either one of the divided commands before the other might be able to march to its relief, then turn and destroy what remained of the American Southern Army in detail. That was simultaneously the most serious and obvious risk, and it was a risk not to be taken lightly.

But the potential rewards were worth that risk. If one of the commands were removed west to the area Cornwallis previously wanted Ferguson to patrol, the British general would be forced to deal with that intrusion before making any move into North Carolina on his own, for his left flank would once again be in grave and obvious danger. If, on the other hand, Cornwallis were to march directly against Greene with a force remaining in his rear, he would invite assault on both of the British posts at Augusta and Ninety Six, or even the potential destruction of his line of supply. Then, again, if he moved with his whole force to attack the newly deployed western Continentals, he would open the door to the interior of South Carolina all the way to Charleston, which Greene might then take advantage of. Nathanael Greene understood one thing for sure: The divided American command would certainly give Cornwallis pause and force him to rethink any plans he had in the offing.

Meanwhile, Greene, at Cheraw, would be centrally located, and while 150 miles from his separated force, still within reasonable marching distance for reinforcement purposes. It would also allow the Continentals to provision themselves from two different areas, thus improving the likelihood of sustaining themselves over the winter months. Like a game of chess with but a few pieces left on the board, this divided deployment would force Cornwallis to think, and in the end, Greene speculated, it would probably force the British commander to send a smaller detachment off to attack in the west while remaining firm with most of his army at Winnsboro. Then, if successful, Cornwallis' strategy would be to reunite with the smaller command then fall upon Greene, now greatly reduced in strength. If that be the British general's most logical and probable choice, Greene realized that any force he sent off to the west would have to be as strong as he could possibly make it, and handled by a skilled commander. The choice for that post was obvious.

On the 16th of December Nathanael Greene drafted these orders for Daniel Morgan: "You are appointed to the command of a corps of Light Infantry, a detachment of Militia, and Lt. Col. Washington's Regiment of Light Dragoons. With these troops you will proceed to the West side of the Catawba river, where you will be joined by a body of Volunteer Militia under the command of Brig. Gen. Davidson of this State, and by the Militia lately under the command of Brig. Genl. Sumter. This force, and such others as may join you from Georgia, you will employ against the enemy on the West side of the River, either offensively or defensively as your own prudence and discretion may direct, acting with caution, and avoiding surprises by every possible precaution. For the present I give you the entire command in that quarter, and do hereby require all Officers and Soldiers engaged in the American cause to be subject to your orders and command."[23]

This was in essence an independent command for Daniel Morgan and, knowing that Cornwallis would probably be forced to attack that independent command, Greene shaped Morgan's corps with the finest troops he could patch together. "Composed of the troops Gates had given him previously and two companies of Maryland Continentals, it also included 250 veteran Virginia militia."[24] Most of that Virginia militia had had previous experience as Continentals, and could be counted on to fight in a pinch. Morgan had every reason to be pleased. This was the cream of Greene's army, as good a light force as he could put in the field, and it was, without question, a testimony to the faith and confidence Nathanael Greene had in Daniel Morgan.

In a deadly game of cat-and-mouse, Daniel Morgan's corps was to serve as bait, a thorn in Cornwallis' side the British general could not long ignore nor tolerate maneuvering unimpeded on his flank or rear. Thus it seemed only a matter of time and logic before Cornwallis would be forced to act, and being Cornwallis it seemed obvious that when he struck he would strike with appropriate force. In that sense it can be readily discerned that Nathanael Greene had bet everything on Daniel Morgan; for if Morgan's new corps were destroyed, Greene, with what little remained of the Southern Army, could not long survive. But no one expected Morgan to be bested. Greene knew his man and had confidence in his troops. Built for firepower, maneuverability, and speed, from that day forward Morgan's light corps would be known with pride as the Flying Army.

CHAPTER TEN

TARLETON

As Nathanael Greene assumed command of the Southern Army in early December – taking inventory of the army's wants and needs, and beginning a detailed assessment of his strategic options – for weeks General Cornwallis despaired of the sudden increase in partisan opposition throughout the region, and took action in an attempt to quell those disconcerting interruptions. Light Horse Harry Lee reminds us that "Marion and Sumter, continuing unchanged amid the despondency which the disasters of August had produced, boldly pushed their disturbing inroads into the enemy's territory."[1] Sumter had managed rather like a phoenix to rise from the ashes of Fishing Creek, and again had a sizeable force under his command that threatened the British garrison in western South Carolina at the settlement named Ninety Six. Francis Marion meanwhile, with far fewer men but with considerably greater aptitude, had managed to utterly disrupt British operations in that eastern region of South Carolina north of Charleston.

Indeed, so successful and aggravating had Marion become, the British presumed his strength far greater than it actually was, and judged Marion, therefore, to be the more serious threat. "He [Marion] not only kept in check all the small parties of the enemy," Light Horse Harry tells us, "whom the want of forage and provisions, or the desire of plunder, occasionally urged into the region east and south of Camden, but he often passed the Santee, interrupting the communications with Charleston, and sometimes alarming the small posts in its vicinity. To such a height had his interruption reached, that Cornwallis turned his attention to the subject."[2] When Tarleton returned from his mission to Camden in order to confront Morgan, whom, it can be recalled, had withdrawn prior to Tarleton's arrival, the cavalryman suggested to Cornwallis that he be allowed to go after Marion, and to this the British commander readily agreed. "I received yours yesterday," Cornwallis wrote to Tarleton on November 5, "and most sincerely hope you will get at Mr. Marion. I am always sanguine when you are concerned."[3]

Francis Marion, small in frame but large in ability, certainly evoked far more fear and consternation than his stature might ever have suggested, and with good cause he would soon rise to fame as the intrepid "Swamp Fox" of American Revolutionary lore. He had been born in 1733 on his family's plantation near Georgetown, South Carolina, his parents having fled persecution as Huguenots (French Protestants) in Europe. The family originally settled along the Cooper River near Charleston, but later moved to the more advantageous location outside of Georgetown. Francis was the youngest of five sons and he grew up on the plantation, favored with only the most minimal of educations. After trying his luck as a sailor at the age of sixteen, he returned from a nautical disaster in which he had almost been drowned, and discarded the sail for a plow. There on the plantation he remained until 1759 when he was appointed lieutenant in a militia expedition commanded by William Moultrie against the Cherokee, and two years later he again served as a captain in a similar mission.

When war broke out between Britain and her North American colonies, Marion was assigned a captaincy in a South Carolina corps, and was soon promoted to major. In time and with good service he rose to the rank of Lt. Colonel. Francis Marion served in both British sieges of Charleston, and was well respected as an officer and fighter. Injured due to a fall prior to the surrender of Charleston in 1780, Marion was thus able to avoid capture, and after recovering from his injury, began his own partisan activities designed to annoy the British in the vicinity of his boyhood home near Georgetown.

Marion hardly fit the romantic picture of either a gentleman or a soldier of the period. Harry Lee describes him as "in stature the smallest size, thin as well as low. His visage was not pleasing, and his manners not captivating. He was reserved and silent, entering into conversation only when necessary, and then with modesty and good sense." During the course of the war virtually nothing distracted Marion from his duty. "He possessed a strong mind," Lee recalled, improved by its own reflection and observation, not by books or travel. His dress was like his address—plain, regarding comfort and decency only."[4]

For months during the late summer and early fall of 1780 the diminutive Marion accompanied by a small band of partisan raiders, had become an irritating itch that Cornwallis could not scratch. In August, only days after the American disaster at Camden, for instance, Marion got wind of a British detachment escorting a fair number of Continental prisoners who had been captured at the battle. That detachment was encamped at Great Savannah on the Santee River, not far from where Marion was then maneuvering. The following morning Marion's small band attacked at first light, taking the British by complete surprise. All of the Continentals were freed and 26 British regulars killed or captured in the action. Marion suffered but two men wounded.[5] While that victory was small; it had an enormous bolstering effect on American morale, and the defeat and loss of American prisoners drove Cornwallis to distraction.

Marion quickly became a master of guerrilla tactics, striking only when the odds for success appeared dramatically in his favor, and disappearing into the swamps and thickets when they did not. Generally riding with a band of no more than twenty to forty men, he rapidly developed a reputation that far exceeded his actual strength. He hit British and Tory patrols alike, and word of his accomplishments spread like wildfire. "In the short space of two weeks, at widely separated points, Francis Marion had first defeated British and provincial regulars, then routed a Tory force that had a five-to-one superiority. Following that coup, sixty new men rode into his camp and volunteered to follow him."[6] In the fall of 1780 Francis Marion was rapidly becoming a legend in the low country of South Carolina.

Even Banastre Tarleton, hardly one to lavish praise on his adversaries, paid grudging respect to Francis Marion. "Mr. Marion," wrote Tarleton, "by his zeal and abilities, shewed himself capable of the trust committed to his charge. He collected his adherents at the shortest notice, in the neighbourhood of Black river, and, after making incursions into the friendly districts, or threatening the communications, to avoid pursuit, he disbanded his followers. The alarms occasioned by these insurrections frequently retarted(sic) supplies on their way to the army; and a late report of Marion's strength delayed the junction of the recruits, who had arrived from New York for the corps in the country."[7] In short, Francis Marion was causing havoc in north east South Carolina.

This, then, was the itch Cornwallis desperately wanted scratched. Light Horse Harry recalls the moment in time. "With a force fluctuating from fifty to two hundred and fifty men, Marion held himself in his recesses in the Pedee and Black rivers whence he darted upon the enemy whenever an opportunity presented itself... To such a height had his interruption reached, that Cornwallis turned his attention to the subject."[8] In the hard riding, hard charging Banastre Tarleton, Cornwallis had the very instrument for projecting royal strength at a distance, and the youthful Lt. Colonel, ever alert to opportunity, was always eager to comply with the general's needs. Thus, when the Tory commander in the region pleaded for help to thwart Marion, Cornwallis readily complied. Tarleton left on November 5 with his entire British Legion, numbering over 400 horse and foot, the infantry recently mounted for the increased speed and maneuverability Tarleton knew he would need to corner the elusive Marion. Armed with two pieces of artillery, Tarleton commanded a substantial force, far greater than anything Marion could possibly raise in a moment's notice to oppose him.

All the couriers who had ridden into Winnsboro from the area near Georgetown that fall had arrived with reports vastly overestimating Marion's strength, thus the usually aggressive Tarleton proceeded initially with great caution, moving "his corps, for a short time, in a very compact body, less the Americans should gain any advantage over patroles or detachments," that might be individually surprised and routed. But once it became clear that Marion was not going to meet the British head-on, Tarleton naturally presumed that Marion was, in fact, weaker than his own force, and had no intention of meeting his pursuer in a fight on even terms. Marion obviously was no Buford, given to tactical miscues, nor was he a Sumter, lazy in security and asleep at the switch as Tarleton approached, and the hard riding British commander soon realized that his favorite tactic of immediate frontal assault against all odds was not going to get him anywhere against the likes of Francis Marion. No, Marion was wily and slippery and cautious, not about to play the game according to Tarleton's playbook. Something else, some other plan, something a bit craftier, would have to be devised.

To Tarleton's credit, he soon hatched a cagey plan of his own, dividing "his corps into several small parties, publishing intelligence that each was a patrole, and that the main body of the King's troops had countermarched to Camden." Tarleton's plan was simple. By spreading wide the deceit that the majority of the Legion had returned to Camden, and by sending out small, individual patrols, he intended to lure Marion into a trap. Carefully, however, he "took care that no detachment should be out of reach of assistance; and that the whole formed, after dark every evening, a solid and vigilant corps during the night. This stratagem," Tarleton later recalled "had not been employed more than three days before General Marion was on the point of falling a sacrifice to it."[9]

Tarleton had taken up a position on the plantation of the deceased American General, Richard Richardson, secreting his force at night in hidden locations advantageous to the surprise attack he hoped to spring. Marion, through various means, soon got word that Tarleton's main force had allegedly returned to Camden, and began inching closer on the morning of the 10th,[10] the hope of inflicting damage to the remaining British obviously dancing through his thoughts. Indeed, Marion was about to fall prey to Tarleton's well-laid trap when Mrs. Richardson, risking all, sent her son to warn the American partisan of the danger lurking ahead. Grasping at once the superiority in numbers he actually faced, Marion promptly turned his small band around and headed for the swamps with all dispatch.[11]

Now, Tarleton was well aware of Marion's initial approach, and when nothing came of it, he naturally grew suspicious. So he "dispatched an officer with a few men to find out the cause, who soon obtained information how the project was betrayed, which had already caused Marion to retreat with confusion and rapidity (sic)."[12] Contrary to Tarleton's fanciful recollections, however, Francis Marion was not retreating in confusion, but was most certainly moving with haste through the back country he knew only too well in order to avoid a collision with a force vastly outnumbering his own. Tarleton, furious that his well-laid plan had been foiled, immediately mounted his men and took off after the fleeing American partisans at top speed, chasing them for the better part of the day. The elusive Marion led the weary British Legion across creeks and through woods and across miles of uncharted swamp until even the usually indomitable Banastre Tarleton had had enough. “Come my Boys!” he called out, “and we will find the Gamecock [Thomas Sumter]. But as for this damned old fox, the Devil himself could not catch him.”[13]

Tarleton’s dismay quickly gave birth to legend. The Swamp Fox would continue to harry and flummox the British in South Carolina until the end of the war, and never would they come close to catching him. Tarleton in his *history of the campaigns* could not bring himself to admit this failure, however, and states rather that he was forced to call off the search for Marion at the very height of the chase, indeed just when he was about to “bring the enemy to action” and that “an express from Earl Cornwallis, who had followed the tracks of the march, recalled Lieutenant colonel Tarleton.”[14] Thus in Tarleton’s version of history, Marion was spared at the last moment by a fortunate change of orders, but this is little more than self-serving fiction. Light Horse Harry, interpreting Tarleton’s pursuit in a less favorable light, suggests that Marion simply “skillfully withdrew to his unassailable position, leaving Tarleton to deplore the inefficacy of his wiles and toils.”[15]

Whether Tarleton's report on the conclusion of the chase was fiction or mere whimsy is a question for debate, but what is not fiction nor open to debate, however, was the wanton and mindless destruction the Legion perpetrated against helpless civilians in the area as they departed. Sadly, it was neither the first nor would it be the last instance of this sort of inhumanity (for rebel or Tory alike), and it would be precisely this sort of barbarity for which "Bloody Ban" would be remembered in the South, long after the guns had ceased firing and the last British man-of-war had sailed for England. Modern apologists might endeavor to polish his image, but they cannot eliminate the facts. "He burned thirty plantation homes, their outbuildings, and their harvests. The women, the children, and the old literally were allowed only the clothes on their backs and were seen gathered under the sky around campfires."[16] For her cunning, Mrs. Richardson would watch her home, animals, and barn go up in roaring balls of flame. This sort of insensible carnage had become Banastre Tarleton's unfortunate calling card, and it was a reputation that would be firmly recalled in the future, especially when both sides finally came to blows on more or less even terms in the weeks to come.

Lord Cornwallis, however, was quite impressed by the embellished report of Tarleton's scattering of Francis Marion's small force. As a result, Tarleton was rapidly becoming the British general's most trustworthy officer, and the apple of his martial eye. To Tarleton's credit, he got things done, no matter how savage his tactics, and in war success rarely goes unnoticed – or, for long unrewarded.

On December 3, for instance, Cornwallis reported to Henry Clinton in New York regarding the Marion affair, appreciation for his hard-driving Lt. Colonel only too apparent: "Colonel Marion had so wrought on the minds of the people," wrote Cornwallis, "partly by the terror of his treats and cruelty of his punishments, and partly by the promise of plunder, that there was scarcely an inhabitant between the Santee and Pedee, that was not in arms against us. Some parties had even crossed the Santee, and carried terror to the gates of Charles town. My first object was to reinstate matters in that quarter, without which Camden could receive no supplies. I therefore sent Tarleton, who pursued Marion for several days, obliged his corps to take to the swamps, and by convincing the inhabitants that there was a power superior to Marion, who could likewise reward and punish, so far checked the insurrection, that the greatest part of them have not dared to appear in arms against us since his expedition."[17]

Cornwallis was wrong, of course, and within the week Marion would be up to his old tricks again. But at the moment the British general had larger fish to fry – Sumter was once again threatening the British left at Ninety Six. One recent attempt to deal with the Gamecock had already ended in utter failure, thus Cornwallis had little choice but to turn again to his trump card, the intrepid Tarleton. "I wish you would get three legions," Cornwallis wrote, flattering Tarleton, "and divide yourself into three parts: We can do no good without you, I trust to your coming immediately, unless you see something more materially pressing."[18] This was high praise indeed from any commander to a subordinate, and only served to underscore how much Cornwallis had come to lean upon his young cavalry officer in matters of importance.

Why was Cornwallis so agitated? Well, it seems that on November 9 Major James Wemyss had marched north from Winnsboro with about 150 troops consisting of the 63rd Foot and a few additional dragoons to confront Sumter, who was rumored to have advanced to a posting a mere 30 miles north and west of British winter quarters. It was Wemyss' intention to fall upon Sumter at daylight, but the assault was horribly bungled. Wemyss, who like Tarleton had a proven penchant for brutality, attacked in the dark of night at the head of his troops and managed little except to immediately get himself shot off his horse by Sumter's sentries. "At one o'clock in the morning Major Wemyss, at the head of his corps," Tarleton later explained, "charged the picket, when, out of five shots which were fired, two took place in the arm and knee of the British commanding officer: This event rendered the surprise useless; and General Sumpter owned, perhaps, his own and the safety of his people to the personal misfortune of Major Wemyss."[19] The second-in-command of the British force, a young lieutenant, had not been properly briefed by Wemyss of the ground, the enemy's strength, or even the rough plan that was to be employed, and thus, having no grasp of the situation, ultimately ordered the British column into retreat. Wemyss had managed to get himself and some twenty other British officers and men killed or wounded; all now captured. The operation proved a complete fiasco.

Cornwallis subsequently theorized that Sumter would be largely emboldened by Wemyss' defeat and fretted for his post at Ninety Six. He immediately picked up his pen and wrote Tarleton, lamenting the disaster, and ordering Tarleton back from his foray east: "Must beg of you to return immediately," he said, "leaving some horses for mounting men at Camden. I am under the greatest anxiety for Ninety Six, and trust you will lose no time in returning to me."[20] The plan was simple. Tarleton was to rendezvous at Brierley's Ford on the Broad River with what remained of Wemyss' 63rd Foot and a battalion of the 71st. From there he was to find and destroy Thomas Sumter.

This was just the sort of mission that Tarleton both loved and excelled at, and the cavalryman had his Legion turned around and on the road at a moment's notice. "Although the light troops had made a laborious march of twenty-four hours," he tells us, "through a very difficult country, they returned ten miles the same evening the express arrived from Earl Cornwallis."[21] Pushing his men and mounts alike on a grueling three-day march, Tarleton arrived at Brierley's Ford on the 18th of November where he took command of the waiting infantry. Typically, he did not dally. Because Sumter's pickets were stationed on the opposite river bank observing the movements of the infantry, and Tarleton did not want them to spot the arrival of his British Legion, he had his green jacketed Legion take measures to cover their uniforms, while two artillery pieces fired shots across the river to disperse the watching Americans. That accomplished, "a detachment of British infantry took possession of both shores."

The Broad River runs south and east across the state of South Carolina, from its northwestern border with North Carolina to the center of the state near present day Columbia where the Broad becomes the Congaree. North of Winnsboro three tributaries of the Broad – the Enoree, Tyger, and Pacolet, in order from south to north – angle off the larger river like ribs projecting from a backbone, and this group of interwoven rivers would more than once come into play as various columns chased, retreated, and toyed with one another during the course of the American Revolution. Shallows, fords, and potential crossing points thus became critical features in a deadly game of cat and mouse, and a game Tarleton and Sumter were about to engage in once more. The fording of a river in the face of an enemy in pursuit is one of the most difficult and dangerous of military maneuvers, and that fact would play into the plans and behaviors of both sides in the coming days, weeks, and months.

At Brierley's Ford, Tarleton wanted Sumter to believe that British infantry alone was maneuvering in the area, thus "The appearance of the 63rd and 71st in red clothing, tended to corroborate the enemies information, and lull them into security, which circumstance had a reasonable chance of producing future advantages to the light troops, who had marched with so much celerity from the eastern part of the province, that no intelligence of their return had reached Sumpter." After the infantry had successfully crossed over the Broad at Brierley's Ford that afternoon, Tarleton with the Legion slipped downriver to another ford where they passed over unobserved. Both crossings were well planned and well executed. Tarleton was once again on the hunt, this time heavily reinforced, and after a prey that was unaware of his presence. After crossing the river Bloody Ban put scouts out in every direction, and by late on the 18th had solid information that Sumter "with upwards of one thousand men, was moving towards Williams' house, a post occupied by friendly militia, fifteen miles from Ninety Six."[22]

At first light Tarleton was once again on the march. All that day the British moved ever closer to Sumter's position, and that night camped "with secrecy and precaution" at Indian Creek near the banks of the Ennoree River. It was Tarleton's aim to move up the river the next morning and surprise Sumter in his camp, but then misfortune struck. A regular from the 63rd Foot deserted in the dark and stole away to Sumter's camp north of Indian Creek. By midnight he was briefing the American general as to Tarleton's presence and precise location – something, as at Fishing Creek, Sumter had been entirely unaware of – and Sumter had to decide quickly just how to respond. This was, after all, not simply some slow units of British infantry trudging through the backwoods on the hunt for him, but the British Legion under Banastre Tarleton, heavily reinforced to boot. Sumter's subordinates urged him to fight, but the land along the Enoree was not particularly favorable for a defensive stand. A superior position was suggested, however, not too far north at William Blackstock's farm on the Tyger River, and Sumter readily agreed to the movement. There, it was confirmed by all, Sumter would meet Tarleton and have it out with this ruthless, relentless adversary, now the most hated man in the south.[23]

Tarleton pressed on again at dawn, and it was not long before his scouts brought him news of Sumter's movement toward the Tyger. At that point the British commander assumed the Americans were on the run, and would simply, like Marion, disband their operation if pressed, only then to regroup once the emergency had past. So, if he was going to find and destroy Sumter, Tarleton presumed he would have to move very quickly. Not long thereafter the British van arrived at a ford on the Enoree where "he found that the advanced guard and main body of the enemy had passed the river near two hours, and, that a detachment to cover the rear was waiting the return of a patrole."[24] The Legion dragoons quickly crossed the river and dispatched the American rearguard, killing many and taking several prisoners.

From the prisoners it was determined that the British deserter, who had fled overnight, had made his way to Sumter and had thus foiled the secrecy of Tarleton's approach. It became painfully clear at that point that Sumter now knew who was giving chase along with the precise count of the troops opposing him, but this dispiriting news did not slow Tarleton even for a moment. On the hunt he was ferocious, regardless of the odds, regardless of the situation, and like a wolf on the scent of fresh blood, he immediately renewed the quest, pressing forward with his entire corps. Knowing that Sumter outmanned him considerably, Tarleton was careful to keep all of his troops together, "unwilling to divide his corps, and risk an action against a great superiority with his dragoons and the 63rd, pressed forward his light and legion infantry, and three pounder, in a compact body, till four o'clock in the afternoon, at which time it became evident, that the enemy would have an opportunity of passing the Tyger river before dark, if he did not alter his disposition."[25]

Tarleton was still operating under the misconception that the Americans were frantically trying to avoid combat and get across the river ahead of him, while the exact opposite was actually the case. At the moment Sumter had taken up a strong position on a hill at Blackstock's farm, and was waiting for Tarleton without even the slightest thought of retreat. Tarleton kept up the pace until late in the afternoon when it became clear that, with light fading, Sumter might get across the Tyger if he did not rush on ahead with his light troops and draw Sumter into some sort of action. Thus the artillery and the 71st infantry were left behind to continue their march with all dispatch, while Tarleton with the Legion horse and the mounted 63rd pressed ahead.

At about five o'clock in the afternoon Tarleton's van mounted a slight ridge that descended to a creek then rose again to another hill opposite where he finally found Sumter's partisan band waiting for him spread-out across the hilltop, apparently prepared to give battle. Banastre Tarleton sat his horse and gazed out over the American position. This is what he saw: "He [Sumter] posted the center of his troops in some houses and out-houses, composed of logs, and situated on the middle of an eminence; he extended his right along some rails, which were flanked by an inaccessible mountain, and he distributed his left on a rugged piece of ground that was covered by a bend of the river; a small branch of water ran in front of the whole rising ground, which was called Blackstock's hill."[26]

In his *history of the campaigns* Tarleton made it clear that he could view the entire American position from his own vantage point opposite, and he thought it had a "formidable appearance."[26] At that moment Tarleton had with him at best 270 men. He was facing, he knew, about 1,000, and these, he also knew, were not untested militia, but tough frontier fighters, most armed with the long rifle, and many posted behind walls or in buildings. These were troubling odds, even for the usually brash Tarleton. To charge head-first into such a defensive arrangement while so outnumbered was to court disaster. So he decided to wait for the 71st and his artillery to come up, or at least in his recollections he so declares, but he at once had the 80-odd men of the 63rd dismount, and take up a position on the down slope of the hill he had just then occupied. Whether this was intended as a defensive arrangement or simply as a show of force is not clear, but it appears Sumter interpreted the posting as aggressive, and responded immediately.

Sumter sent a detachment of his own down Blackstock's hill out toward the deployed British infantry. The Americans let loose an ineffective volley, then turned and fled before the stout bayonets of the British 63rd, who responded to the American assault and sudden retreat with an advance of their own. Rather than remaining in a defensive posture, as we can presume Tarleton intended, the 63rd, its ardor apparently up at the sight of fleeing Americans, continued to advance until they came within easy range of the riflemen arrayed across the crest of Blackstock's hill. Once they moved into rifle range, all hell broke loose. A sheet of flame and a cloud of smoke rose across the crest of Blackstock's hill, and the men of the 63rd Foot toppled to the ground as if cut down by a reaper, officers the first to fall. Realizing that the British were now in trouble, Sumter ordered an attempt made against the British left flank, an attempt which was spotted and routed when, Tarleton tells us "a troop of cavalry, under Lieutenant Skinner, bravely repulsed the detachment which threatened the flank."[27]

The British 63rd remained pinned down, however, and in danger of being chopped to pieces. So now it was Tarleton's opportunity to respond, and respond he did, immediately employing his favorite tactic, the hell-bent-for-leather frontal assault. Leading the charge himself, Tarleton took his galloping legion straight down the ridge, splashed across the creek then rode straight up Blackstock's hill into the waiting muzzles of the American riflemen. "Though the undertaking appeared hazardous," Tarleton later admitted, in order to cover the withdrawal of the 63rd, which was being cut to ribbons before his eyes, he took the column of dragoons straight at the American position. But this was not Waxhaws, where Buford's Continentals had been deployed foolishly in an open line, but Blackstock's, where most of the American riflemen were hidden behind walls or fences or inside buildings where the slashing cavalry could not get at them. Nevertheless, according to Tarleton his charge proved a great success. "The attack was conducted with great celerity, and, was attended with immediate success," he insisted, this causing the American line to implode and the riflemen to immediately "disperse."[28]

Others, however, were not so fast to crown Tarleton with all the laurels he so quickly claimed for himself. Indeed many eyewitness accounts insisted that the charge never made it to the American line at all, and that the Legion horse was shot down in great numbers, well short of the American riflemen. Light Horse Harry, who was not at Blackstock's hill but studied thoroughly the accounts of the war, concluded that

Tarleton failed in his attempt to break the American line, and was forced to retreat well short of his objective.[29] Far more damning than Lee, however, was the account later written by Lt. Roderick McKenzie of the 71st Highlanders. While it can be stated with certainty that McKenzie was certainly no fan of Tarleton's, nevertheless, after interviewing numerous participants of the action, McKenzie insisted that "Lieutenant Colonel Tarleton, observing their situation [the dilemma faced by the 63rd Foot] charged with his cavalry; unable to dislodge the enemy, either from the log barn or the height upon his left, he was obliged to fall back,"[30] leaving the Gamecock in full possession of the field.

While Tarleton dare not falsify his casualty report of the action, which could later be challenged, he most certainly could embellish the tactical results of the engagement, and this he wasted no time in doing. In his *history of the campaigns* Bloody Ban wrote that "An express was sent to acquaint Earl Cornwallis with the success of his troops," almost immediately after the contest, but Tarleton concedes curiously as well that he thought a pursuit of the enemy "not advisable in the night." Thus a defensive position was assumed by the British Legion "adjoining the field of battle," in order to await daylight, but the truth of the matter was Tarleton retreated a good two miles from Blackstock's before going into bivouac, hardly "adjoining" as he claimed, but far removed from the field where the fight had taken place.

The truth of the matter appears to be that Tarleton, while hardly defeated, did in fact suffer a bloody repulse at Blackstock's hill, a repulse that he later tried to paint as a triumph of arms. And while Tarleton had in all probability suffered a repulse, the martially challenged Sumter, as if unwilling to be out-blundered, would nevertheless punctuate Tarleton's bloody mistake with an equally foolish error of his own. To get a closer look at the retrograde movement of the British 63rd, the Gamecock, ill-advisedly rode down Blackstock's hill to within easy musket range of the retreating Redcoats. For his imprudence he would be rewarded with a chest full of buckshot, surviving a mortal wound by only the slimmest of margins. Severely wounded, the Gamecock would be out of action for months as a result, and Tarleton was well aware of Sumter's wounding at the time. That night Thomas Sumter was laid upon a hide slung between poles, then dragged over land and across water for miles to the safety of another partisan camp. That he survived the episode gives credence to his remarkable vitality, but offers little for his wits. Tarleton wrote: "Three of the enemy's colonels fell in the action, and general Sumpter received a severe wound in the shoulder."[31]

That Tarleton had accurately reported his own casualty count while embellishing his success at Blackstock's can be inferred from Cornwallis' response dated November 22: "I most heartily wish you joy of your success," wrote the general, "But wish it had not cost you so much."[32] The Earl, accepting Tarleton's version of events, later wrote Henry Clinton in New York, advising him of the action at Blackstock's and once again singing Tarleton's praises. "Lieutenant-colonel Tarleton, to save them [the 63rd] from considerable loss, was obliged to attack, although at some hazard, and drove the enemy with loss over the river: Sumpter was dangerously wounded, three of their colonels killed, and about one and twenty men killed, wounded, or taken... It is not easy for Lieutenant-colonel Tarleton to add to the reputation he has acquired in this province; but the defeating of one thousand men, posted on very strong ground, and occupying log houses, with one hundred and ninety cavalry and eighty infantry, is a proof of the spirit and those talents which must render the most essential services to his country."[33] Tarleton's report of the outcome at Blackstock's was, of course, pure baloney. "The best estimate of Rebel casualties is three killed and four wounded. Tarleton lost ninety-two killed and seventy-six wounded, or sixty-two percent of his command that engaged the enemy."[34]

The clash at Blaskstock's was a minor affair, but, regardless of the facts, it firmly established Lt. Colonel Banastre Tarleton in Cornwallis' mind as the most bold, intrepid, fearless, hence useful officer of light troops under his command. As a consequence, whenever and wherever trouble reared its ugly head in the provinces, Cornwallis was sure to send Tarleton and his British Legion to confront any threat or disturbance. And it just so happened that by late December of that year a significant threat, one far more serious than Sumter or Marion could ever have mounted, had, in fact, been reported. For it was then that Cornwallis got wind of Nathanael Greene's arrival and the subsequent division of the American Southern Army into two separate commands, one moving toward the Peedee River, the other toward the Catawba.

Naturally, Cornwallis immediately notified Tarleton by dispatch on December 26 of the impending problem: "A man came this morning from Charlotte town; his fidelity is, however, very doubtful; he says, that Greene marched on

Wednesday last towards the Cheraws, to join General Caswall, and that Morgan, with his infantry and one hundred and twenty-four of Washington's light horse, crossed Biggar's ferry, on Thursday and Friday last, to join Lacey. I expect more certain intelligence before night, when you shall hear again from me."[35]

In just that manner, then, from a galaxy of potential outcomes and adversaries, two commands, one American under Morgan, the other British under Tarleton, were soon to emerge from the backdrop of war and sectional conflict to suddenly take center stage. Considering the chessboard as the pieces were then arranged, their clash appeared inevitable.

CHAPTER ELEVEN

MORGAN

On December 21, 1780 the clatter of horses, the jokes of marching men, and the rhythmic jangle of canteens and powder horns filled the air; the Flying Army was on the move. Just the day before Nathanael Greene had marched off toward Cheraws with his half of the Southern Army, and now it was Morgan's turn to take his posting west of the Catawba River. Above all else, Morgan realized, he had to remain vigilant, for Cornwallis was sure to try and strike at one of the divided American forces, and, with the necessity of protecting Ninety Six at all hazards, most informed observers believed that the hammer would soon fall on Morgan.

The long column, heading off to the south-west, "tramped over hills and through swamps,"[1] mucked its way through heavy rains, and took the better part of five days to cover some sixty miles.[2] As they were neither pursued nor pursuer, speed was not a priority, and Robert Kirkwood, leading the Delaware troops on the long march, noted in his journal that on the first day the Flying Army "March'd to Biggon Ferry on the Catawba River." On the second day the army "Crossed the Ferry and March'd," while on both the 23rd and 24th the column simply "March'd" then "March'd" again. Finally, on Christmas day, the 25th of December, the Flying Army arrived at its destination, Grindal's Shoals on the north, or eastern bank of the Pacolet River, having put both the Catawba and Broad Rivers behind them.[3]

With the Pacolet in front, and Thicketty Creek not far behind, the camp was cold and barren and uninviting, but it was, at least, on the grounds of a plantation owned by the Tory, Alexander Chesney, and the Americans helped themselves to Mr. Chesney's grain, corn, blankets, and trees for firewood.[4] But the area was still reasonably barren, uncultivated country, and the promise of ample food for the men and forage for the horses, while better than at Charlotte, was still meager. So over time Morgan divided the camp even further, with a number of units and recently arrived militia moving off to winter at various locations nearby.

Almost like a gift at Christmas, upon their arrival at Grindal's Shoals the Flying Army received a contingent of sixty men under the local militia leader Andrew Pickens, who had marched to cast their lot with Morgan.[5] Far more than numbers alone, these men represented a significant addition, for in the backcountry of South Carolina, the name Andrew Pickens carried considerable weight. By December of 1780, Pickens had proven himself a tough backwoods fighter and commanding leader of men, and Morgan was thrilled to welcome both Pickens and his men aboard.

Born in Paxton Township, Pennsylvania on the 19th of September, 1739 to a family of Irish immigrants, Pickens' family moved south to Virginia when Andrew was small, then on to Waxhaw, South Carolina in 1752. There the family farmed while young Pickens hunted in the woods and fought the Cherokee on the frontier. He served in the French and Indian War, and later volunteered in the same expedition against the Cherokee as had Francis Marion. In 1765 he married Rebecca Calhoun, aunt of John C. Calhoun, and together they raised a considerable family consisting of six daughters and nine sons. As a leader of militia in the Revolutionary War, Pickens had already defeated a force composed of Tory infantry and their Indian allies outnumbering him two to one at the battle of Kettle Creek. Then when Charleston fell to Clinton and Cornwallis in May of that year, Pickens thought it prudent to take the British oath of allegiance, as rebel resistance in the state suddenly seemed a doomed proposition. But when his family was allegedly threatened by Tory militia, Pickens renounced his oath, and took up arms against the crown again. "His frame was sinewy and active," Light Horse Harry Lee recalled of Andrew Pickens, "his habits were simple, temperate, and industrious. His characteristics were taciturnity and truth, prudence and decision, modesty and courage, disinterestedness and public spirit." Pickens was known for speaking little, and for choosing his words with great care whenever he did. Far less flamboyant than the Gamecock, Andrew Pickens was nevertheless a solid, dependable, cooperative, and fearless fighter.[6] He would prove an enormous asset for Daniel Morgan in the coming days.

The division of the Southern Army into two separate components was intended to accomplish a number of objectives. First and foremost, it was designed to stall Cornwallis, for if he advanced against one component he would have immediate problems with the other (true, unless Cornwallis were to be heavily reinforced, in which case he could advance as he pleased). Secondly, the division would allow the Americans to better subsist in areas that were not already picked clean by marauding bands and marching armies. Finally, it was hoped that word of Morgan's movement west would unite the scattered militia bands operating in that region under his singular command. The jury remained out as far as the first two objectives were concerned, but for days after establishing his camp at Grindal's Shoals, small bands of partisan militia had filtered in. Just two days, for instance, after Pickens' arrival, General Davidson marched into camp with 120 North Carolinians then set off again for North Carolina intent on bringing back another 500.

Many of the militia units that arrived were from Georgia, and while Morgan was happy to welcome them under his wing, he also realized that the hit-and-run form of partisan warfare to which they had all become accustomed would never work against a larger foe such as Cornwallis. Fighting as two or four or ten different groups, with no coordination or comprehensive strategy – as many were still doing – could annoy the British but never defeat them. Joining together as one, centrally directed force was critical to the success of the American cause, and Daniel Morgan, a frontier fighter himself, knew how to put that message to the volunteers in terms they would understand and appreciate, a crafty combination of praise and common sense. So Morgan carefully put his message down in writing, and sent it out with riders to the various groups still operating independently. It read:

"Gentlemen: Having heard of your sufferings, your attachment to the cause of freedom, and your gallantry and address in action, I had formed to myself the pleasing idea of receiving in you, a great and valuable acquisition to my force. Judge then of my disappointment, when I find you scattered about in parties subjected to no orders, nor joining in any general plan to promote the public service. The recollections of your past achievements, and the prospect of future laurels should prevent your acting in such a manner for a moment. You have gained a character and why should you risk the loss of it for the most trifling gratifications. You must know, that in your present situation, you can neither provide for your safety nor assist me in annoying the enemy. Let me then entreat you by the regard you have for your fame, and by your love to your country, to repair to my camp, and subject yourselves to order and discipline. I will ask you to encounter no dangers or difficulties, but what I shall participate in. Should it be thought advisable to form detachments, you may rely on being employed on that business, if it is more agreeable to your wishes: but it is absolutely necessary that your situation and movements should be known to me, so that I may be enabled to direct them in such a manner, that they may tend to the advantage of the whole."[7] Fortunately, Morgan's message was well received, and over the following days and weeks militia units continued to arrive in Morgan's camp on the Pacolet, his numbers slowly swelling.

Several days after establishing camp Morgan received his first correspondence from Nathanael Greene. Dated December 29, the commanding general brought Morgan up to date as to the army's movements, and added some unsettling news. "Dear Sir—We arrived here on the 26th inst., after a very tedious and disagreeable march, owing to the badness of the roads and the poor and weak state of our teams. Our prospects with regard to provisions are mended, but this is no Egypt.

"I have this moment received intelligence that General Leslie has landed at Charlestown, and is on his march to Camden. His force is about 2,000, perhaps something less. I also am informed Lord Cornwallis has collected his troops at Camden. You will watch their motions very narrowly, and take care and guard against a surprise. Should they move in force this way you will endeavor to cross the river and join us. Do not be sparing of your Expresses, but let me know as often as possible your situation. I wish to be fully informed of your prospect respecting provisions, and also the number of militia that have joined you."[8]

Leslie's arrival at Charleston was the unsettling news, the fly in the ointment, so to speak, that Nathanael Greene had not the prior knowledge of to properly calculate into his strategic outlook, and for the divided Americans, it was the sort of news that changed everything. For once Leslie joined with Cornwallis at Camden the combined British force would be sufficiently strong to hold off one of the separated American divisions, while marching on the other. In short, the unexpected arrival of substantial British reinforcements under Leslie negated the logic of the divided American deployment, and in that sense contained within it the germ of disaster. The good news was that Leslie had only begun his march from Charleston toward Camden, and in transit was now having to deal with the same wet, soggy weather that had impeded both Morgan and Greene during the course of their own deployments. The roads had turned to mud and the going was very slow. Still, time appeared short. It was not yet a moment for panic, but it was indeed time for the greatest care and the most meticulous observation of the enemy.

One day after Nathanael Greene wrote his first dispatch to Morgan, Otho Holland Williams followed-up in writing himself from Greene's camp on the Pee Dee, further clarifying the situation as to Leslie's arrival, and speculating as to Cornwallis' probable intent. Williams, no fool when it came to discerning the enemy's intentions, clearly grasped the dangerous situation that suddenly confronted the separated elements of the American Army, as well as its probable outcome. A single misstep over the coming days might prove fatal, he knew, not only for the Southern Army, but for the very cause of independence. It was, therefore, time for the greatest care, deliberation, and vigilance, a fact Otho Williams was painfully aware of. "Col. Marion writes the General that Gen. Leslie landed with his command at Chas. town on the 20th inst., and that he had advanced as far as Monk's Corner," wrote Williams. "You know Lord Cornwallis has collected his force in Camden, probably they mean to form a junction and attempt to give a blow to a part of our force, while we are divided, and most probably that blow will be aimed at you, as our position in the centre of a wilderness is less accessible than your camp. I know your discretion renders all caution from me unnecessary, but my Friendship will plead an excuse for the impertinence of wishing you to run no risque(sic) of a defeat."[9]

The danger to Morgan's command now appeared amplified considerably, thus reliance upon his fighting abilities suddenly far more critical to the fate of the aspiring nation than perhaps originally calculated when American forces had been initially divided, just days before. Put simply, with Leslie's arrival a great deal now rode on the Old Wagoner's shoulders, and while all were aware of Daniel Morgan's reputation, one nagging question no doubt persisted: Was he up to this newly complicated task? Everyone knew Dan Morgan could fight, but was he as well an excellent commander? Would he blunder in the face of a significant force sent for no purpose other than to destroy him? Would his temper, ego, illness, or his lack of formal military training get the better of him? No one knew the answers to these questions, but it certainly appeared that the time was rapidly approaching when the answers would be revealed, for better or worse.

Meanwhile, the ever vigilant Cornwallis had not been sitting on his thumbs as Greene and Morgan initiated their scheme. The day after Christmas he received information concerning the dual American movements, news that he immediately passed on to Tarleton, advising his favorite cavalryman that "Morgan and Washington have passed Broad river."[10] Tarleton would later put into writing the general grasp of the situation the British high command held at the moment: "During the preparations for the second invasion of North Carolina, emissaries had been dispatched into that province, to obtain intelligence of the force and designs of the Americans. Near the end of December information was received, that General Greene had made a division of his troops, who did not exceed one thousand four hundred men, exclusive of the militia; and, that he had committed the light infantry and colonel Washington's cavalry to General Morgan, with directions to pass the Catawba and Broad rivers, in order to collect the militia in the districts through which he marched, and afterwards to threaten Ninety Six; whilst he conducted the other division of the continentals to Haley's ferry, on the river Pedee, to form a junction with General Caswall, and give jealousy to Camden. This appeared to be the outline of the American designs previous to the arrival of General Leslie's reinforcements."[11]

While Cornwallis had scouts out searching for Morgan, Morgan already had scouts of his own out scouring the entire region, monitoring the country on a wide arc, and one soon returned with unpleasant news – a band of Tory militia was wreaking havoc just twenty miles or so south of Grindal's Shoals. Morgan knew that the only way to gain the confidence of local rebel militia was to prove a worthy commander, and in the frontier districts that proof meant *action*. "He added 200 mounted militiamen under Major James McCall to William Washington's dragoons and ordered the hard-riding cavalryman to advance against the raiders."[12]

The Tory band got word of Washington's approach, however, and rapidly withdrew toward Ninety Six, but Washington pursued them vigorously, finally hunting them down at a place called Hammond's Store on December 30.[13] Again the loyalists fled, but Washington, like Tarleton before him, pursued them with a vengeance, and this time it was the saber-wielding Americans who attacked with brutality. "One hundred and fifty Loyalists were hacked to death or badly mutilated and forty taken prisoner. Washington then dispatched some of his horsemen against the Loyalist stronghold at Williams' Plantation fifteen miles from Ninety Six, only to discover that its occupants had fled."[14]

But Williams' Plantation was dangerously near the critical British post of Ninety Six, and any American operations in that area as a direct consequence had to be taken seriously by Cornwallis. Something would have to be done to counter Washington's sudden appearance at Williams', and done immediately to restore strength and confidence in the British left. Cornwallis turned at once to Tarleton. He wrote on January 2nd: "I sent Haldane to you last night, to desire you would pass Broad river, with the legion and the first battalion of the 71st, as soon as possible. If Morgan is still at Williams', or any where within your reach, I should wish you to push him the utmost: I have not heard, except from McArthur, of his having cannon; nor would I believe it, unless he has it from very good authority: It is, however, possible, and Ninety Six is of so much consequence, that no time is to be lost."[15]

Morgan had, in fact, done little more than respond to local Tory provocations by sending Washington south, but from small acorns mighty oaks do grow. Now Tarleton had been given his marching orders to "push" Morgan to the "utmost," and the aggressive cavalry commander lost no time responding. "On receipt of this letter [Cornwallis' instructions]," Tarleton explained, "he [Tarleton] directed his course to the westward, and employed every engine to obtain intelligence of the enemy." But by the time Tarleton arrived near Williams' Plantation Morgan's cavalry had already withdrawn from the area, so Tarleton halted his command, and allowed "time for the junction of the baggage of the different, corps."[16] Once he was sure of Morgan's whereabouts and strength, Tarleton devised his own plan for the destruction of the Flying Army, a plan which he confidently presented to Cornwallis via dispatch on January 4:

"Morgan, with upwards of one thousand two hundred men, being on this side Broad river, to threaten Ninety Six, and evade your lordship's army whenever you may move, I beg leave to offer my opinion how his design may be prevented.

"I must draw my baggage, the 71st and legion's are deposited at my old camp, to me. I wish it to be escorted by the 17th Light dragoons, for whom horses are ready; by the yagers, if to be spared; and by the 7th regiment. The 7th I will send, as soon as I reach Ennoree, with the field piece, to Ninety Six. My encampment is now twenty miles from Brierley's, in a plentiful forge country, and I can lay in four days flour for a move. When I advance, I must either destroy Morgan's corps, or push it before me over Broad river, towards King's mountain. The advance of the army should commence (when your lordship orders this corps to move) onwards for King's mountain. Frequent communication by letter can pass the Broad river. I feel myself bold in offering my opinion, as it flows from zeal for the public service, and well-grounded enquiry concerning the enemy's designs and operations."[17]

There it was, a simple, compact plan to either destroy Morgan's Flying Army, or else drive it like a heard of cattle into the waiting clutches of the rest of the British Army, once, that is, Cornwallis had marched up the east bank of the Broad towards King's Mountain and taken position thereabouts. There was nothing unruly, overly elaborate, or fanciful about Tarleton's thinking, and he requested quality reinforcements enough to strengthen his column sufficiently for the task as he saw it. It was a good plan.

And Cornwallis was simply thrilled by Tarleton's suggestion. After reading over the dispatch, the British general responded approvingly: "You have exactly done what I wished you to do, and understood my intentions perfectly. Less my letter of this morning should miscarry, I repeat most material paragraph. Your baggage is ordered to Brierley's, under care of seventh regiment. I propose to march on Sunday."[18] Cornwallis intended to march on Sunday, thus Tarleton would begin his advance toward Morgan at the same time, both columns moving up opposite sides of the Broad River like the twin faces of a vise hoping to catch and flatten Morgan between them. Events had now been put in motion; the die had been cast – both Tarleton and Cornwallis would march on Morgan.

At the same time, at Morgan's camp on the Pacolet, the good news that American effective strength was steadily growing due to the arrival of the local militias, was in turn offset by the fact that Morgan now had to feed a growing contingent with food he did not have and could not find anywhere in the local area. As Morgan saw it, he had but two options. He could return to North Carolina in order to better subsist his command, but that, he feared, would smack of retreat and discourage those remaining frontier militias still on the fence when it came to commitment. The other option

– and the one that far better suited Morgan's aggressive temperament – was to go over to the offensive and deliver a blow somewhere.

Morgan's aggressive instincts took a further boost after his own Captain Chitty returned from a meeting with Thomas Sumter's partisans, a meeting in which Morgan had attempted to establish a positive working relationship with the Gamecock. Although Morgan carried orders from Nathanael Greene empowering him to take command of all militia west of the Broad, Morgan, aware of Sumter's infinitely delicate sensibilities, had decided to try and coax the South Carolinian into cooperation rather than bludgeon him with orders. Greene had been confident the Gamecock would work with Morgan by supplying the much needed provisions for his troops, but Chitty returned empty-handed. Indeed, the Gamecock – still recuperating from the wound he had suffered at Blackstock's in November –had refused to cooperate with Morgan in any way, and was in fact brooding over the Old Wagoner's deployment in an area he considered, operationally speaking, his, and his alone.

Morgan, to his credit, let the matter drop, but the Gamecock's refusal to help provision the Flying Army only served to underscore in Morgan's mind the need to move on. Looking over a map of the area, he finally decided upon a march through the backwoods to attack Savannah in northern Georgia, a movement that would take him far from Greene and the other half of the American forces. Morgan was first and foremost a fighter, and the fact that such a move would remove the Flying Army from its strategic position west of Cornwallis, did not appear to weigh heavily, if at all, in his calculations. Considering the fact that both Greene and Morgan were then aware of Leslie's arrival, and that the British reinforcements greatly undermined the already precarious status of the American's divided commands, Morgan's impatient idea, from a practical perspective, was not only unwise, but dangerous.

Fortunately, Morgan was a man of far greater character than Thomas Sumter. Rather than brood or pout or march his corps without approval, on January 4 he laid out his thoughts in writing to Nathanael Greene, hoping the American general would concur with his reasoning and approve the movement. After reporting on Washington's success near Ninety Six, Morgan got down to business: "My Situation is far from being agreeable to my Wishes or Expectations," he pointed out. "Forage and Provisions are not to be had. Here we cannot subsist so that we have but one alternative, either to retreat or move into Georgia. A retreat will be attended with the most fatal consequences. The Spirit which now begins to pervade the People and call them into the Field will be destroyed. The Militia who have already joined will desert us, and it is not improbable that a Regard for their own Safety will induce them to join the Enemy.

"I shall await with impatience for your directions on the subject of my letter by Colonel Malmady, as till then my operations must be in a manner suspended."[19]

To Morgan's inquiry Nathanael Greene responded on January 8 with both good nature and good sense. Among many various suggestions, he laid out the obvious reasons that a movement of Morgan's Flying Army into Georgia would create far more problems than it could ever hope to solve: “I have maturely considered your proposition of an expedition into Georgia,” he wrote, “and cannot think it warrantable in the critical situation our Army is in. I have no small reason to think, by intelligence from different quarters, that the enemy have a movement in contemplation, and in all probability it will be this way, from the impudence of the Tories, who are collecting in different quarters in the most inaccessible swamps and morasses. Should you go into Georgia and the enemy push this way, your whole force will be useless.”[20] Useless indeed. So the expedition into Georgia was out, and as a consequence Morgan had no choice, for the time being at least, but to seek forage and provisions near his base on the Pacolet, and await further developments.

Unknown at the time, of course, to either Morgan or Nathanael Greene, Banastre Tarleton had already halted his column at Brooke’s Bush River Plantation near Brierley’s Ford while awaiting his baggage and reinforcements from Cornwallis.[21] His intention was to procure four days rations and forage, then on Sunday cross over Indian and Dunken creeks while driving north toward the Enoree River with all his usual vigor. Somewhere north of the Enoree it can be safely presumed that Tarleton, not only expected to find Morgan, but to promptly engage and destroy the Flying Army.

CHAPTER TWELVE

TARLETON

At Brierley's Tarleton awaited only his reinforcements and baggage train before heading north to confront Morgan. His plan, although specific to Morgan, had been accepted heartily by Cornwallis because it fit comfortably within the British Model, that bit of elitist fantasy previously referenced in Chapter Eight that governed British strategic rationale at the time. The principle notion contained in the model, it may be recalled, was that a legion of eager Loyalists waited only the arrival of British arms in order to rise against their rebel tormenters and march hand-in-hand with their red-coated friends through the Southern states, thus destroying the rebellion. That this wave of Loyalist sentiment was, in fact, essentially illusory never seems to have dawned on British war planners, thus its continued inclusion in all designs concerning regional maneuver remained unchanged.

That abundant evidence existed to contradict the British Model – militia forces, ambuscades, rampant disrespect and disloyalty, as examples – was simply ignored, just as the young romantic ignores the wayward ways of his heart's desire until all is lost. In his *history of the campaigns* Tarleton readily admits to the powerful effect of this recurring delusion: "The strength of the royal army in South Carolina, near the end of the year 1780, allowed Earl Cornwallis the experiment of an enterprise, which the loyalists and British troops in America, as the administration in England, supposed he could with facility accomplish. The superiority of his force, when compared with General Greene's, gave every reasonable assurance, that with proper care the latter might be destroyed or driven over the Roanoke; when it was imagined that the loyalists, who were computed to be the greater proportion of the inhabitants, would make indefatigable exertions to render themselves independent of Congress. Such was the opinion of thousands when the King's troops prepared for this expedition: But their expectations were not verified... "[1]

It can be recalled that Tarleton's plan called for a convergence of two separate columns, his own advancing up the south (or west) side of Broad River while Cornwallis, with the larger portion of the British Army, marched up the north (or east) bank of the Broad. Moving more or less in tandem on opposite sides of the river, Cornwallis was to take up a defensive position somewhere near King's Mountain. Tarleton then planned on either destroying Morgan outright – which, we can presume, for obvious reasons was his first choice – or else driving him into Cornwallis' waiting clutches. Either way, Morgan would be destroyed and the pathway into North Carolina opened for offensive maneuver. With Morgan's Flying Army dispatched, Nathanael Greene would have no hope of standing before Cornwallis' combined force – now additionally reinforced by Leslie – and would be forced to flee with all dispatch with what little remained of the Southern Continental Army. The entire South would then fall to the strength of British arms, and the American revolution soon collapse for want of support not long thereafter – this, at least, appears to have been the thinking.

The plan was good, but almost all combat plans seem good until the elements of time, geography, weather, egos, logistics, provisions, personal conflicts, human frailty, etc., etc. are suddenly injected like aggressive viruses into their shallow, intellectual structures. Often then, those same plans, which appeared virtually foolproof only days or even hours before, unravel like wet tissues in the rain, only then to disintegrate entirely, suddenly taking on the stark appearance of mindless blunder or incomprehensible fiasco; the work, not of professionals, but of amateurs, idiots, or fools. Such is, and has always been, the maddening, unpredictable nature of warfare. Indeed, the coordination of two separated columns over space and time with the object of converging simultaneously on a distant target – although basic in concept, and seemingly simple in execution – has been proven time and again one of the most difficult of military maneuvers to achieve, and neither Tarleton or Cornwallis were at the time immune from this reality. Nevertheless, initially, at least, both commanders appeared completely sanguine of success. On January 8 Cornwallis confidently advised Tarleton: "I shall remain here to-morrow, march to cross roads on Wednesday, halt Thursday, and reach Bullock's-creek meeting house Saturday."[2]

Tarleton, no doubt, was equally confident of success, for his force had been substantially augmented with veteran reinforcements. According to historian Lawrence E. Babits, "Tarleton's command in January 1781 included infantry, artillery, and cavalry, making up what would be called a combined arms group today. It combined rapid movement with heavy firepower and included all of Cornwallis' light infantry. Both the British Legion infantry and the 71st Regiment were known for their rapid marching and ferocity in battle."[3] When fully assembled, and with the addition of the 17th Regiment, Tarleton's force, including some fifty royal artillerymen to work two light field pieces, would number approximately 1,100 effective troops.[4] Surely it was a powerful force, yet it was also a command substantially larger than anything the young cavalrymen was used to handling. Thus, while Morgan might be at the head of an independent command for the very first time, Tarleton as well was riding off into uncharted waters, facts that enliven our drama with the unpredictable element of inexperience on both sides of the equation.

While Tarleton laid in his forage and flour for the four days he presumed adequate to either drive or destroy the Flying Army, Nathanael Greene alerted Morgan that the Americans at their camp on the Pee Dee had gotten wind of Tarleton's errand, and suggested his lieutenant stand firm near his base on the Pacolet. "It is my wish also that you should hold your ground if possible," Greene wrote, "for I foresee the disagreeable consequences that will result from a retreat... Col. Tarleton is said to be on his way to pay you a visit. I doubt not but he will have a decent reception and a proper dismission. And I am happy to find you have taken every precaution to avoid a surprise... "[5]

As the situation slowly resolved into greater clarity over the coming days, however, it appears Nathanael Greene began to notice dark clouds suddenly tumbling along the horizon of his well-crafted plan, rising omens of disaster that increasingly he could not brush aside. He took the time, once again, to put his thoughts into writing for his distant subordinate, for it seems to have become painfully clear to Greene at this point that Morgan was, in fact, the target of all British maneuvers. Greene also appears to have suddenly realized just how hazardous the situation was becoming for Morgan, potentially caught as he might be between two converging enemy columns. "I was informed of Lord Cornwallis' movements before the arrival of your letter," he wrote, "and agree with you in opinion that you are the object; and from the making of so general a movement it convinces me he feels a great inconvenience from your force and situation."

This sense of "inconvenience," of course, was precisely what the twin American deployments was supposed to inspire in the enemy's mind, and Greene was seeing nothing more than his strategy coming to fruition, but now, it seems, with an almost frightening immediacy. "He would never harass his troops to remove you," Greene went on to Morgan, "if he did not think it an object of some importance. Nor would he put his collective force in motion if he did not have some respect for your numbers." Then, almost as if it suddenly dawned on Nathanael Greene as he was writing that his own strategy had in fact inaugurated this dangerous state of affairs, he seemed to grow wary; to back away from the seemingly ominous consequences of what he had wrought.

One can almost see Nathanael Greene's brow furrow deeply as he continued to write: "I am sensible your situation is critical," he continued, "and requires the most watchful attention to guard against surprize. But I think it is of great importance to keep up a force in that quarter, nor can I persuade myself that the militia alone will answer the same valuable purposes as when joined by the Continental troops." Now, suddenly, the stark nature of the reality he had created became manifestly clear to Nathanael Greene – Tarleton *and* Cornwallis were both after Morgan, and if Morgan were to blunder, all would be lost. Suddenly, calamity was staring Nathanael Greene right in the face, and he immediately turned away from the confrontation he had just days before welcomed. "It is not my wish you should come to action unless you have a manifest superiority and a moral certainty of succeeding."

Now, this suggestion of Greene's is all well and good, but it is also obvious that Morgan's command was not about to have a manifest superiority over Tarleton's column anytime soon, and a moral certainty of success in warfare is something only a fool might profess. Morgan was aggressive and a fighter to the core, but he was no fool. It seems clear that Nathanael Greene at this point was beginning to feel the heat of the situation he, himself, had created, and his advice to Morgan was of the greatest caution. No longer does he seem assured that Morgan will provide Tarleton a "proper dismission," as he so confidently predicted just days before, but virtually pleads instead for Morgan to consider withdrawal and inaction. "Put nothing to the hazard," he warned, "a retreat may be disagreeable but not disgraceful.

Regard not the opinion of the day. It is not our business to risque too much, our affairs are in too critical a situation and require time and nursing to give them a better tone."

Then in closing, as if he had not as yet made his preference for caution clear enough, General Greene decided to leave nothing to doubt. "Before they can possibly reach you I imagine the movements of Lord Cornwallis and Col. Tarleton will be sufficiently explained, and you obliged to take some decisive measure. I shall be perfectly satisfied if you keep clear of a misfortune, for, tho' I wish you laurels, yet I am unwilling to expose the common cause to give you an opportunity to acquire them."[6]

Nathanael Greene can be forgiven for his sudden bout of anxiety. It was, in the final analysis, little more than the normal self-questioning any intelligent person undergoes when their happy plans are suddenly seized and shaken by the angry fist of an unforgiving reality. Greene was an able fighter and a brave man, qualities he had already established during the course of the war, and qualities he would prove time and again. Still, it was fortunate for the American cause that Morgan did not receive this dispatch of Greene's until after he had already met Tarleton on the field of battle, for an earlier reception may well have critically injured any prospect for success, had Morgan acted on Greene's anxious concerns, and not his better instincts.

Stuck now at Grindal's Shoals, Daniel Morgan's temper was deteriorating. He had been ordered not to advance, yet he dared not withdraw. Men were coming and going to and from his camp like flies from a dish of sugar water, such that a proper count was something that was often impossible. And now he had been informed of Leslie's advance toward

Camden, and that Tarleton and Cornwallis both were probably soon to be headed in his direction. If true, those facts promised troubling odds. Morgan was no amateur, and while he relished a crack at Tarleton, he also realized that any clash would have to take place distant enough from Cornwallis and the main body of the British Army to prevent Tarleton from being strengthened even further by additional reinforcements; or worse, Cornwallis marching directly to Tarleton's support. Additionally, Morgan realized that any retreat the Flying Army might have to make would have to be northward, not east toward Greene and Cornwallis, and that any such movement would have to be made with the greatest speed in order to avoid being either cut off or crushed entirely; the very outcome Tarleton had sketched out for Cornwallis and was even then preparing to administer. To say the least, at the moment Daniel Morgan and his Flying Army faced a dicey situation indeed.

To avoid entrapment or a surprise from Tarleton, Morgan dispatched much of his cavalry and the South Carolina militia under Pickens to points south in order to monitor the fords and roads in that direction. Andrew Pickens, now in command of a full brigade of South Carolina militia, was to hopefully perform as a screen between Tarleton's advance and Morgan.[7] It was an assignment of the greatest importance. With the Broad River flowing along his left then turning north along his rear, and with Tarleton maneuvering somewhere south of Grindal's Shoals, Morgan was surely in a precarious position. With time and information he might maneuver his way out of trouble, but any surprise might easily produce calamity.

By the 11th of January Tarleton had received his baggage and reinforcements and was prepared to move north from Brierley's Ford. At the moment he was operating on the original timetable laid out by Cornwallis, and he had every expectation that it would be adhered to by both advancing columns. But the inclement weather had already impeded Leslie's advance to the point that Cornwallis was himself forced to delay. On January 9 the commanding British general sent this dispatch off to Lord Rowdon at Camden: "I think it prudent to remain here a day or two longer, otherwise by the corps on my flanks being so far behind, I should be in danger of losing my communication. I have not heard from Tarleton this day, nor am I sure whether he has passed the Enoree."[8] It is clear from this correspondence that communication – thus coordination – between Cornwallis and Tarleton had already broken down.

But Tarleton, unaware that Cornwallis had delayed his march, dashed ahead on the 11th, moving with his usual speed north to a position near Newberry, South Carolina, still south of the Enoree River, but only about forty miles below Grindal's Shoals. Then on the 13th, through muck and mud and swollen creeks, Tarleton's long column labored all the way north to the Enoree, where he immediately initiated measures to begin crossing over his troops. Unknown to Morgan, the game was on.

CHAPTER THIRTEEN

MORGAN

On January 11, as Banastre Tarleton made his camp just south of the Enoree River, Andrew Pickens' South Carolina brigade remained camped above the river with pickets out observing the fords along the river for any sign of enemy activity. Pickens may have been frontier bred, but he understood his business, and he had created an effective system of scouts that, like a spider's web, was capable of detecting the slightest alien tremor. When Tarleton broke camp early on the 12th and started for the Enoree, his movement was spotted by one of Pickens' scouts and promptly reported.[1] In turn Pickens sent a rider back to Grindal's Shoals with the news. It was news that Daniel Morgan, initially at least, did not care to hear, but he wasted no time in pouting. He immediately recalled Washington's cavalry and all the small units that had been wintering near Grindal's Shoals. He also recalled Andrew Pickens' South Carolina Brigade, asking Pickens to screen the Flying Army as it slipped back toward Morgan's main camp on the Pacolet. All reports indicated that Tarleton was nearing rapidly with some 1,200 men, a force Morgan knew at the time he could not match.[2] Nevertheless, sensible steps had to be taken, and Morgan dispatched riders north along the Broad to hold the important fords, while also sending out riders to enjoin all the local militias to immediately march to his aid.

It is not clear precisely when Morgan adopted the plan he did, but it is reasonable that he did so early on, and not as a harried response to sudden necessity. His basic idea was to move toward the northwest on the Green River Road, drawing Tarleton farther away, mile-by-mile, from Cornwallis into a territory that had already been picked clean of forage and food. Morgan knew that Tarleton marched hard, spared no one, and would drive his men to the extreme to achieve the twin elements of shock and surprise. Thus every additional mile north toward the North Carolina line that Morgan could draw Tarleton represented one more mile farther from help for the British, an extra mile of hard marching, and a mile deeper into terrain that could not well support them. In contrast, all the while Morgan would be moving increasingly into friendly territory. Morgan's battle plan appears to have been simple. Not far above the North Carolina line Dan Morgan planned on gaining the hills on or near Thicketty Mountain where he could make a defensive stand, perhaps fighting Tarleton much as he had Johnny Burgoyne's troops at Freeman's Farm so many years before; his rifleman firing from behind trees and rocks while the Continentals covered his flanks and responded to British bayonets with bayonets of their own.

No doubt Morgan had also by then developed a clear idea as to what he might expect from Tarleton, should their commands ever come face-to-face. William Washington, his cavalry chief, for instance, was well acquainted with the British Colonel, and Tarleton's tactics had by then become almost legend throughout the South. It might be recalled that Washington had more than once been surprised by a charging Tarleton, and in that sense had a score to settle with the British cavalryman. Many of the local militia had fought against Tarleton at Blackstock's as well, and it can be presumed that Morgan knew Tarleton would chase him to the ends of the earth, and then, if successful, attack frontally and at once. Known for speed, persistence, ferocity, and barbarity, there was nothing terribly sophisticated or cerebral that might be expected from Banastre Tarleton in his manner of deployment or design of attack. In a sense it would be like one of the Old Wagoner's now almost forgotten barroom brawls back in Battletown, Virginia, standing toe-to-toe and throwing fists and elbows at one another until one man was knocked to the floor, the other left standing. Indeed, Morgan would later write that "I knew my adversary, and was perfectly sure I should have nothing but downright fighting."[3] In that sense, at the time Morgan appeared to have had a very clear grasp of both Tarleton the man and Tarleton the soldier. The question was did Tarleton have any real grasp of Morgan?

Meanwhile, Tarleton had his men construct rafts to float his infantry over the Enoree, while simultaneously having scouts out in search of the best fords for crossing the Tyger. Typically, his march was organized, efficient, and relentless. Moving ever west, Tarleton "continued his course on the 12th to the westward," he wrote, "in order to discover the most practicable fords for the passage of the Ennoree and Tyger, and that the infantry might avoid the inconveniencies they had undergone in crossing the other waters." This constant westward movement disguised, thought Tarleton, the basic British plan of ensnaring Morgan between Tarleton and Cornwallis as both moved north. Tarleton explained: "In proportion to the approach of the [British] light troops to the sources of the rivers, and the progress of the main army to King's mountain, General Morgan's danger would increase, if he remained to the westward of Broad river."[4] Like a cowboy herding cattle, it was Tarleton's notion that by staying to the west he would be pushing Morgan into a sort of corral between Cornwallis and his own column where, once cornered, the Americans would be ripe for slaughter.

On January 14 Tarleton crossed both the Enoree and Tyger rivers, the Loyalist Alexander Chesney serving as his local guide. He then continued his march west in order to cut off any movement Morgan might make in that direction, in that manner keeping his adversary trapped between the two closing British columns. From his advanced scouts Tarleton had secured intelligence as to Morgan's location, and he was wasting no time in closing the gap. As the Redcoats splashed across the Tyger, they were less than thirty miles from Grindal's Shoals, and closing rapidly, but they were also now a hard three days out on the march, and burning quickly through what remained of their four day's rations. If fatigue was not yet a factor as the British marched, it soon would be if they maintained the same labored pace.

Fortunately for Morgan, his scouts were by the 14th watching Tarleton's movements very closely, and shortly after the British splashed across Tyger River, he had word of the British advance. By now Morgan had little doubt that the Flying Army was Tarleton's objective, and he began a series of moves in preparation. First he dispatched militia to points along the Pacolet fords to block Tarleton's advance across the river, or at least report promptly if a crossing should be forced. Then he packed his camp and moved northwest toward Burr's Mill on Thicketty Creek where a temporary camp was constructed, thus forcing Tarleton to continually advance in order to catch up, and this over a territory already stripped of food and forage. Morgan explains his strategic thinking: "My former position subjected me at once to the operations of Lord Cornwallis and Colonel Tarleton, and in case of a defeat my retreat might easily have been cut off."[5] As historian Lawrence Babits notes, "The flying Army grew stronger as detachments came in, but Morgan continued marching northwest, sending units ahead to gather supplies and protect the route."[6] The weather was cold and wet and Morgan knew that a spirited advance over a number of days like the one Tarleton was pressing, would eventually take a severe toll on his men and animals alike. If there was going to be a fight, it was clearly an aspect of Morgan's strategy that if and when that fight took place, his men would still be reasonably fresh while Tarleton's would be suffering from the effects of hunger and exhaustion. It would prove a cagey, veteran strategy.

After crossing over the Enoree and Tyger rivers, Tarleton's scouts discovered that Morgan's pickets were guarding all the fords along the Pacolet, thus complicating his advance.[7] The British cavalryman also received a dispatch from Cornwallis, bringing him up to date as to the rest of the army's movements. "About the same time," wrote Tarleton, "Earl Cornwallis advertised Tarleton, that the main army had reached Bull's run, and that General Leslie had surmounted the difficulties which had hitherto retarded his march." Cornwallis' dispatch, dated January 14 read: "Leslie is out of the swamps. I have not heard of Morgan's moving; but conclude he will not cross Broad river: I hear it has fallen very much."[8] After reading the dispatch from Cornwallis Tarleton must have imagined his plan to trap Morgan blossoming toward fruition, for he wrote back directly to Cornwallis, requesting that both columns move quickly on the timetable they had previously agreed upon. "At this crisis Lieutenant-colonel Tarleton assured Earl Cornwallis that he would endeavor to pass the Pacolet, purposely to force General Morgan to retreat towards Broad river, and requested his lordship to proceed up the eastern bank without delay, because such a movement might perhaps admit of co-operation, and would undoubtedly stop the retreat of the Americans."[9]

No doubt Banastre Tarleton could at that moment envision his plan of a convergence upon Morgan's Flying Army working almost to perfection. All that was needed now was to somehow get across the Pacolet, and then force Morgan – who Tarleton knew to be only a few miles ahead – to fight or flee. The sun rose on a bitterly cold January 15, the fifth day of Tarleton's harried advance, and it can be recalled that he had packed away only enough food and forage for a four day adventure. In that sense, if Tarleton intended to make something happen, it would have to be done very soon, or else he would be forced to stop to rest his men while scouring the area for additional provisions – all this while

Morgan happily escaped his trap. "On the 15th," Tarleton advises us, "circumstantial intelligence was procured... of the different guards stationed on the Pacolet. A march was commenced in the evening towards the iron works, which are situated high upon the river; but in the morning the course was altered, and the light troops secured a passage within six miles of the enemy's camp."[10]

In short, Tarleton had managed to slip away from the fords guarded by the Continentals under the cover of darkness, faking an encampment while, unbeknownst to Morgan, crossing his force undetected at Easterwood Ford, a mere six miles distant from Morgan's camp.[11] Morgan's pickets had fallen for Tarleton's charade. For a weary commander driving weary troops, it was a clever and well-executed maneuver in the cold and dark of a January night. It was by then the early morning hours of January 16, and Tarleton wasted no time dispatching his scouts directly to locate and occupy a camp previously constructed in the area by Patrick Ferguson when he had campaigned in the area. "As soon as the corps were assembled beyond the Pacolet Lieutenant-colonel Tarleton thought it advisable to advance towards some log houses, formerly constructed by Major Ferguson, which lay between the British and Americans, and were reported to be unoccupied by General Morgan."[12] Not knowing precisely where Morgan was at the moment, or the American's intentions at the time, taking temporary possession of a potential defensive position was for Tarleton a wise move.

But for Morgan, Tarleton's crossing the Pacolet smacked of disaster. The one thing he could not allow had now happened – a surprise! At Burr's Mill the Americans were quietly cooking their breakfasts, smoke trailing gently up between the lofty trees, when a scout on horseback came bounding into camp with the terrible news. Tarleton was across the Pacolet! The report must have struck Morgan like a bolt of lightening, but in fact it was just the sort of thing that brought out the best in the Old Wagoner. Known for his cool under fire, he responded immediately. "Morgan shouted for the wagons to be loaded. The men, preparing breakfast around small fires, scrambled to their feet, and soon the little army was ready to move."[13] Leaving a screen of North Carolina militia behind to both watch and try and delay Tarleton's advance, then ordering Washington's cavalry to cover his flanks and rear, Morgan had the Flying Army on the road toward the North Carolina line in short order. He probably realized by then that a fight with Tarleton was inevitable, and that when and where that engagement would take place were really the only questions that remained unanswered. With luck he might still be able to get the Flying Army across the Broad River and take up a position near Thicketty Mountain as he had originally planned. But if his luck didn't hold, well, he would have to make do.

CHAPTER FOURTEEN

TARLETON

Tarleton immediately had his dragoons on the move, searching for the log huts Patrick Ferguson had previously constructed while campaigning in the area. The British cavalryman's thinking was clear. He "intended to take post, with his whole corps, behind the log houses, and wait the motions of the enemy."[1] There he would be able to rest and feed his weary troops while assuming a strong defensive position, should Morgan move to attack. His only real fear at the time was that Morgan would get to the huts first and take up that same position, thus flipping the defensive scenario in Tarleton's face. But his scouts soon returned with welcome news. Not only were the huts unoccupied, but the Americans had hastily deserted their own camp at Burr's Mill and appeared to be fleeing north. For Tarleton this could have meant only one thing, and the news must have warmed his heart: He had Morgan on the run.

So there would be no break for his weary troops; not with the Flying Army racing away. No, Morgan could not be allowed to elude his trap! So Tarleton ordered everyone back up and onto the mud soaked Green River Road again, and the exhausting march was renewed once more. Late in the afternoon his column finally approached Morgan's now abandoned camp at Burr's Mill, and it can be assumed that the British cavalryman was more than pleased by what he found there.[2] The American's campfires were still smoldering, and there were half-cooked rations everywhere in abundance – clear evidence of just how badly the Americans had been surprised!

Imagine that! Tarleton must have been euphoric. He had come close to catching the famous Morgan napping, if not literally, then at least figuratively, just as he had surprised Thomas Sumter at Fishing Creek, not to mention the entire American command at Monck's Corner before that. Perhaps, Tarleton may well have reasoned, with Morgan on the run, he would soon chase down this new American general just as he had Buford at Waxhaws and wreck Morgan without the need of Cornwallis' assistance at all. Everything at that moment appeared to be going as planned. Tarleton was the great wolf once again, chasing down a wounded prey, the famous Morgan now running just as Buford had run before him.

As they entered the abandoned American camp Tarleton noted that "the British light troops were directed to occupy their position, because it yielded a good post, and afforded plenty of provisions, which they had left behind them, half-cooked, in every part of their encampment."[3] One can easily imagine the hungry British troopers falling upon the deserted food throughout the camp, for they had been pushing hard, often both day and night, in the wet and cold, for five days, and already they may have been nearing the limit of their endurance. As his men devoured the food around them and rested as best they could, Tarleton finally found time to dash off a quick dispatch to Cornwallis, his first since the 14th. "My Lord," he wrote, sounding almost breathless, "I have been most cruelly retarted by the waters. Morgan is in *force and gone for Cherokee Ford.* I wish he could be stopped."[4] Thus did Tarleton conclude his short report, expecting that Cornwallis would march with all dispatch for Cherokee Ford on the Broad River in order to block Morgan's harried retreat. But unbeknownst to Tarleton, Cornwallis was still far south waiting for Leslie to catch up with his reinforcements. Tarleton didn't know it then, but for the time being at least, he was on his own.

But since Tarleton could be sure of nothing at the moment, "Partoles and spies were immediately dispatched to observe the Americans: The dragoons were directed to follow the enemy till dark, and the other emissaries to continue their inquiries till morning, if some material incident did not occur." Later that evening the dragoons returned with news that Morgan had "struck into byways, tending towards Thickelee [Thicketty] creek."[5] What was Morgan up to? Tarleton could not be sure at the moment, but it appeared from the dragoon's reports that the Americans had left the Green River Road for some other local roadway that was better known by the local militia, or perhaps in better condition than the main turnpike.

Then Tarleton had a stroke a good fortune. An American militia colonel had foolishly left the column and was in turn swept up by Tarleton's Tory scouts and promptly delivered to the British camp where Tarleton was able to question him in detail. According to the colonel, Morgan was then in the process of being heavily reinforced. Whether this was fact or deliberate disinformation is not clear, but Tarleton grasped its meaning and decided to move with some caution. "The examination of the militia colonel," said Tarleton, "and other accounts soon afterwards received, evinced the propriety of hanging upon General Morgan's rear, to impede the junction of reinforcements, said to be approaching, and likewise to prevent his passing Broad river without the knowledge of the light troops who could perplex his design, and call in the assistance of the main army if necessity required." Late that night still other reports filtered into camp, and Tarleton listened carefully to them all, trying to fathom Morgan's intentions. He would later comment that "Other reports at mid-night of a corps of mountaineers being upon the march from Green river, proved the exigency of moving to watch the enemy closely, in order to take advantage of any favorable opportunity that might offer."[6]

Clearly, at this point in time Tarleton believed that Morgan would be trying to get his army across Broad River come morning and the "favorable opportunity" he referred to was probably the hope of catching the Americans in mid-career. He had just that evening written to Cornwallis that Morgan was headed for Cherokee Ford, and Tarleton's only real concern was that Morgan might cross over before Cornwallis could get there. Tarleton had a reasonable idea of Morgan's strength – although he would naturally have been uncertain of the recently mentioned reinforcements – but regardless of the numbers, if he could catch a portion of Morgan's column on the west side of the Broad after the other portion had already crossed over or was then in the process of crossing, he could dash down and crush a sizeable part of the Flying Army almost helplessly against the bank of the river. It was a classic military tactic, old as the hills and proven as gold, and one that no doubt sent sparks of delight dancing through Banastre Tarleton's mind as he contemplated it. If he played his cards right he could cut Morgan's numbers in half while forcing the Americans to turn and defend themselves, only then to face about and find Cornwallis closing on their rear. Indeed, it was the very trap Tarleton had suggested to Cornwallis so many days ago, yet now so near completion he could almost reach out and touch it. But one thing was certain: He could not allow Morgan to get the Flying Army across Broad River unopposed, and to avoid that possibility Tarleton clearly intended to "perplex his design" with an assault that would hold the Americans in place or – should God grant such a wondrous opportunity – destroy them in detail himself.

Out on the Green River Road, a narrow, muddy, rutted track of sand and dirt, the Flying Army was now slipping and stumbling through the same conditions that had inhibited the British columns for the past few days. Morgan had been directed off onto another route (the byway Tarleton's scouts had spotted), but it proved even worse than the main road, and if conditions did not radically improve, Morgan knew he would never get his column across the Broad by nightfall. Morgan, like Tarleton, was well aware of the carnage that could ensue if he were to be caught crossing the Broad by his hard charging adversary, and no doubt it was a picture he cared not to contemplate. And he knew that Tarleton would be coming on strong at first light, no matter the conditions, so if he could not get across the river that day, then he would have to fight somewhere between the army's current position and the Broad River tomorrow. It was as simple as two plus two. Once it became more or less clear that the Flying Army was not going to be doing any flying that day, Morgan decided to depart the column with some of his staff to see what ground could be found ahead that might conform to his requirements for battle.

A few miles ahead he met Captain Dennis Tramell who lived not far from a crossroads, some six miles south and west of the Broad. Tramell was naturally well acquainted with the area, and promptly gave Morgan a tour of the grounds.[7] Even then Morgan must have had an idea of the sort of ground he would require to deploy his men in the new battle configuration he had recently conceived for his militia, and the land that Tramell showed him, while far from perfect, seemed to meet the basic criteria. John Eager Howard, then leading the Continentals through the long afternoon shadows back on the Green River Road, would later describe the land selected as "where pens were made, as was the custom at the time, for the purpose of collecting the cattle once a year to give them salt and more especially to mark the ears of the young to distinguish the property of different owners, and to alter the males. This was all the attention given to them. Hence the name Cowpens."[8] It was a location well known throughout the area, and as it was situated at a crossroads it could easily serve as a rallying point for militia units from far and wide.

Morgan chose the position with care, apparently with one eye toward the tactics he intended to employ, the other to comply with the essential strategy of getting away rapidly across Broad River, which now ran at his back. "The Cowpens was a long, gently sloping ridge covered with open woods of red oak, hickory, and pine. Beyond the crest of the ridge was a swale extending northward for eighty yards. Then came a smaller ridge behind which the ground gradually leveled into a plain, stretching toward the Broad River."[9] Morgan did not expect Tarleton to attempt to flank his position, but rather to come straight at him, at once, and probably with almost everything he had. That was Tarleton's style, he knew, and that was what he was preparing a defense to receive. As far as the river at his back was concerned, should he defeat Tarleton, he could still dash across the Broad and march rapidly to reunite with Greene. Should he lose, well, then it probably wouldn't matter. But Morgan, being Morgan, did not expect to lose.

Late that afternoon and on into the evening the Flying Army slogged its way into the Cowpens. There they found level ground at or around the crossroads, and settled in for the night. Soon dinner fires began dotting the scene like fireflies on a summer night. Slowly, during the remainder of the afternoon and on into the early evening, the army grew as groups of militia, large and small, drifted into camp, all eager to finally take on the hated Tarelton. Indeed, the movement up the Green River Road that afternoon, which had appeared to many a hasty retreat from the closing British (just, no doubt, as it appeared to Tarleton himself), had many of the men grumbling in the ranks. They did not care to run. They wanted to fight, and they were disappointed in Morgan, the one man above all whom they thought could be trusted to stand up to Bloody Ban. Thomas

Young, a young partisan raider, recalled clearly that, "We were very anxious for battle, and many a hearty curse had been vented against General Morgan during that day's march for retreating, as we thought, to avoid battle."[10] But once the decision to stand had been made, and the army halted for the evening at Cowpens, the men grasped clearly Morgan's intent, and the grumbling was replaced with a firm resignation. Morgan had not been running after all, and soon they would have Tarleton and his dragoons in their rifle sights. Come morning there would be scores to settle. The inexhaustible Robert Kirkwood leading the tough Delaware Continentals on the long march, ended the difficult day with this simple, descriptive note in his journal: "March'd to the Cowpens."[11]

Back at Burr's Mill, Banastre Tarleton probably slept very little as the early hours of January 17, 1781 began to accumulate. There were scouts still coming in, guards that had to be posted, and intelligence that had to be digested. It was a cold, damp, and uncomfortable night, but everything he had been striving to accomplish now seemed suddenly within his reach; and for a man like Tarleton that alone must have animated his being. In the early hours he would get his men up and put them on the road toward Morgan's camp. The great wolf would mount his horse and ride again, once more on the trail of wounded prey, this time an American named Morgan, but the name really did not matter. Morgan like Buford at Waxhaws was on the run, and soon the wolf would catch and devour him too, just as he had all the other pitiful American officers and men who had tried to evade him. Every fact, every movement, every detail no doubt seemed to confirm the accuracy of that picture in Tarleton's ever calculating mind, but this time Tarleton was wrong.

Morgan was not running and he would never be prey. In a subsequent report to Nathanael Greene he spelled out his movements and rationale. "On the 14th, having received intelligence that the British army were in motion, and that their movements clearly indicated the intention of dislodging me, I abandoned my encampment at Glendale Ford, and on the 16th, in the evening, took possession of a post about seven miles from Chroke on Broad River. My former position subjected me at once to the operations of Lord Cornwallis and Colonel Tarleton, and in case of a defeat my retreat might easily have been cut off. My situation at Cowpens enabled me to improve any advantage that I might gain and to provide better for my security should I be unfortunate. These reasons induced me to take this post, not withstanding it had the appearance of a retreat."[12]

While Morgan appears to have developed a clear picture of what he might expect from Banastre Tarleton, Tarleton himself seems to have had precious little idea just what sort of an adversary he was about to come face-to-face with; how fierce, how cunning, how frightening an opponent Daniel Morgan could actually be. When the American attack upon Quebec years before had fizzled, for instance, and Morgan and his command had been pinned down by British muskets on the city's snowy streets, the rifleman George Morison saw Morgan at his wildest, fiercest best and it was a sight Morison would never forget. "Betwixt every peal the awful voice of Morgan is heard, whose gigantic stature and terrible appearance carries dismay among the foe wherever he comes."[13] That is the sort of opponent Banastre Tarleton had never dreamed of, better yet faced, and ahead, indeed just ahead, *that* Daniel Morgan had now stopped and turned on ground of his own choosing. The wolf was waiting.

CHAPTER FIFTEEN

MORGAN

Daniel Morgan may have chosen the ground he intended to fight upon with great care on the afternoon of the 16th, and he may already have conceived a new method of deployment that would greatly enhance the Flying Army's capabilities, but many of the other elements that were now conspiring to bring him to battle were still very fluid, thus beyond his reckoning or control. Yes, Tarleton was driving hard up the Green River Road but just when, in what numbers, and in what condition the British would make their appearance remained speculations at best. Likewise, Morgan had chosen to encamp near the Cowpens because it was a well-known landmark in that section of South Carolina, thus he hoped the local militias would find it easy to flock to his standard, but just how many would answer his pleas, and in what timeframe they might arrive, remained elements of pure conjecture. Indeed, how the numerous militia bands would respond, and then again how they might fight, were the thorniest questions of all. Ammunition, swords, horses, rations, etc. could all be counted and sensibly dispersed, but just how many men would actually show up to fight was anyone's guess.

Unlike the more traditional conflict that had been fought in the American North, the war in the South had been principally a partisan affair, bitterly contested between Tory (loyalist) and Whig (rebel), far more reminiscent of civil war than the struggle between Continental and Redcoat that had played out in places like Boston, New York, or Philadelphia. It was a war of bitter and evolving hatreds, grudges nursed a hundred times over until actions were often predicated on revenge rather than even the vaguest military necessity. The Southern conflict thus devolved into a series of bloody and remorseless tit-for-tat strikes that had no more to do with revolutionary thought or independence than did the bitter struggle between the Hatfields and McCoys. It was blood and hate that drove the war in the South, and it is impossible to understand the men who were then gathering to fight for Daniel Morgan without grasping that one essential fact.

Thomas Young and James Potter Collins were then two young members of partisan militias that were converging on the Cowpens to fight alongside Morgan on the evening of the 16th, and it is instructive to delve, if even briefly, into their stories and motivations. Thomas Young, for instance, recalled years later with brutal clarity in his "Memoir" the hatred that drove him throughout the course of the war. It was spring of 1780, and a Whig party under a Colonel Brandon had captured a Tory by the name of Adam Steedham. "By some means Steedham escaped during the night," Young tells us, "and notified the Tories of Brandon's position. The Whigs were attacked by a large body of the enemy before day and completely routed. On that occasion, my brother, John Young, was murdered. I shall never forget my feelings when told of his death. I do not believe I had ever used an oath before that day, but then I tore open my bosom, and swore that I would never rest till I had avenged his death. Subsequently a hundred Tories felt the weight of my arm for the deed, and around Steedham's neck I fastened the rope as a reward for his cruelties. On the next day I left home in my shirt sleeves, and Joined Brandon's party."[1]

Fifty-four years after the engagement at Cowpens, James Potter Collins appeared before the Third District Court Parish of East Feliciana, Louisiana, where he then resided, and testified as to his activities during the course of the Revolutionary War, all of which began when he was little more than a boy. The hearing was to establish Collins' claim to a military pension and his testimony provides an intriguing glimpse into the life and activities of a Southern partisan. "I never was called into service of my country on any tour of duty," Collins testified. "In the early part of the revolution there was a great enmity between the Whigs and Tories and they mutually armed against each other. My father was a Whig and like the rest became very obnoxious to the Tories. Before it was thought that I was able to carry arms, I was often employed by the Whig leaders, and particularly by Colonel Moffet to carry and fetch news – Confidence was placed in me. I was a good rider, and knew the byways through the woods, by which I was able to elude the vigilance of the Tories, who were always on the watch."

Yet in the bloody, bitter contest the American Revolution in the South had become, Collins' youth, he realized, would hardly shield him from immediate retribution if captured by the other side. "It became known to the Tories how I was employed and a mark was set on me," he explains. "If I had fallen into their hands I have no doubt I should have been killed. Young as I then was, my father thought it prudent that I should enter the service he was in."

Collins then goes on to describe in some detail the harried life of a militia partisan. "This service was what was called minute men. We armed ourselves, and generally marched on horseback. We furnished our own equipment: we got swords, butcher knives, and war spurs made by the blacksmiths... Sometimes we were permitted by our officers to disperse, when we knew of no enemy near. We have been at home sometimes four or five days at once. Sometimes we would not be at home a day before our officers went again [and] called us out – sometimes we did not get home before we were again ordered to rendezvous and go in pursuit of the enemy. This is the only kind of service I was in and it lasted from long before I entered it until nearly a year after Cornwallis surrendered at Yorktown... I was never in garrison during that period – my services were all active. I say with great confidence that from the time I entered the service in 1780, until I was discharged [1783], I never was at home in ten days at one time but was on active duty as I have before stated." Collins saw action at Fishing Creek, Williamson's Plantation, and later was heavily engaged at King's Mountain in a small, local band that often formed then melted away in days or even hours only, before being summoned to Cowpens by Morgan. "We never were attached to any Troops but our own, or more than three or four days at a time that I remember, and that was always for our own safety (for the odds were against us) or to assist in checking the Progress of the enemy."[2]

Thomas Young, who would eventually rise to the rank of major in the militia service before the end of the war, was often involved in minor actions that suddenly embroiled friends or even family members from opposite sides of the war. These sorts of engagements and entanglements were not at all uncommon. In one of these, for instance, Colonel Brandon led one section of militia while Captain Love led another against a Tory encampment at Stallions' farm. "Mrs. Stallions was a sister of Capt Love," wrote Young, "and on the approach of her brother she ran out, and begged him not to fire upon the house. He told her it was too late now, and that their only chance for safety was to surrender. She ran back to the house and sprang upon the door step, which was pretty high. At this moment, the house was attacked in the rear by Col. Brandon's party, and Mrs. Stallions was killed by a ball shot through the opposite door. At the same moment with Brandon's attack, our party raised a shout and rushed forward. We fired several rounds, which were briskly returned. It was not long, however, before the Tories ran up a flag, first upon the end of a gun, but as that did not look exactly peaceful, a ball was put through the fellow's arm, and in a few moments it was raised on a ram-rod, and we ceased firing....

"The loss of the Tories was two killed, four wounded, and twenty-eight prisoners whom we sent to Charlotte, N.C. After the fight, Love and Stallions met and shed bitter tears; Stallions was dismissed on parole to bury his wife and arrange his affairs."

Thus did the war play out in the American South. Young would go on to fight at King's Mountain where numerous Tory prisoners were taken. Most of these were horribly mistreated and nine hung after a "court martial" found them guilty of crimes of an "outrageous and bloodthirsty character." The militia then marched off, and Young describes their arduous journey: "After the battle [King's Mountain] we marched upon the head waters of Cane Creek, in North Carolina with our prisoners, where we all came nearly starving to death. The country was very thinly settled, and provisions could not be had for love or money. I thought green pumpkins, sliced and fried, about the sweetest eating I ever had in my life. From this point we marched over into the Dutch settlements in the fork of Catawba and recruited, until we joined Gen. Morgan at Grindal Shoals."[3]

These, then, were the men who were marching to join the Flying Army on the night of January 16th. By and large they were tough frontier fighters, good with a rifle, knife, and horse, perfectly capable of living off the land, but certainly unskilled as soldiers in the traditional mold. In that sense, these were the same sort (and in some cases, the same men) who had flocked to Horatio Gates' army in August, only then to flee without firing a shot at the first glimmer of British bayonets. They were brave enough, but they were hardly fools, and since they were entirely untrained in close order drill or the basics of battlefield maneuver, they could hardly be expected to acquit themselves admirably when facing veteran British troops on the field. Yet once assembled, by sheer numbers alone the militia would comprise the majority of Morgan's force when he finally came face-to-face with Tarleton, just as they had Gates' army at Camden. Morgan knew that Tarleton's column consisted of the finest light troops under Cornwallis' command, all well trained in the art of rushing American militia with the bayonet, so the obvious question was: What was Morgan going to do different than Gates had done in order to avoid another disaster like Camden?

Fortunately, it appears Daniel Morgan had already spent some time turning that conundrum over in his mind, and indeed he had already struck upon a brilliant and novel solution. In fact, his answer was so well conceived that it would not only utilize the militia's finest features while hopefully shielding them from the prospect of British bayonets, but the novel deployment he was considering would simultaneously prey upon Banastre Tarleton's generally over-aggressive instincts. Tarleton might be tough, brave, and relentless, but on more than one occasion he had also relied almost exclusively on the shock of his appearance and the suddenness of his attack to carry the day without ever stopping to once consider the odds deployed against him or the obvious fact that a headlong dash against an unexamined position might well spell disaster. In that sense, a shrewd commander might use Tarleton's own tendencies against him by drawing him into a well-laid trap. Reviewing the action at Fishing Creek, for instance, the intrepid North Carolinian, William Davie commented that: "Col. Tarleton with only 160 men, presented himself before the American camp, without either information, or a moments reflection proceeded to charge them, had the Commanding officer taken any of the ordinary precautions to resist an attack, Tarleton must have suffered severely for his boyish Temerity;

the conflict was nothing, the fighting was entirely on one side, and the slaughter among the defenceless."[4] As Davie notes, Tarleton's attacks were generally furious but they were often reckless, and there seems little doubt that Morgan perceived in Tarleton's rashness the potential for opportunity.

Andrew Pickens' arrival at Cowpens with his corps apparently cemented in Morgan's mind the decision to stand and fight, and word quickly spread throughout the American encampment. Thomas Young would later declare that "We arrived at the field of the Cowpens about sundown, and were told that there we should meet the enemy. The news was received with great joy by the army."[5] Still, deciding and doing were two very different things, and Daniel Morgan realized that – with no time for drill or practice – the employment of his new scheme would require a great deal of work and explanation, and he straight away began doing just that. Beef were slaughtered on the site; campfires lit so that every man would be warm, rested, and well-fed come dawn. Orders were issued to ensure that every militiaman had twenty-four rounds prepared and ready for the coming fight. [6] Then Morgan called all of his officers to a meeting – we can assume around a blazing campfire – where he explained in detail the deployment he intended to use come morning.

They were all – like Thomas Young – weary of running, and every man was anxious to finally stand and have it out with Banastre Tarleton. Here around the fire sat John Eager Howard, Robert Kirkwood, Andrew Pickens, and William Washington, to name but a few. Every one of them had seen action, and every man had a score to settle with the British. For Howard and Kirkwood in particular, the bitter defeat and rout at Camden must still have been something they could almost taste, and an opportunity to reverse that score a coveted opportunity. Beyond that, Tarleton's reputation for barbarity alone was enough to inspire and motivate the Americans. So as the fire crackled and light from the flames danced in the trees overhead, the officers fell silent as Daniel Morgan, one of the few American officers with an unblemished reputation for skill and hard fighting, explained what he wanted them to do.

Yes, the militias were all good fighters, but they could not be asked to stand up to a British frontal assault, and every officer present was aware of that fact. So Morgan had decided to deploy them differently. Far out in front he would place 120 or so hand-picked skirmishers, and on this advanced line only the best with the long rifle would do. These men would take cover on a small rise; force the British to deploy, peppering them as they did so, but firing only two or three rounds each before executing a controlled withdrawal to a second line of militia located 150 yards behind the advanced skirmish line. Here Morgan would post Andrew Pickens with the remainder of his militia, a total of about 400 men, all formed in line of battle in a slight swale so that they would be largely hidden from the British as they approached. Here again, Morgan did not want this militia line to stand and fight, only to fire two or three volleys before executing a controlled withdrawal themselves, back to yet the third, main line, composed of his Continentals and Virginians another 150 yards behind Pickens.

Morgan realized that the British Army was organized and fought like a fine machine, but like any human organization it relied upon order and that order was supplied by the chain of command. So he asked his militia riflemen to concentrate their fire on the officers and non-commissioned officers first; if the head was severed, the body would falter. Both advanced lines of militia would then withdraw back through the main American line and take up positions on the flanks where they would lend their firepower to the final stand while shielded by the Continental's bayonets. These planned withdrawals, if properly performed, would maximize the militia's finest abilities, while freeing them of the necessity of standing firm before a British bayonet advance – the best of both worlds. Then, behind the main line Washington would wait with the cavalry, forming a general reserve ready to lend support to any part of the field at a moment's notice.

If executed properly, Morgan's plan would accomplish a number of tactical objectives. First and foremost, the militia fire was designed to limit and demoralize the British advance, leaving many of their troops and officers dead or wounded on the field before the British even encountered the main Continental line, also somewhat hidden from view. Secondly, the triple line arrangement would work to physically exhaust the already wearied British regulars, forcing them to fight through two lines of battle before even encountering the third and strongest American line; ready, prepared, and waiting for them. And finally, if Morgan had read Tarleton correctly, the British commander would no doubt interpret each American withdrawal as a sure sign of victory and respond by driving his command even harder and further into the teeth of Morgan's trap. The coordination of the British assault would become increasingly unglued, only then to realize – much to their horror – that they had been duped, and that the hard fighting was only about to begin. All of these elements, if properly executed, would play heavily in Morgan's favor. But would they be properly executed by untrained militia? That was the question.

If Morgan's plan was to work, the militia had to fire their two to three volleys accurately, and the withdrawals had to be performed in a controlled manner lest panic might ensue and Camden be repeated. Morgan knew that terror was contagious, that the sight of fleeing men on a battlefield could cause an instant panic throughout the ranks, thus every man on the field had to be made aware of the fact that the front line withdrawals were part of his plan, and not a forced retreat or evidence of fiasco.

At this Morgan was instantly seen at his backwoods best, for he understood his men, and in particular he understood militia. He was, after all, a frontier fighter himself, thus the mind of the militia fighter was hardly a mystery to him. Thomas Young recalled years later just how the Old Wagoner went about his business. "It was upon this occasion I was more perfectly convinced of Gen. Morgan's qualifications to command militia, than I had ever before been. He went among the volunteers, helped them fix their swords, joked with them about their sweet-hearts, told them to keep in good spirits, and the day would be ours. And long after I laid down, he was going about among the soldiers encouraging them, and telling them that the old Wagoner would crack his whip over Ben (Tarleton) in the morning, as sure as they lived. 'Just hold up your heads, boys, three fires, he would say, and you are free, and then when you return to your homes, how the old folks will bless you, and the girls kiss you, for your gallant conduct!' I don't believe he slept a wink that night!"[7]

One of the stories Morgan reportedly repeated as he made the rounds that evening, was of a troubling experience he'd had at the hands of the British years before. It seems that during the course of the French and Indian War, Morgan had been contracted by the British to haul supplies along the route of Braddock's March out toward the Ohio Territory. For some reason – it is not known why – Morgan and a British lieutenant became embroiled in an argument, and the young lieutenant was foolish enough to strike the then young wagoner with the flat of his sword, which in those days was somewhat akin to trying to kiss an enraged wolverine on the lips. Morgan instantly knocked the officer out cold, and he was then, of course, immediately tried and found guilty for the transgression.

The penalty in those days for striking an officer of the king's army was severe indeed, and Morgan was ordered to undergo 500 lashes, a punishment that for many men would have been tantamount to a death sentence. According to Morgan's rendition of the tale, however, not only did he remain conscious throughout the entire ordeal, but he calmly counted each and every lash as the flesh on his back was whipped and torn to a bloody pulp. But, as Morgan recounted it, the penalty ultimately totaled only 499 lashes, one short of the required number, and from then on, Morgan was occasionally known to quip that the king still owned him one good lash. The story was true, the scars all there to be seen, and it is easy to understand how it would have impressed the young frontiersmen then gathered around the smoking fires with a deep appreciation for the Old Wagoner's sheer physical stamina, ferocity, and indomitable spirit. The man who intended to lead them into battle come daylight was clearly no prima donna or shrinking violet, but rather a leader of proven worth. Indeed, here was a man who would gladly do battle with the devil himself.[8]

So campfire-to-campfire Morgan moved throughout the long night, constantly explaining his plan, greeting new militia units as they arrived, and reminding everyone over and over again that he needed at least two or three good shots from every rifle. This was a task far beyond either the desires or capabilities of a Horatio Gates or, for that matter, most officers in the Continental Line, but for Daniel Morgan it was simply old hat. He had hauled too many loads, after all, hoisted far too many tankards of rum and told too many a tall tale in country taverns to feel anything less than comfortable around these simple, frontier men, and they drew strength and confidence from his effort. And still there was more work to be done; scouts to post and debrief; (the American scouts were posted some three miles from camp, and Tarleton was reported to have gone into bivouac at Burr's Mill another nine miles east of the scouts) rounds to be counted, beef to fire for the late arrivals, and so on.

The cavalry too had to be augmented, for Tarleton's dragoons far outnumbered Washington's, and once again Thomas Young found himself square in the mix. "Night came upon us," he wrote, "yet much remained to be done. It was all important to strengthen the cavalry. Gen. Morgan knew well the power of Tarleton's legion, and he was too wily an officer not to prepare himself as well as circumstance would admit. Two companies of volunteers were called for. One was raised by Major Jolly of Union District, and the other, I think, by Major McCall. I attached myself to Major Jolly's company. We drew swords that night, and were informed we had authority to press any horse not belonging to a dragoon or an officer, into our service for the day."[9]

Thus passed the long night, Morgan slowly, confidently preparing the Flying Army for the test that was to greet them once Tarleton arrived – as was now expected – with the coming dawn. Fire-to-fire, story after story, Morgan moved and joked and prepared his little army until most of the men had bedded down for at least a few hours rest. Darkness brought with it a miserable dampness, and the temperature dropped below freezing. Light from the campfires played and danced against the stark, leafless trees of the Cowpens, and as the long winter's night slowly began to fade into the first light of day, Daniel Morgan readied himself for what he must have known was going to be the fight of his life.

Light Horse . Henry Lee

Battle of Cowpens

Daniel Morgan

CHAPTER SIXTEEN

TARLETON

Like Morgan – who now waited some twelve miles distant – during the early morning hours of January 17, Banastre Tarleton got little if any rest and, indeed, in all probability he slept not at all. He allowed his men to grab what little sleep they could manage at the abandoned Continental camp at Burr's Mill, but the Americans were now within striking distance, the road between the two adversaries, he knew, slow and rough going. So if he was going to hit them before they could slip across Broad River, Tarleton knew he would have to be on the road long before dawn. Moreover, Tarleton had been warned by the American militia colonel he had detained earlier that Morgan was expecting substantial reinforcements, so if the British were going to strike before Morgan was heavily complimented, time was surely of the essence.

At 2:00 A.M. the British troops were roused and by 3:00 they were on the road.[1] Marching through the cold and impenetrable darkness of the Carolina backcountry at night, the British could do little more than slip, slosh, and stumble their way up the Green River Road. “Three companies of light infantry,” wrote Tarleton, “supported by the legion infantry, formed the advance, the 7th regiment, the guns, and the 1st battalion of the 71st, composed the center; and the cavalry and mounted infantry brought up the rear.”[2] All of the baggage and the command’s train of wagons were ordered to remain behind until dawn before proceeding forward, all guarded by a small detachment comprised from each of the British corps. It was a column built for speed and ready deployment, but in the early hours of January 17 and the black night of the American frontier, speed proved impossible.

“The ground which the Americans had passed being broken, and much intersected by creeks and ravines,” Tarleton later complained, “the march of the British troops during the darkness was exceedingly slow, on account of the time employed in examining the front and flanks as they proceeded.”[3] Morgan had posted a number of scouts and videttes well in front of the Flying Army to track and delay Tarleton as he approached, and a constant fear of ambush eventually caused the British commander to employ his dragoons to screen the advance while also scouring the ground on his flanks for potential trouble. This precaution, like the darkness, ravines, mud, and creeks, also served to slow the march, and an exhausting struggle it proved to be. Even in the best of conditions, a marching column has a tendency to bunch and lurch; to stop and then rush forward again, like modern automobiles on a heavily traveled highway. But in the cold, wet, dark conditions of this January 17th this odd phenomena could only have been greatly amplified, generating exhaustion and distress amongst the already weary troops, all, of course, to Morgan's eventual benefit. The first five miles of the long twelve mile march were covered in about three hours, notes historian Lawrence Babits, clear testimony as to the hazards of the terrain and the difficulty of the march.[4] "Before dawn," Tarleton recalled, "Thickelle [Thickety] creek was passed, when an advanced guard of cavalry was ordered to the front."[5] These British dragoons swept forward, and soon encountered American scouts on the Green River Road.

Thomas Young recalled that "Our pickets were stationed three miles in advance. Samuel Clowney was one of the picket guard, and I often heard him afterwards laugh at his narrow escape. Three of Washington's dragoons were out on a scout, when they came almost in contact with the advanced guard of the British army; they wheeled, and were pursued almost into camp. Two got in safely; one poor fellow, whose horse fell down, was taken prisoner."[6] That unfortunate cavalryman was Lawrence Everhart, and Tarleton's own account of the action states that "The enemy's partole approaching, was pursued and overtaken: Two troops of dragoons, under Captain Ogilvie, of the legion, were then ordered to reinforce the advanced guard, and harass the rear of the enemy."[7]

Everhart was severely sabered by the British dragoons, and he was captured and brought to Tarleton for questioning. But Everhart, who had been in the Continental cavalry on an intermittent basis since August, 1776, was hardly intimidated by the British commander. Like Otho Williams, Everhart was originally from Frederick County, Maryland, and had fought with the Continental Line at the battles of Long Island, White Plains, and later Fort Washington where he and several others had managed a gallant escape across the Hudson River to Fort Lee thus avoiding the captivity which befell Williams and the rest of the fort's unfortunate garrison. He returned to Frederick in 1777, but after the harvest of 1778 reenlisted with William Washington's cavalry at Frederick City and took part in much of the Southern Campaign, from Charleston to Monck's Corner. The small cavalry corps then marched north, only then to return in December of 1780 to reinforce what remained of Horatio Gates' shattered army.

In April of 1834 Everhart provided testimony for his pension application, and it is by means of that document that his story and encounter with Banastre Tarleton have been retained. According to that application and those documents attached therein, "about dawn of the day on the 17th of January 1781 you [William Washington] selected Sergeant Everhart from your Regiment and twelve men, whom you sent to reconnoiter Lt. Colonel Tarleton's Army." Tarleton's dragoon, however, had impressed some of the fastest horses in the area for their use, and due to the speed of these animals the British were able to run down Sergeant Everhart and disperse the Continental scouts with little effort. Everhart's horse was shot out from under him, and he was left essentially defenseless before the charging dragoons. In his own words, Everhart recalled that "Petitioners horse being shot he was captured early in the morning by quarter master Wade of the British army with whom he had some previous acquaintance & by him taken to Col Tarleton, Our army at this point of time being perhaps three miles in the rear. Dismounting from his horse, that officer asked this petitioner, after some previous conversation if he expected Mr. Washington & Mr. Morgan would fight him that day." (It can be inferred from the tone of Everhart's application that at the time he was not aware of the fact that he was actually talking with Tarleton himself, but presumed him to be some other British officer.) "Yes," Everhart responded fearlessly, indeed almost sarcastically, "if they can keep together only two hundred men. Then said he [Tarleton], it will be another Gates' defeat. I hope to God it will be another Tarleton's defeat, said this petitioner. I am Col Tarleton Sir [said Tarleton]. And I am Sergeant Everhart."[8]

Testifying some fifty-three years after the fact, Everhart can be forgiven if he slightly embellished the boldness of his response to Tarleton's query for posterity's sake; the truth of that will never be known. But it is Tarleton's, not Everhart's state of mind at the time that is of particular interest for our story. For Everhart had no reason to embellish the British commander's statements, and they seem to reveal a Tarleton utterly confident of victory, apparently concerned only with whether the Americans were floundering in retreat or willing to stand and fight. And if they be foolish enough to stand and fight, then it appears Tarleton had every confidence he would run right over them and inflict "another Gate's defeat" just as Cornwallis had administered at Camden, and that speaks volumes to the British commander's mental state as his column closed in on the Flying Army that morning. Trap, deception, decoy, defeat; these possibilities seem to have been utterly foreign to Tarleton at the time, and precisely because he refused to even consider them, he remained open to them all. And what was Tarleton's immediate response to his conversation with Everhart? As previously stated, the British commander wasted no time going over to the offensive: "Two troops of dragoons, under Captain Ogilvie, of the legion, were then ordered to reinforce the advanced guard, and to harass the rear of the enemy."[9] The great wolf, emboldened by his conversation with the captured American, was now closing on the prey with all dispatch.

Sergeant Everhart was then taken off to the British surgeon where his wounds were treated, but his treatment at the hands of his captors would turn foul, and we shall hear from him again.

As the British dragoons galloped off it was then approximately first light, true sunrise still an hour off, and the British column, driven hard as always by Tarleton, began to gain speed. As Lawrence Babits calculates, "The British vanguard was moving at the rate of a mile every twenty-five minutes. The British still had an hour's marching to cover the last five miles, but now they were marching on higher ground, following drier roads over a more level course without crossing a major stream. They moved even faster because dragoons were checking for ambushes."[10]

Not long thereafter one of the dragoons dashed back to Tarleton with a report from far out in front; the Americans had been spotted in strength ahead, forming, it appeared, for battle! "The march had not continued long in this manner," Tarleton recalled, "before the commanding officer in front reported that the American troops were halted and forming. The guides were immediately consulted relative to the ground which General Morgan then occupied, and the country in his rear. These people described both with great perspicuity: They said that the woods were open and free from swamps; that the part of Broad river, just above the place where King's creek joined the stream, was about six miles distant from the enemy's left flank, and that the river, making a curve to the westward, ran parallel to their rear."[11]

We can easily imagine that to Tarleton at the time these facts must have sounded almost too good to be true. The foolish Americans had taken up a position with the Broad River covering not only their left, but flowing behind them as well, thus blocking any rapid retreat. To take up a defensive position with a river at one's back was a military mistake made only by a novice or a fool, yet it appeared Morgan had made just such a mistake. So, which was Morgan, Tarleton may well have wondered; the novice or the fool? For once the enemy's lines were broken – as broken they surely would be! – Tarleton's Legion need only chase them down and crush the survivors against the banks of the river. Any of the Americans who managed to get away and cross the river would be gobbled up as Cornwallis closed on the other side of the Broad with the remainder of the army. Tarleton's plan to destroy Morgan between two converging columns appeared to be materializing right before his eyes, yet he had to credit Morgan for playing his part to perfection. Had Tarleton drawn an "X" on the map where he wanted to fight when the chase had begun, it could not have been far from where the Flying Army now stood.

Tarleton leaped at the opportunity. "Lieutenant-colonel Tarleton, having attained a position, which he certainly might deem advantageous, on account of the vulnerable situation of the enemy, and the supposed vicinity of the two British corps on the east and west of Broad river," Tarleton explained, "did not hesitate to undertake those measures which the instructions of his commanding officer imposed, and his own judgment, under the present appearances, equally recommended."[12] Now he need only ride forward and slam the door on the Americans, and the British commander wasted no time issuing orders to locate Morgan and initiate battle. Everything, every small detail seemed to have fallen into place, just as he had planned it. Yes, the wolf was again on the hunt, and for Banastre Tarleton the smell of blood must surely have been in the air.

CHAPTER SEVENTEEN

MORGAN

The scout flew passed the posted videttes – his horse lathered, its nostrils hissing steam – and galloped into the American camp about an hour before dawn with news that Tarleton's column was on the move, now only five miles shy of the Cowpens. Major Joseph McJunkin, then camped with Morgan, would later recall that "The Cols. Brandon and Roebuck, with some others, had the special charge of watching Tarleton's movements from the time he reached the valley of the Pacolet. They sat on their horses as he approached and passed that stream and counted his men and sent their report to headquarters. They watched his camp on the night of the 16th until he began his march to give battle. Morgan appears to have had the most exact information of everything necessary."[1] Daniel Morgan grasped without a second thought what the scout's report meant: The British would be on his front within the hour, and the fight would in all probability commence at once. It was time to move! He and Andrew Pickens mounted their horses and began to awaken the slumbering troops. "Boys, get up," Morgan's deep voice boomed across the dark, frozen landscape, "Benny's coming!"[2]

In his report of the battle, Morgan explained to Nathanael Greene his pre-dawn decisions and subsequent preparations. "On the evening of the 16th, the enemy occupied the ground we had removed from in the morning. One hour before daylight one of my scouts informed me that they had advanced within five miles of our camp. On this information the necessary dispositions were made. From the activity of the troops we were soon prepared to receive them."[3]

Slowly men began to crawl out from under their blankets amongst a dark grey panorama of black tree trunks and smoky campfires. Dry logs and small kindling were tossed onto the fires, the embers stirred, and the campfires began again to crackle with flame and warmth. Quickly, very quickly, pans were greased and placed on the fires and a rushed breakfast had by all. On this cold January morning, as the weary British troops struggled through the morning hours of a fatiguing march, the Americans, at least, would be both rested and fed; no small advantage. Yet there was no time to lose. The men had to be moved into position and told again of their duties and obligations, and the Flying Army rapidly deployed into the three-line configuration Morgan had conceived. James Collins recalled the rushed events of the early morning "for Tarleton came on like a thunder storm, which soon put us to our best mettle. After the tidings of his approach came into camp, - in the night, - we were all awakened, ordered under arms, and formed in order of battle by daybreak."[4] All night long militia units had come in from the surrounding countryside, and Morgan's ranks had swollen (the exact numbers were not known at the time, and are not to this day) to a number somewhere between 1,000 and 1,100 men. They were all anxious for a fight; for the opportunity to redeem the debacle at Camden; to destroy the hated Tarleton, and every man knew that those opportunities would very soon be upon them.

The officers understood their instructions, and in the cold, grey light before dawn the men checked their rifles, their ammunition, and the army quickly deployed. Thomas Young, then mounting his horse and taking position with Washington's dragoons, recalled that: "The morning of the 17th of January, 1781, was bitterly cold. We were formed in order of battle, and the men were slapping their hands to keep warm – an exertion not long necessary. The battle field was almost a plain with a ravine on both hands, and very little under growth in front or near us. The regulars, under the command of Col. Howard, a brave man, were formed in two ranks, their right flank resting upon the head of the ravine on the right."[5] The Cowpens was dotted with trees, but the undergrowth had been grazed away by years of herding, thus the ground was open for cavalry and maneuver. Morgan's flanks, for the most part, were covered by swampy ground and heavy undergrowth.

The line of Continental regulars and the militia, just 150 yards ahead of them, were the first to form. The men picked for the advanced line of rifleman then departed the militia line for their positions, still further in front. Joseph McJunkin later recalled the entire deployment clearly. "Three lines of infantry were drawn across the plain. First the regulars and some companies of Virginia militia are posted where the final issue is expected. In front of these the main body of militia under Gen. Pickens are drawn up at the distance of 150 yards. Still in front of these at the distance of 150 yards a corps of picked riflemen is scattered in loose order along the whole front."[6] Meanwhile, William Washington moved the cavalry to the rear where it was out of sight. At that point they also held the horses the militia had ridden in on, while ready to lend their support to any part of the field at a moment's notice.

Unlike Horatio Gates, who had commanded at both Freeman's Farm and Camden from a considerable distance in the rear, Morgan was immediately out in front, cheering his men on and watching as the British came up. He first rode out to the men on the skirmish line. Here Major Joseph McDowell had placed approximately sixty North and South Carolina crack shots to the right of the Green River Road. To the left of the road Major Charles Cunningham had deployed the same number of expert Georgia riflemen.[7] Morgan went among them, urged them to take good aim, insisted they not fire until the British were within fifty yards of them, and then to aim for officers first. Two shots he demanded, and then they would be free to fall back in good order into Andrew Pickens line of militia that was waiting to receive them, 150 yards further to the rear. The riflemen on the skirmish line took cover where they could find it so as not to present clear targets for the British dragoons, or so that their numbers could be easily counted. Morgan, reining his horse to a stop before leaving, volunteered hearty praise then offered a challenge: "Let me see," he called out, "which are most entitled to the credit of brave men, the boys of Carolina or those of Georgia."[8]

Next Morgan rode directly back to the militia line where once again "he delivered a fiery speech, pounding his fist into his palm as he spoke. He expected to see their usual zeal and courage, and he reminded them not to withdraw until they had fired twice at close range."[9] Light Horse Harry Lee provides a convincing rendition of Morgan's impassioned performance as he rode amongst the assembled militiamen. "On the verge of battle, Morgan availed himself of the short and awful interim to exhort his troops. First addressing himself, with his characteristic pith, to the line of militia, he extolled the zeal and bravery so often displayed by them, when unsupported by the bayonet or sword; and declared his confidence that they could not fail in maintaining their reputation, when supported by chosen bodies of horse and foot, and conducted by himself. Nor did he forget to glance at his unvarying fortune, and superior experience; or to mention how often, with his corps of riflemen, he had brought British troops, equal to those before him to submission;... [he] exhorted the line to be firm and steady; to fire with good aim; and if they would pour in but two volleys at killing distance, he would take upon himself to secure victory."[10]

Lastly, Morgan moved on to the trustworthy Continentals and Virginians who formed his last and main line, tough veterans of many a fight that would not require, he knew, any grand speeches or excessive motivation to account themselves well that morning. John Eager Howard, in command of this last line, and riding next to Morgan as he spoke, even years later recalled Morgan's visit. "He reminded them of the confidence he had always reposed in their skill and courage; assured them that victory was certain if they acted well their part; and desired them not to be discouraged by the sudden retreat of the militia, that being part of his plan and orders."[11]

The coming contest would be an event of great importance, and Morgan knew well that the very fate of the Revolution might well be determined, for better or worse, that morning on the fields of the Cowpens. He did not speak down to the troops like other officers might; that would never have been his style. Rather he spoke to them as worthy compatriots, brothers in arms. "My friends in arms," he called to them all, his deep voice booming above the assembled line of soldiers, "my dear boys, I request you to remember Saratoga, Monmouth, Paoli, Brandywine, and this day you must play your parts for your honor & liberty's cause."[12] Yes, it was short and sweet and straight to the point and every veteran standing there understood what he meant. The losing and maneuvering and endless retrograde movements were now a thing of the past. Today they were going to whip Banastre Tarleton and the cream of Cornwallis' army and send them packing on the fields of the Cowpens. Or they would die in the attempt.

Then Morgan turned his horse and rode back to a point slightly behind the Continental line, a position from where he could look out and over the entire deployment: to the roughly five hundred Continentals and Virginians; ahead of them the 400 militia under Pickens, and 150 yards in front of them the skirmish line deployed in small groups and knots of men behind trees. Everything was in waiting. Everything was set. Not far behind Morgan's position there was another small rise, not really a hill at all, but a small eminence where the Flying Army might retire if pressed, there to make its final stand if it came to that. There, then, behind the blue-coated Continentals, General Daniel Morgan sat his horse and waited patiently for the enemy to appear. It was just slightly before 7:00 A.M. and the sun was just beginning its creep over the eastern horizon sending long shadows across the quiet, undulating fields of the Cowpens. The army waited in quiet readiness, steam rising from the cold mouths of a thousand and more men.

The wait was not long. Shots were heard, a staccato popping off to the south, and then again, and just as rapidly, a sudden silence consumed the morning. Joseph McJunkin, standing cold and impatient in the militia line ahead with Andrews Pickens recalled the moment with great clarity. "The guns of the videttes, led by Capt. Inman announce the approach of the foe, and soon the red coats stream before the eyes of the militia."[13] Suddenly there was movement, a flash of color, and then, yes, the enemy was seen moving up the Green River Road into position upon the Cowpens. First on horseback rode the dragoons sporting green jackets and white leggings, then behind them the infantry in their famous red coats, all coming on now with speed and precision. It was the British Army, the finest fighting force in the world at the time, and they had no fear of American guns or American militia. A youthful James Collins, standing in the line of militia, and peering down at the British as they arrived, would never forget the moment. "About sunrise on the 17th January, 1781," he recalled, "the enemy came in full view. The sight, to me at least, seemed somewhat imposing."[14]

Morgan waited and watched as the British troops filled the small field in front of his skirmish line and began their deployment, knowing all the while they could not see either his militia or Continental lines from their position afar. No, for the Redcoats those lines would come as a surprise. Morgan later vividly recalled the moment in a report to Nathanael Greene, citing the order of battle and giving credit to every unit he deployed: "The light infantry commanded by Lt. Col. Howard, and the Virginia Militia under Major Triplett, were formed on a rising ground. The Third Regiment of Dragoons, consisting of about 80 men, under command of Lt. Col. Washington, were so posted in the rear as not to be injured by the enemy's fire, and yet to be able to charge them should an occasion offer; the Volunteers from North Carolina, South Carolina and Georgia, under the command of Col. Pickens were posted to guard the flanks. Major McDowal, of the North Carolina Volunteers, were posted on the right flank in front of the line 150 yards. Major Cunningham, of the Georgia Volunteers, on the left, at the same distance in front, Colonels Brannon and Thomas, of the South Carolina Volunteers, on the right of Major McDowal, and Colonels Hays and McCall of the same corps to the left of Major Cunningham. Capts. Tate and Buchanan, with the Augusta Riflemen, were to support the right of the line. The enemy drew up in one line four hundred yards in front of our advanced corps."[15]

Then suddenly there arose the unmistakable pop of rifle fire, and even from a distance Morgan could see the small puffs of gunpowder drift up into the air. The skirmish line had come to life, and now British riders could be seen tumbling from their horses; not many, but enough to create problems, confusion, and anger. Then in the center of the British column a small knot of riders could be seen moving forward, scanning the ground before them, and in the center of that knot of riders a short officer with broad shoulders and a stern expression on his face. That stern rider, of course, was Banastre Tarleton, taking his position at center stage, eyes eagerly scanning ahead for Morgan and his men.

CHAPTER EIGHTEEN

TARLETON

An impatient Banastre Tarleton rode across the British front for a quick inspection of the American position, but in the grey light of early dawn, precious little could be discerned. As historian Lawrence Babits notes, there may well have been some mist clinging to the ground in the swales and low-lying areas to additionally obscure the British commander's vision, thus beyond the vague and partially concealed appearance of the skirmish line some 150 yards distant, little of value could be discovered. The normal military procedure on such an occasion was to "feel out" an enemy's position in order to develop an accurate idea of both strength and disposition so that a sensible tactical plan could then be crafted. In the 18th Century this was often achieved through the use of cavalry – which could move quickly across the front, thus cover more ground and see farther and better than infantry – or an infantry feint that would force a concealed enemy to fire and reveal both their numbers and position. Initially, at least, Tarleton opted for his cavalry to carry out this objective, and he "ordered the legion dragoons to drive in the militia parties who covered the front, that General Morgan's disposition might be conveniently and distinctly inspected."[1]

The sound of horse's hooves and jangling sabers suddenly reverberated across the Cowpens as British cavalrymen took their positions, disrupting the early morning stillness. The dragoons formed immediately, steam hissing from their mounts' nostrils, and the command to charge was shouted, shrill and ominous in the chill morning air. They drove straight toward the skirmish line, determined to drive the American militia from the top of the small rise they occupied directly ahead. Sabers flashing, the fifty or so green-clad horsemen initially created an impressive spectacle of power and determination, the thunder of hooves suddenly exploding across the frozen ground. But as they closed to within some fifty yards of the skirmishers, the American riflemen, their sights trained steadily on the British riders as they approached, opened fire. It was an unexpected and disagreeable reception to say the least and numerous dragoons were instantly unhorsed, tumbling in bloody confusion across the hard, frozen ground. So accurate was the American fire that the charge was at once forced to veer away from the top of the hill and, thinking better now of exposing themselves and their mounts to another volley from the crack American riflemen, the magnificent advance that had begun with such spirit, returned to the British lines, bloodied for the effort while having accomplished almost nothing of value.

But the charge had at least given Tarleton the opportunity to get a sense of the volume of rifle fire from the American line, and the number of shots apparently did not impress him. And now too it could be seen that some of the men that formed the American skirmish line were already making for the rear, abandoning their position, apparently dispirited by the mere show of British might and determination. As he watched some of the riflemen disappear from view Tarleton had to have been thinking: *surely this is nothing more than a scanty rearguard, some backwoods militia ordered to try and harass and annoy our advance as Morgan makes good his escape across Broad River. And now, look, already the wretches are running!* Banastre Tarleton, impatient and aggressive as ever, would have none of it. He had seen this script before, and he certainly knew how to deal with backwoods militia in flight. He would quickly deploy his infantry, make short work of the force on his front – whatever trifle it amounted to – then quickly find and roll over the fleeing Morgan. The notion that just beyond that ridge, behind the retreating skirmishers, there awaited two more solid lines of American infantry poised and waiting was something Tarleton never once entertained. He had not, and would not, properly develop the enemy's strength and position – a basic to any military operation – and this fundamental failure would soon prove his undoing.

One of the officers marching with the British column that day was Roderick Mackenzie, a lieutenant in the 71st Regiment, and to say the least no fan of Banastre Tarleton's. In 1787, and in direct response to Tarleton's self-serving account of his experiences during the American Revolution, Mackenzie published his own scathing denouncement of Tarleton, and Mackenzie had much to say about his commander's decisions at Cowpens. "Without the delay of a single moment," he pointed out angrily, "and in despite of extreme fatigue, the light-legion infantry and fusileers were ordered to form in line. Before this order was put in execution, and while Major Newmarsh, who commanded the latter corps, was posting his officers, the line, far from complete, was led to the attack by Lieutenant colonel Tarleton himself."[2] Impatient and overconfident, Tarleton could not even await the proper deployment of his infantry before leading them forward into what for virtually all of them would very soon amount to death, injury, or capture. It is an odd fact of human nature that people often see what they expect to see, and expecting weakness, Tarleton had seen just that and wrongly expected to run roughshod over it, precisely as he had done so many times in the past. It seems that Morgan had correctly read and prepared for his opponent with uncanny insight.

As the British infantry formed, their artillery moved forward into position along the Green River Road in the center of the Redcoat deployment, employing two light field pieces called grasshoppers. At once they went into action, belching shots far down the road into the trees, doing little if any harm, but forcing the American cavalry under William Washington to shift position. As the artillery boomed and the infantry formed, the last of the American riflemen on the skirmish line fired, then turned and headed back toward Pickens' line behind them. To Tarleton it undoubtedly looked as though they were all now abandoning their position on the run, this only serving to energize him all the more.

"The British lieutenant-colonel, urging forward, was at length gratified with the certainty of battle;" wrote Light Horse Harry Lee, "and being prone to presume on victory, he hurried the formation of his troops. The light and Legion infantry, with the seventh regiment, composed the line of battle; in the centre of which was posted the artillery, consisting of two grasshoppers; and a troop of dragoons was placed on each flank. The battalion of the seventy-first regiment, under Major McArthur, with the remainder of the cavalry, formed the reserve. Tarleton placed himself with the line, having under him Major Newmarsh, who commanded the seventh regiment. The disposition was not completed, when he directed the line to advance, and the reserve to wait further orders."[3] Thomas Young, then sitting his horse with Washington's cavalry watched the entire scene unfold and was quite impressed. "About Sunrise," he later recalled, "the British line advanced at a sort of trot, with a loud halloo. It was the most beautiful line I ever saw."[4]

John Buchanan rightly notes that Tarleton was generally candid and accurate when describing his own victories, but self-serving and downright deceitful when recounting his failures, and there is little doubt that Cowpens represented his greatest failure, hence his greatest literary deceit. It is clear that at no time did the British commander properly reconnoiter the American position, better yet detect the two main infantry lines concealed behind in the trees, yet that fact would not stop him from later claiming that he had. Tarleton simply lied, insisting that he "discovered that the American commander had formed a front line of about one thousand militia, and had composed his second line and reserve of five hundred continental light infantry, one hundred twenty of Washington's cavalry, and three hundred back woodsmen. This accurate knowledge being obtained,

Tarleton desired the British infantry to disencumber themselves of every thing, except their arms and ammunition."[5] This is pure nonsense, fabricated long after the fact to cover Tarleton's failures and negligence, for at the moment he was leading his troops straight into the jaws of a trap he had failed to discern and had no knowledge awaited.

All the British officers and men, Tarleton later insisted, displayed the utmost confidence that they would drive the Americans from their position, and the day would soon be theirs. "During the execution of these arrangements, the animation of the officers and the alacrity of the soldiers afforded the most promising assurances of success," he wrote. That may well have been the case, for across their front all the British officers and men could really see at the time were the few men of the American skirmish line, and these were already withdrawing back to join Pickens' militia. "The disposition being completed," wrote Tarleton, "the front line received orders to advance, a fire from some of the recruits of the 7th regiment was suppressed, and the troops moved on in as good a line as troops could move at open files."[6] When the British troops stepped off they let out a tremendous shout, a design of pure intimidation, but on the opposite end of the field Daniel Morgan was waiting for just that moment, and was ready to respond in kind. Thomas Young recalled that "When they [the British] shouted, I heard Morgan say, 'They give us the British halloo, boys, give them the Indian halloo, by G--- [']] and he galloped along the lines, cheering the men, and telling them not to fire until we could see the whites of their eyes."[7]

Wait, Wait! Morgan was surely imploring, and all of the American officers were shouting the same. Hold your fire! It was imperative that the militia deliver a killing volley, and that meant firing at a distance of no more than fifty yards. The two shots Morgan wanted could not be squandered ineffectively at a distance. That could not happen. So up and down the militia line Morgan rode, fiercely preaching patience and inspiring confidence wherever he went.

Anxious men stood and waited as the deadly, cold steel of British bayonets rushed closer, approaching at the quick step. The Redcoats surged forward, up a small incline, over and through what had been the ground occupied by the advanced American skirmish line. Here and there an American rifleman lingered, pulled the trigger, and sent a Redcoat toppling, but for the most part the small hill was now vacant, and the British were in turn sensing an easy victory. As the red ranks advanced the two grasshoppers were booming their charges up and over the American position; far more unnerving than they were effective, but unnerving nevertheless. Thomas Young, at the time watching from horseback with Washington's dragoons, recalled that "Every officer was crying don't fire! For it was a hard matter for us to keep from it. I should have said the British line advanced under cover of their artillery; for it opened so fiercely upon the center, that Col. Washington moved his cavalry from the center towards the right wing."[8] Daniel Morgan, now dismounted, was moving back and forth amongst the militia, joking with the men, insisting over and over again that they take their time and fire only once they could see the whites of the Redcoat's eyes. It was Morgan at his best, calming unsteady nerves and itchy trigger fingers.

Still the British came on at the quick step, rapidly closing the gap between their front rank and the waiting militia, but until they came upon Andrew Pickens's partially hidden line, the extent of the opposing force now facing them directly ahead remained obscure. Indeed, many of the Redcoats thought they were chasing a beaten foe, but that calculation soon took a radical change.

As the British closed, Morgan sent out small detachments of riflemen just slightly ahead of the main militia line to harass the oncoming enemy. Joseph McJunkin was among them, and he recalled the moment when the Redcoats neared, and the first shots rang out from the militia. "A column marches up in front of Brandon's men [on the left of the militia line] led by a gaily dressed officer on horseback. The word passes along the line, 'Who can bring him down?' John Savage looked Col. Farr full in the face and read yes in his eye. He darted a few paces in front, laid his rifle against a sapling, a blue gas streamed above his head, the sharp crack of a rifle broke the solemn stillness of the occasion and a horse without a rider wheeled from the front of the advancing column."[9] Thomas Young later agreed with McJunkin's version of the battle's flash point. "I have heard old Col. Fair say often, that he believed John Savage fired the first gun of this battle. He was riding to and fro, along the lines, When he saw Savage fix his eye upon a British officer; he stepped out of the ranks, raised his gun—fired, and he saw the officer fall."[10]

Historian Lawrence Babits describes the British rapid, disciplined approach: "The British Legion infantry and the light infantry came on quickly, grimly confident, moving steadily at the quick step, more certain of success now that they were going forward. The trap Morgan created was already starting to close on Tarleton's men. The full extent of the South Carolina militia line was revealed only after the British came over the crest of militia ridge. Now, as the last of the skirmishers took their positions, a new, much more deadly phase of the battle began."[11]

Suddenly, then, the British line came within effective rifle range of the militia line, and the Americans opened on them, sporadically at first, but then with a furious thunder. Daniel Morgan was waiting, carefully gauging the British approach until he had them right where he wanted them. According to riflemen Richard Swearingen, it was Morgan who bellowed the order to open fire.[12]

Fire! Fire!

"The militia fired first," said Thomas Young. "It was for a time, pop-pop-pop and then a whole volley."[13] A sheet of flame and a billowing cloud of smoke erupted between the opposing lines. By all accounts, the militia fire was deadly, and many British officers and men tumbled from the ranks.[14] The initial volley, long awaited and well prepared for, was generally the most effective volley in any Revolutionary engagement, and at fifty yards the capable militia riflemen could hardly miss.

The British advance recoiled, stunned by the volume and accuracy of the militia volley. This was a greeting no one had expected or been prepared for. Then the Redcoats recovered, brought their muskets to their shoulders and responded with a blistering volley of their own. But Morgan had prepared the American position with great skill, for while the American militia was firing uphill from the bottom of a slight swale, the

British were firing down, and Morgan knew that British infantry had a tendency to fire high. Thus the American accuracy had been enhanced by the position they occupied, while the British fire flew even higher than usual. John Buchanan notes the fact. "They [the British] fired their volley but as usual it did little if any damage, for most of the balls flew high over the Americans' heads, to be found many years later imbedded in trees as high as thirty feet off the ground."[15]

Rather than firing the two volleys Morgan had requested, however, according to both Collins and Young, most of the men in the militia line fired only once, and then began a controlled withdrawal. Thomas Young states clearly that, "After the first fire, the militia retreated, and the cavalry covered their retreat."[16] But other sections stood and fired at least one more volley. Indeed the British tried to advance with the bayonet on the militia, only to be staggered and driven back for their efforts. "The light infantry was the first British unit to charge. They recovered from their initial shock and started forward to give Brandon the bayonet after Hayes fired. Unfortunately for the light infantry, Brandon's men completed reloading before Hayes fired. As the light infantry advanced, the Fair Forest men got off a second volley which stopped the British dead in their tracks."[17]

Then the militia fighters started back toward the Continental line, but with good order and discipline. Some moved tree-to-tree, loading and firing parting shots as they did, taking a still greater toll on the staggered line of Redcoats. Morgan, having thought every small detail through in advance, had arranged for individual units of the Continental line to step backward slightly. Once properly executed, the movement opened avenues of egress for the militia so they could move through the Continentals quickly and reform while at the same time not disrupting the main battle line before the next phase of fighting had begun. At this the militia behaved admirably.[18]

The red-clad formations had suffered terribly as a result of the first two engagements. Not only were many men and officers down, but shock and exhaustion were already taking a significant toll on British fighting effectiveness. Roderick Mackenzie observed that at this point: "The infantry were not in condition to overtake the fugitives; the latter had not marched thirty miles in the course of the last fortnight; the former, during that time, had been in motion day and night. A number, not less than two-thirds of the British infantry officers, had already fallen, and nearly the same proportion of privates; fatigue, however, enfeebled the pursuit much more than loss of blood."[19] The well-directed fire of both the skirmish and militia lines had taken a major toll on British morale, stamina, and fighting capability. So far, Morgan's trap was working precisely as originally envisioned.

Tarleton attempted to dress the British lines again, but some of his infantry, seeing the militia withdrawing before them, again fancied victory suddenly within their grasp, and struck out after the Americans in disjointed order. The iron discipline of the British advance was becoming unglued. In some disorder, then, the Redcoats continued on after what they presumed – once again – to be a beaten, fleeing foe, only then to run headfirst – and much to their shock – into the main line of Morgan's Continentals. With muskets loaded, the American regulars stood shoulder-to-shoulder directly in the path of the approaching Redcoats, ready and waiting.

CHAPTER NINETEEN

HOWARD

John Eager Howard sat his horse behind the Continental line and watched as the British reformed on the ridge the American militia had just moments before vacated. From his position he could hear the British officers shouting their commands and the wail of the enemy wounded, already distinct and alarming. The Redcoats had paid dearly for what little ground they had gained. And while it was clear that Morgan's plan for savaging the British attack by forcing them to fight their way through a defense in depth had so far been successful, it was also obvious that the British were far from defeated and that the curtain was very soon to be drawn on the main event. Howard would later write that the British "shouted and made a great noise to intimidate, and rushed with bayonets upon the militia who had not time, especially the riflemen, to fire a second time. The militia fell into our rear, and part of them fell into the rear of my right flank."[1] Morgan's clever design of having several infantry units move slightly backward in order to open small gaps in the Continental line through which the militia could pass had worked without hitch or confusion. Once the militia had passed through the line, the Continentals stepped forward smartly and reestablished a solid front. All of this had been accomplished without prior drill, and the success of the maneuver was a testament to the American fighters and the confidence they had in their leader. Some of the militia was then ushered off to the left flank of the American line, while the rest was redeployed on the right.

James Collins, who had been stationed on the far right of the militia line when he fired his one shot,[2] scampered back through the line of Continentals to a position behind the extreme left flank along with many of his compatriots. Said Collins, "We gave the enemy one fire, when they charged us with their bayonets; we gave way and retreated for our horses."[3] Whether he intended to stay and fight or mount his horse and ride away as fast as he could ride, Collins does not say, but events would soon have their own way with him and his cohorts for, noting the retrograde movement of the militia, Tarleton quickly ordered the fifty dragoons he had stationed on the British right flank to advance on the militia. "The cavalry on the right were directed to charge the enemy's left:" wrote Tarleton. "They executed the order with great gallantry."[4]

The dragoons had not fared so well when charging the American skirmish line earlier that morning, but chasing down retreating militia was another story entirely. Suddenly the thunder of horse's hooves on frozen sod was clearly heard again, and Collins and his mates turned for a quick look, only to see the British cavalry, sabers flashing in the morning sunlight, come sweeping down upon them. Major

Joseph McJunkin recalls the dash of the cavalry upon the retreating Americans. "The sharpshooters fall behind Pickens and presently his line yields. Then there is a charge of the dragoons even past the line of regulars after the retreating militia. Numbers are cut down." The militiamen were entirely surprised by the British cavalry and, caught in the open, were easy prey for whirling British steel. "Two dragoons assault a large rifleman," McJunkin recalled, "Joseph Hughes by name. His gun was empty, but with it he parries their blows and dodges round a tree, but they still persist. At the moment the assault on Hughes began John Savage was priming his rifle. Just as they pass the tree to strike Hughes he levels his gun and one of the dragoons tumbles from his horse pierced with a bullet. The next moment the rifle carried by Hughes, now literally hacked over, slips out of his hands and inflicts such a blow upon the other dragoon that he quits the contest and retires hanging by the mane of his horse."[5]

Another militia private standing nearby watched in amazement as Joseph Hughes responded to the cavalry attack. "He was not only a man of great personal strength, but of remarkable fleetness on foot. As his men, with others, broke at Cowpens, and fled before Tarleton's cavalry; and though receiving a sabre cut across his right hand, yet with his drawn sword, he could out-run his men, and passing them face about, and command them to stand, striking right and left to enforce obedience to his orders; often repeating with a loud voice: 'You d—d cowards halt and fight—there is more danger in running than in fighting, and if you don't stop and fight, you will all be killed!'"[6] James Collins, making for his horse with the rest of the militia, turned to spot the dragoons pounding down upon him, and would never forget the sight. "Tarleton's cavalry pursued us; ("now," thought I, "my hide is in the loft;") just as we got to our horses, they overtook us and began to make a few hacks at some, however, without doing much injury."[7]

The dragoons had come on in such a fury that for the most part they overrode the militia, and had to come about for a second go. But it was not to be. For two American officers were watching the mayhem as it developed behind their left flank, and both would take immediate action. The first of those two was William Washington, watching from his position with the cavalry. It can be recalled that the cavalry had been placed in the rear as a general reserve, and Washington had Morgan's confidence to strike whenever and wherever he deemed necessary. Washington did not hesitate. Spotting the dragoons descend upon the militia, he ordered an immediate charge, and Collins was one of the happy recipients of Washington's vigilance. "They [the British dragoons] in their haste," said Collins, "had pretty much scattered, perhaps, thinking they would have another Fishing creek frolic, but in a few moments, Col. Washington's cavalry was among them, like a whirlwind, and the poor fellows began to keel from their horses, without being able to remount. The shock was so sudden and violent, they could not stand it, and immediately betook themselves to flight; there was not time to rally, and they appeared to be as hard to stop as a drove of Choctaw steers, going to a Pennsylvania market." In a few moments the clashing of swords was out of hearing and quickly out of sight.[8]

The second watchful officer was Morgan himself. Spotting the dragoons manhandling the retreating militia, Morgan immediately spurred his horse to that quarter to provide assistance and restore order. Perhaps somewhat dispirited from the British cavalry attack, and naturally given to scatter in confused circumstances, Morgan sensed the need to calm and rejuvenate his militia fighters before they had a chance to mount their horses and disperse, and Collins saw him coming: "by this time, both lines of the infantry were warmly engaged and we being relieved from the pursuit of the enemy began to rally and prepare to redeem our credit, when Morgan rode up in front, and waving his sword, cried out, "Form, form, my brave fellows! Give them one more fire and the day is ours. Old Morgan was never beaten."[9] Responding to Morgan, Pickens, and their better angels, the militia reformed and began a movement around the rear of the Continental line in order to take up a position on their extreme right flank.

Meanwhile, the British infantry had reformed, and begun their assault upon the line of Continentals standing directly across their path. "Captain Andrew Wallace's Virginia Continentals were posted on Howard's right, their flank guarded by a small force of North Carolina state troops. The veteran Maryland and Delaware Continentals occupied the center, with the experienced Virginia militia to their left along with some South Carolina militiamen under Samuel Hammond. Howard rode back and forth along the rear of the line, encouraging his troops to stand fast."[10] The British advanced steadily upon Morgan's main line, and it was immediately evident that neither side had any intention of running. "The British advanced until my regiment commenced firing,"[11] Howard reported, and when the Americans opened fire they did so in sections, from right to left. Thomas Young thought the initial volley a thing of martial perfection, for "when the regulars fired," he remembered vividly, "it seemed like one sheet of flame from right to left. Oh, it was beautiful!"[12] The British fired in return, and the Americans offered volley after volley, holding the British in place with a well-delivered rolling fire, section-by-section.

The action became intense, both sides trading volleys. However it soon appeared that the Americans – well rested and well fed – had the better of these exchanges, while the British infantrymen were firing regularly but inaccurately; a product, in all likelihood, of the fact that they were nearing physical and mental exhaustion. Sheets of flame and torrents of smoke poured from the opposing lines, as men toppled from the ranks. The intensity of the fight was stern, the sound deafening. Tarleton, riding behind his main line observed the ferocity of the contest. "The fire on both sides was well supported and produced much slaughter,"[13] he wrote, and Joseph McJunkin agreed, later recalling that "Meanwhile the British infantry and the regulars under Col. Howard are hotly engaged; the fight becomes desperate."[14] Howard knows he cannot be beaten nor can he withdraw. The Continentals were at that moment giving the British everything they could handle. In the center of the Continental line, Captain Robert Kirkwood was demonstrating the skill and determination of his Delaware troops. Morgan, watching confidently from behind the line observed that "When the enemy advanced on our lines they received a well-directed and incessant fire."[15]

On both British and American lines the order of firing was fundamentally the same, officers shouting the repetitious commands over and over again, trying to be heard above the thunder of battle that was rising and booming all around them. "Prime and load! Shoulder; Make Ready; Take Aim!; Fire!"[16] The disciplined Continental troops were every bit a match for the finest soldiers the British Army had to offer.

An expert with a musket could get off several shots per minute, but it became far more difficult under the intensity of battle conditions, where the guns might foul due to powder residue, mishandling, or simple mechanical breakdown. Loading a flintlock weapon was no easy task even in the best of times. First, the butt was dropped to the ground and powder deposited in a charger. The powder was then poured down the muzzle of the weapon and a patch placed over the open bore. A ball was then seated in the patch and pushed down into the muzzle and the excess patch cut quickly away. The ball was then rammed down the barrel with a ramrod until it sat firmly in place in the powder charge. Then the weapon had to be primed by pulling the hammer back to the half-cocked position, opening and cleaning the frizzen, clearing the vent, pouring a small dose of powder into the firing pan, closing the frizzen, and pulling the hammer back to full-cock.[17] It was a laborious and meticulous process, and every step had to be done correctly each and every time, or the weapon might jam or fail. And along both lines of battle, the muskets and rifles were cracking away with startling regularity.

Light Horse Harry Lee describes the combat as the British and Americans slugged it out along the main line. "Tarleton pushed forward, and was received by his adversary with unshaken firmness. The contest became obstinate; and each party, animated by the example of its leader, nobly contended for victory. Our line maintained itself so firmly, as to oblige the enemy to order up his reserve."[18] It appeared the Continentals could not be dislodged by volleys of musket fire alone, thus Tarleton was forced to improvise on the spot. "As the contest between the British infantry in the front line and the continentals seemed equally balanced," he confided, "neither retreating, Lieutenant-colonel Tarleton thought the advance of the 71st into line, and a movement of the cavalry in reserve to threaten the enemy's right flank, would put a victorious period to the action. No time was lost in performing this maneuver."[19] Tarleton ordered his reserve infantry, the 71st to move beyond the 7th before opening fire and likewise to be careful "not to entangle their right flank with the left of the other battalion. The cavalry were ordered to incline to the left, and to form a line, which would embrace the whole of the enemy's right flank."[20]

It was Tarleton's intention to turn the American right flank, and what's more, he realized this movement had to be made quickly, for his infantry was then taking a heavy pounding. Savaged by both the skirmish and militia lines, the British were now in all probability outgunned all along the front. Lawrence Babits explains: "The reduced light and legion infantry faced a numerically superior, rifle-armed force at close range. The Virginians were not vulnerable in this fight because they had rifles. They were protected by the cycle of firing which left one company always loaded, and by the bayonets of adjacent Continentals."[21]

John Eager Howard watched as the 71st began maneuvering toward his right flank and immediately feared for the worst. On Howard's far right the reformed militia under McDowell had taken up a position just slightly forward of the main line from which they were directing a severe and enfilading fire at the British. Across their front the British 71st now appeared, and then stepped off to advance upon the American flank as Tarleton had ordered. The 71st was a unit of veteran Scottish Highlanders, and as their lines lurched forward the wail of Scottish bagpipes blossomed over the Cowpens like the high-pitched squall of some disembodied fiend, a shrieking message calculated to engender fear in any waiting foe. The forward lurch of the 71st was the signal for another general advance of the entire line of British infantry, for according to Tarleton "Upon the advance of the 71st, all the infantry again moved on."[22]

Along the American line the muskets responded with renewed fury as the British infantry again began to close the distance between the two opposing ranks, but Howard still had much concern for his exposed right flank, and rightly so. The 71st was approaching across his right front while British dragoons were also maneuvering on ground beyond his flank. There he "soon observed, as I had but about 350 men and the British about 800, that their line extended much further than mine particularly on my right, where they were pressing forward to gain my flank."[23] Riding to that quarter, Howard struck upon a sensible solution. He would have the extreme company of Continental's under Captain Wallace turn and refuse the line as they did; a maneuver by which they would face the approaching threat directly, thus securing the flank. The order was promptly given to Captain Wallace and just as promptly either misunderstood or completely mishandled. Rather than turning and repositioning as ordered, the end Continental unit did an about-face and began to retreat! It was a disaster, indeed just the sort of self-inflicted calamity that often occurs during the confusion and tumult of battle. Howard was thunderstruck. "Whether my orders were not well understood or whether it proceeded from any other cause," said Howard, "in attempting this maneuver some disorder ensued in this company which rather fell back than faced as I wished them."[24]

Howard watched in horror as his flank company turned and began a retrograde movement directly away from the line of battle. And then lighting struck. His entire line of battle, observing the movement of Wallace's Virginians, presumed the order to withdraw in order had been given, though not heard, and company-by-company began to follow suit, initiating a general withdrawal of the entire Continental line! Howard latter explained that "Seeing my right flank was exposed to the enemy, I attempted to change the front of Wallace's company (Virginia regulars); in doing it, some confusion ensued, and first a part, and then the whole of the company commenced a retreat. The officers along the line seeing this, and supposing that orders had been given for a retreat, faced their men about, and moved off."[25]

The thunder of musketry and artillery, the swirling smoke of battle, the screams of the wounded and dying, the wail of Scottish bagpipes had all seemingly conspired to produce a horrible mistake along the American line. Or had it? Great officers respond with calm and clear thinking in times of extreme stress, and John Eager Howard was about to demonstrate his greatness on the field of battle. Rather than panicking, he realized at once that the retrograde maneuver of his entire line was in fact removing it from the British threat on his far right, thus if accomplished with speed and discipline, he could simply redeploy the line at a more advantageous position and resume the contest. The confused maneuver was not necessarily a disaster at all, indeed quite possibly a gift, but a gift only if properly understood and immediately executed.

Just then Morgan galloped up and expressed his dismay. What in the world was happening? Were the Continentals beaten?

John Eager Howard later recounted the hurried exchange between these two calm and unflappable commanders. "Morgan, who had mostly been with the militia, quickly rode up to me and expressed apprehensions... but I soon removed his fears by pointing to the line, and observing that men were not beaten who retreated in that order. He then ordered me to keep with the men until we came to the rising ground near Washington's horse, and he rode forward to fix on the most proper place for us to halt and face about."[26]

Daniel Morgan rode back up the slight incline that had been designated as a potential spot for a last stand, and carefully selected the most advantageous location for the Continentals to halt and about-face. While a mistake had been made, the Americans had reacted with skill and composure, and if discipline prevailed, the mistake could be turned to their advantage. The Continental infantry had been taught to reload while performing the very retrograde movement they were now executing, thus once brought to a halt and swung about, they would be ready to fire at an instant.

It was the British, not the Americans who now lost all discipline. Once again misinterpreting the American withdrawal as defeat and demoralization, the exhausted British infantry broke forth in a great rush forward in a wild, desperate attempt to drive home their victory. The storied British discipline had all but disintegrated, yet the onward rush alone might still carry the day if they caught up to the Continentals while still in retreat. Tarleton recalled this moment of crisis: "The continentals and back woodsmen gave ground: The British rushed forwards: An order was dispatched to the cavalry to charge;"[27] On the British came, screaming and racing after the retreating American line, gaining on the Continentals with every step, and it was apparent to all that the endgame at Cowpens would be decided by the slimmest of margins; would the Americans be able to stop and about-face before the Redcoats were upon them? That was the question.

Just ahead Morgan had located his spot, marked it clearly, and was waiting for Howard to close with the line of retreating Continentals. With drill field precision the regulars reached Morgan, and there the line was immediately halted by Howard. He later explained that "this retreat was accidental but was very fortunate as we thereby were extricated from the enemy. As soon as the word was given to halt and face about the line was perfectly formed in a moment. The enemy pressed upon us in rather disorder, expecting the fate of the day was decided."[28]

The British were rushing upon the Americans in furor and disorder, coming on as individuals or as raging clumps of men, their front ranks now less than thirty yards from the Continental muskets. The Redcoats expected victory; what they received was disaster. Howard gave the order, and a sheet of flame greeted the charging British infantrymen directly in their faces, some of them only yards from the looming muzzles of the American guns when they went off. A wall of flame and lead at point-blank range utterly staggered the exhausted, charging British, killing many in a flash, blowing the remainder backward or forcing them in confusion to stumble to their knees. In seconds only, the wild British charge had been blown utterly to pieces, and in the aftermath there loomed only the sudden silence of shock and dismay. For the Americans this was a moment ripe with extraordinary potential, and John Eager Howard seems to have grasped that potential in an instant. Unanticipated, and probably never previously discussed with Morgan, Howard understood almost instinctively the dramatic alteration the battle had just undergone, and he reacted with startling aggressiveness.

For at this critical moment John Eager Howard made one of the great, instinctive decisions of the American Revolution, issuing an order that would turn what appeared to be a capable defensive stand into a complete and total rout, and an order that would put the Revolution – a contest that had been at loggerheads for years – on a straight line to victory and independence at Yorktown. Here at last loomed amends for Camden, for the months and years of bad food and foul conditions, for disasters like Charleston, Brandywine, and Fort Washington, for the awful retreat from Charlotte that August; for Monck's Corner and Fishing Creek. Here at long last loomed, not only retribution, but victory, and Howard moved to claim that victory without the slightest hesitation. Riding behind his Continental line, John Eager Howard observed the terrible effect the American volley had had on the British infantrymen, then bellowed the order that was to alter the war. "Charge bayonets!"[29] he screamed and the line of Continentals lowered their bayonets, gave out a mighty roar, and surged forward instantly like a blue tidal wave.

CHAPTER TWENTY

MORGAN

It was Camden in reverse. Indeed, it was everything that men like Robert Kirkwood, Otho Williams, William Washington, and John Eager Howard could have asked for. In the blink of an eye, the British assault had been turned on its head, and before many of the exhausted British soldiers could even draw a breath, the red-coated hunters had become the hunted. Roderick Mackenzie of the British 71st later recalled the nightmare as it unfolded. "In disorder from the pursuit [of the Americans], unsupported by the cavalry, deprived of the assistance of the cannon, which in defiance of the utmost exertions of those who had them in charge, were not left behind, the advance of the British fell back, and communicated a panick to others, which soon became general: a total rout ensued."[1]

Observing the same event while riding directly behind the line of Continentals as they rushed forward, bayonets jabbing at the fleeing foe, Daniel Morgan later described the British collapse and rout after "they gained our flanks, which obliged us to change our position. We retired, in good order, about fifty paces, formed and advanced on the enemy and gave them a brisk fire, which threw them into disorder. Lieut.-Col Howard observing this gave orders for the line to charge bayonets which was done with such address that the enemy fled with the utmost precipitation."[2] As if a switch had been thrown, the Redcoat assault had gone from forward into immediate reverse.

It was not just a defeat, nor even a terrible defeat. It was a complete implosion. Redcoats fell to the ground, surrendered in droves, begged for mercy, or ran as fast as their exhausted legs could carry them. The British infantrymen collapsed in terror and dismay and exhaustion as the lethal phalanx of American steel swept out and over them. Rarely on any field had the fortunes of war changed so rapidly and dramatically. Light Horse Harry describes the British debacle: "Considering the retrograde movement the precursor of flight, the British line rushed on with impetuosity and disorder; but, as it drew near, Howard faced about, and gave it a close and murderous fire. Stunned by this unexpected shock, the most advanced of the enemy recoiled in confusion. Howard seized the happy moment, and followed his advantage with the bayonet. This decisive step gave us the day the reserve having been brought near the line, shared in the destruction of our fire and presented no rallying point to the fugitives. ..Morgan pressed home his success, and the pursuit became vigorous and general."[3]

Even Tarleton years later could not disguise the dimensions of the collapse, noting that just as the rushing British infantry seemed to reach the retreating Continentals with the intention of overwhelming them once and for all,

"An unexpected fire at this instant from the Americans, who came about as they were retreating, stopped the British, and threw them into confusion. Exertions to make them advance were useless. The part of the cavalry which had not been engaged fell likewise into disorder, and an unaccountable panic extended itself along the whole line. The Americans, who before thought they had lost the action, taking advantage of present situation, advanced upon the British troops, and augmented their astonishment. A general flight ensued."[4]

From the small hill in the rear of the American position William Washington had earlier spotted the British charging the main American line in excited disarray and quickly sent off a message to Howard: "They are coming on like a mob. Give them a fire and I will charge them."[5] Washington immediately made good his promise, and Thomas Young was riding among Washington's dragoons and described the cavalry charge with great relish and excitement. "I saw Col. Brandon coming at full speed to the rear and waving his sword to Col. Washington. In a moment the command to charge was given, and I soon found that the British cavalry had charged the American right. We made a most furious charge, and cutting through the British cavalry, wheeled and charged them in the rear. In this charge, I exchanged my tackey for the finest horse I ever rode; it was the quickest swap I ever made in my life! At this moment the bugle sounded. We, about half formed and making a sort of circuit at full speed, came up in rear of the British line, shouting and charging like madmen. At this moment Col. Howard gave the word "charge bayonets!" and the day was ours. The British broke, and throwing down their guns and cartouche boxes, made for the wagon road, and did the prettiest sort of running."[6] Redcoats defeated and running; it was not the sort of thing American troops were used to seeing.

The American cavalry cut through the British dragoons who were riding out on the American right, then circled behind the 71st momentarily cutting them off from further retreat, and virtually surrounding them. The Scottish Highlanders were made of stern stuff, however, and they briefly rallied and tried to make a stand, only then to be attacked on all sides by advancing Continentals on their left and front and militia on their flanks. Andrew Pickens had now returned to the field with his militia freshly assembled and reanimated, and took up a position on the Highlander's left flank; a double envelopment! From that position they poured shots into the dispirited warriors as the Continentals pressed them all across their front with the bayonet. It was the last resistance the British would offer at Cowpens, and it proved noble but entirely futile.

Ahead of the onrushing Continentals, John Eager Howard rode directly into the retreating British ranks, calling upon them to surrender. It was a brave but dangerous thing to do, yet Howard understood that further bloodshed would be useless; the issue had already been decided and adding to the death toll would add nothing to the lopsided American victory but senseless tragedy. "I called to them to surrender," Howard later wrote, and "they laid down their arms, and the officers delivered up their swords."[7] Behind him, however, Howard began to hear the menacing cry of "Tarleton's Quarters! Tarleton's Quarters!" as the American infantrymen approached. It was, of course, a bloodthirsty demand for vengeance, an insistence that no mercy be shown any man wearing red that day. It was a pitiless decree inspired by the cruel acts of Tarleton's own Legion, now apparently come full circle. But fortunately for American posterity, neither Howard nor Morgan would stand for any sort of blood lust. Both men had come to fight, but not to murder, and immediately Howard began shouting that quarter would be honored, and that all British prisoners were to be treated with decency. Morgan's booming voice called out the same, and he later proudly reported to Nathanael Greene that "Not a man was killed wounded or even insulted after he surrendered,"[8] and that fact was a testament to the moral fiber of Morgan and his entire officers corps.

Yet it was also apparent that many of the British officers and men did not believe Howard's promise at face value and presumed, rather, that they were going to be seriously mistreated, quite possibly executed where they stood. In fact, while riding amongst the surrendered British one officer dogged alongside the American officer, and literally tried to topple Howard from the saddle. "Captain Duncanson," Howard explained, "of the 71st grenadiers, gave me his sword, and stood by me upon getting on my horse I found him pulling at my saddle, and he nearly unhorsed me. I... asked him what he was about. The explanation was that they had orders to give no quarter and they did not expect any....I admitted his excuse, and put him into the care of a sergeant."[9] At that both Howard and Morgan grasped just how touchy the situation actually was, and took great pains to assure the British prisoners they were safe, while ordering the victorious Americans to conduct themselves with decency. Both officers worked hard to defuse a potentially dangerous situation that could have easily – with but a single wrong or misunderstood act – turned into a slaughter.

The two British field pieces, each originally at opposite ends and slightly forward of the original line of advance, were now run over by the advancing Continentals. Howard gave orders for each artillery piece to be taken, and officers dashed off to comply. But the Redcoat artillerymen, alone and unprotected now by their own infantry, put up a valiant if suicidal resistance. Many were cut down in and amongst the guns by the closing Continentals. One piece was taken when an American officer literally jumped atop the gun, while Howard spotted one of the British artillerymen near his gun refusing to give up the flaming match that might detonate the charge. Fearing that the man would be bayoneted to death by his approaching Continental troops, Howard galloped forward quickly and intervened. "The men," said Howard, "provoked by his obstinacy, would have bayoneted him on the spot, had I not interfered, and desired them to spare the life of so brave a man. He then surrendered the match."[10]

At this point those British officers and men that had not laid down their arms and surrendered were running as fast as they could for the rear, but American bayonets were hot on their trail, and the reformed militia was rapidly closing on their flanks. The once stout British ranks had simply evaporated and in minutes only it was all over save for the mopping-up. Joseph McJunkin, now racing ahead with the militia, recalled the British collapse and flight: "Howard orders a charge, the militia come back and fall in right and left. The British line is broken, some begin to call for quarters, the voice of Howard is heard amidst the rush of men and clangor of steel: 'Throw down your arms and you shall have good quarters.' One battalion throws down their arms and the men fall to earth. Another commences flight, but Washington darts before them with his cavalry and they too ground their arms. In the conclusion of the last foray you might have seen Major Jackson of Georgia rush among the broken ranks of the 71st Regiment and attempting to seize their standard, while they are vainly trying to form by it; you might have seen Col. Howard interposing for the relief of his friend when entangled among his foes."[11]

Banastre Tarleton might have been utterly dismayed by the sight of his fleeing Legion, but he was hardly undone. The British commander may well have had a cruel streak, but he was first and foremost a fighter, and he still had plenty of fight left in him, even if his men did not. Dashing back toward the rear to order his cavalry into the fray, a crafty American rifleman drew a bead on him and brought down his horse. Tarleton hit the ground with an awful splash, but was somehow uninjured by the fall. A British surgeon gave up his steed, and Tarleton quickly remounted. He then promptly gave orders for his cavalry to form in order to check the American assault while he dashed off and tried in vain to rally his infantry. But nothing he attempted worked. "The cavalry did not comply with the order," he later acknowledged, "and the effort to collect the infantry was ineffectual. Neither promises nor threats could gain their attention; they surrendered or dispersed, and abandoned the guns to the artillery men, who defended them for some time with exemplary resolution."[12]

The American wave washed onward, unstoppable; irresistible, gunning down or gobbling up British fugitives as it swept across the field; a tidal wave of blue and buckskin. When Banastre Tarleton realized that the order he had given for his reserve dragoons – some 200 strong – had not been obeyed, he rode directly back to their location, and in a fury issued the order in person. It did not matter. "In this late stage of defeat," Tarleton admitted, the British leader "made another struggle to bring his cavalry to the charge. The weight of such an attack might yet retrieve the day, the enemy being much broken by their late and rapid advance, but all attempts to restore order, recollection, or courage, proved fruitless. Above two hundred dragoons forsook their leader, and left the field of battle."[13] Such was the magnitude of the American victory that British dragoons simply turned on their horses and galloped off in fear, leaving their enraged commander behind on the field. Roderick Mackenzie of the British 71st watched in horror as "Two hundred and fifty horse which had not been engaged, fled through the woods with the utmost precipitation, bearing down such officers as opposed their flight."[14] This was beyond mere defeat. This was a total breakdown of British morale, discipline, and fighting spirit.

But despite the disaster unfolding before his eyes, the surrender of the majority of his light infantry, even the desertion of his cavalry, Banastre Tarleton, to his credit, still intended to stand and fight. Even Roderick Mackenzie, one of his harshest critics, later applauded Tarleton's valiant effort. "Lieutenant Colonel Tarleton," Mackenzie observed, "with no more than fifty horse, hesitated not to charge the whole of Washington's cavalry, though supported by the continentals; it was a small body of officers, and a detachment of the seventeenth regiment of dragoons, who presented themselves on this desperate occasion."[15] Tarleton himself would trumpet the occasion, writing that "Fourteen officers and forty horse-men were, however, not unmindful of their own reputation, or the situation of their commanding officer. Colonel Washington's cavalry were charged, and driven back into the continental infantry by this handful of brave men."[16]

The actual facts of the situation, however, were far more involved and less self-congratulatory than Banastre Tarleton was later willing to admit. Tarleton did in fact charge with his forty or so companions back onto the field at Cowpens, but it was in an attempt to reclaim the two artillery pieces, and in this he was entirely unsuccessful. The American cavalry, William Washington in the lead, spotted Tarleton's small band and gave immediate chase. Washington, riding far out ahead of his men, stormed into the group and tried desperately to get at Tarleton. In a scene surely worthy of a Hollywood script, horses turned, pistols cracked, and sabers sliced the air as the two commanders came literally face-to-face. Morgan would describe the affair: "Tarleton & two of his Officers Charged Coll. Washington; Tarleton fired both pistols at Washington & wounded his Horse... before two of Washington's men came up & cut the two Officers very much —Tarleton cleared himself by the swiftness of his Horse."[17] Roderick Mackenzie seemed to second Morgan's assessment of the contest more so than Tarleton's, recalling that "the loss sustained was in proportion to the danger of the enterprise, and the whole body [of British horse] was repulsed."[18]

Light Horse Harry describes a similar but more involved encounter between Washington and Tarleton. "In his eagerness of pursuit, Washington advanced nearly thirty yards in front of his regiment. Observing this, three British officers wheeled about, and made a charge upon him. The officer on his right was aiming to cut him down, when a sergeant came up and intercepted the blow by disabling his sword arm. At the same instant the officer on his left was also about to make a stroke at him, when a waiter, too small to wield a sword, saved him by wounding the officer with a ball, discharged by a pistol. At this moment the officer in the centre, who was believed to be Tarleton, made a thrust at him, which he parried; upon which this officer retreated a few paces, and then discharged a pistol at him, which wounded his knee."[19]

Whatever the precise sequence of thrusts, blows, and pistols shots, Tarleton by then had had enough. Barely escaping Washington's furious clutches, he turned and with what remained of his small band of dragoons, raced off for the safety of the woods far beyond the American lines, leaving behind an appalling scene of death and ruin in his wake. Of the roughly 1,100 men who had entered the battle on the British side, few beyond the dragoons who deserted and Tarleton's small party of horse escaped. Almost all of the red-coated infantry who had stepped off that morning were dead, wounded, or taken prisoner. The cream of Cornwallis' light infantry had simply ceased to exist.

Joe McJunkin gazed out over the field of battle after the British had fled and recorded his final thoughts: "At the end of the strife you might have seen the same young man [Major

Jackson of Georgia] introducing Major McArthur, the commandant of the British infantry, to Gen. Morgan and receiving the General's thanks for the gallantry displayed on the occasion. You might have seen some five or six hundred tall, brawny, well clad soldiers, the flower of the British Army, guarded by a set of militia clad in hunting shirts, 'blacked, smoked and greasy.' The plain was strewn with the dead and dying. The scattered fragments of the British Army were hurrying from the scene of carnage....The victory was complete."[20] The Battle of Cowpens was over.

CHAPTER TWENTY ONE

WASHINGTON

The battle may well have been over, but the pursuit of the fleeing British was not. Indeed, for Colonel William Washington, desperate now to track down and have another crack at Banastre Tarleton, the hunt had just begun. Within moments only, Washington, fresh off his violent encounter with the British commander, was back on the road again with a mind to running down the Redcoat leader and dispensing an American form of justice. Hopefully, the form of justice Washington had in mind was far different from that which the British had just administered to poor Lawrence Everhart.

It can be recalled from Chapter 16 that Everhart had been taken prisoner while in advance of the Flying Army where he was sabered by British dragoons, but later sent off to the surgeon where he was properly treated. There he remained until the British collapse, after which his captivity took a grim turn for the worse.

If there is a more dramatic example of the ruthless influence Banastre Tarleton had instilled in his troops, it is hard to imagine. It can be recalled from the previous chapter that the artillery officer Howard captured advised him readily that the British had been given orders to "give no quarter," and we can only presume that the British commander intended to slaughter en masse any Americans who surrendered. Here, while Morgan and Howard were doing their all to give quarter and prevent any unnecessary killing or abuse of the surrendered Redcoats, a truly murderous act took place.

Realizing that the British could no longer hold Everhart prisoner due to the Redcoat flight, an unknown British officer took out a pistol and attempted to execute the American prisoner on the spot, shooting him in the head. The incident was witnessed and later recounted by James Simmons, who in a letter to William Washington noted that "finding they could no longer keep Everhart a Prisoner, Shot him with a Pistol, in the head, over one of his eyes, (I cannot remember particularly which) being then intermixed with the enemy, Everhart pointed out to me the man who shot him, and on whom a just Retaliation was exercised, and who by my order, was instantly Shot, and his horse as well as I can recollect, was given to Everhart, whom I ordered to the Rear to the Surgeons."[1]

While Lawrence Everhart would almost miraculously survive the attempt on his life, he suffered for months from the effects of the head wound, and while remaining in the army, he would never again serve in active combat. "After the battle," Everhart reported, "Col Washington sent two dragoons with me about three miles from the ground to take care of me: Dr Pendell formerly of Hagers Town [sic: Hagerstown] Maryland surgeon of our corps dressed my wounds – remained here until the latter part of February & went thence to Catawba near where I remained a few days with a friend of mine of my name: thence to Salem in North Carolina accompanied by the two dragoons & from this place to Guilford Court House."[2]

James Collins, who once feared that his "hide was in the loft" fought hard and survived the sharp action at Cowpens, although he would never forget the battle. "They [the British] began to throw down their arms," he recalled in his autobiography, "and surrender themselves prisoners of war. The whole army, except Tarleton and his horsemen, fell into the hands of Morgan, together with all the baggage. After the fight was over, the sight was truly melancholy. The dead on the side of the British, exceeded the number killed at the battle of King's Mountain, being if I recollect aright, three hundred, or upwards. The loss, on the side of the Americans, was only fifteen or sixteen, and a few slightly wounded. This day, I fired my little rifle five times, whether with any effect or not, I do not know. The next day after receiving some small share of the plunder, and taking care to get as much powder as we could, we (the militia) were disbanded and returned to our old haunts, where we obtained a few day's rest."[3]

While young James Collins was reflecting on the awful nature of the battlefield as the British disappeared into the woods, Thomas Young, riding, it can be recalled, with Washington's horse, set off on a far different sort of adventure. The American lines from mere pursuit were now almost as broken and disjointed as were those of the British, but in victory, not defeat, and for many it seemed a capital moment to get after the retreating British and loot whatever the Redcoats had left behind worth plundering. After watching the Redcoats run off "Major Jolly and seven or eight of us," Young tells us, "resolved upon an excursion to capture some of the baggage. We went about twelve miles, and captured two British soldiers, two Negroes, and two horses laden with portmanteaus. One of the portmanteaus [a leather trunk or suitcase] belonged to a paymaster in the British service, and contained gold. Jolly insisted upon my returning with the prize to camp, while he pursued a little farther. I did so."

Young turned and headed back toward Morgan's camp, not knowing how far forward his compatriots had gone, and unmindful of any potential danger. He was soon in for a rude awakening. "I rode along for some miles at my leisure, on my fine gray charger, talking to my prisoners, when, all at once I saw coming in advance, a party, which I soon discovered to be British. I knew it was no time to consider now; so I wheeled, put spurs to my horse, and made down the road in hopes of meeting Jolly and his party. My horse was stiff, however, from the severe exercise I had given him that morning, and I soon found that they were gaining upon me. I wheeled abruptly to the right into a cross road, but a party of three or four dashed through the woods and intercepted me. It was now a plain case, and I could no longer hope to engage one at a time. My pistol was empty, so I drew my sword and made battle. I never fought so hard in my life. I knew it was death anyhow, and I resolved to sell my life as dearly as possible. In a few minutes one finger on my left hand was split open; then I received a cut on my sword arm by a parry which disabled it. In the next instant a cut from a sabre across my forehead, (the scar of which I shall carry to my grave,) the skin slipped down over my eyes, and the blood blinded me so that I could see nothing. Then came a thrust in the right shoulder blade, then a cut upon the left shoulder, and a last cut (which you can feel for yourself) on the back of my head – and I fell upon my horse's neck. They took me down, bound up my wounds, and placed me again on my horse as a prisoner of war."

But for Young things were just getting interesting. "When they joined the party in the main road," he later recalled, "there were two Tories who knew me very well – Littlefield and Kelly. Littlefield cocked his gun, and swore he would kill me. In a moment nearly twenty British soldiers drew their swords, and cursing him for a d—d coward, for wanting to kill a boy without arms and a prisoner – ran him off. Littlefield did not like me, and for good reason. While we were at Grindal Shoals with Morgan, he once caught me out, and tried to take my gun away from me. I knocked him down with it, and as he rose I clicked it, and told him if he didn't run I'd blow him through. He did not long hesitate which of the two to choose. I asked Kelly not to tell the British who I was, and I do not think the fellow did."

Now taken prisoner, and with the good fortune of having avoided death at the hands of the British dragoons, Thomas Young was about to meet the infamous Banastre Tarleton, for the British commander was trying to come to grips with the disaster he had just experienced. "Tarleton sent for me," Young recounted many years later, "and I rode by his side for several miles. He was a very fine looking man, with rather a proud bearing, but very gentlemanly in his manners. He asked me a great many questions, and I told him one lie, which I have often thought of since. In reply to his query whether Morgan was reinforced before the battle? I told him 'he was not, but that he expected a reinforcement every minute.' 'He asked me how many dragoons Washington had.' I replied that 'he had seventy, and two volunteer companies of mounted militia, but you know they won't fight' 'By G-d!' he quickly replied, 'they did today, though!' I begged him to parole me, but he said, 'If he did, I should go right off and turn to fighting again.' I then told him he could get three men in exchange for me, and he replied 'Very well, when we get to Cornwallis' army, you shall be paroled or exchanged; and mean while, I'll see that your wounds are taken care of.'"

Tarleton later recorded his thoughts and emotions at the time. After his altercation with Washington and the American dragoons "Another party of the Americans, who had seized upon the baggage of the British troops on the road from the late encampment, were dispersed, and this detachment retired towards Broad river unmolested." On the route Tarleton heard "with infinite grief and astonishment, that the main army had not advanced beyond Turkey creek: He therefore directed his course to the south east, in order to reach Hamilton's ford, near the mouth of Bullock creek, whence he might communicate with Earl Cornwallis."[4]

For the remainder of that long day Thomas Young was held captive as the British dragoons made their way back toward Broad River in hopes of finding Cornwallis and the main body of the British Army. "We got to Hamilton Ford, on Broad River, about dark," wrote Young. "Just before we came to the river, a British dragoon came up at full speed, and told Col. Tarleton that Washington was close behind in pursuit. It was now very dark and the river was said to be swimming. The British were not willing to take water. Col. Tarleton flew into a terrible passion, and drawing his sword, swore he would cut down the first man who hesitated. They knew him too well to hesitate longer."[5]

But the British dragoon who had reported that Washington's cavalry was hot on Tarleton's heels had been entirely in error. Whatever or whoever had been spotted remains unclear, but Washington had by then been deliberately misdirected, and as a result had lost Tarleton's trail. What actually happened, was that in the course of his retreat Tarleton discovered much to his "astonishment" that Cornwallis had not yet passed Turkey Creek, thus he had to redirect his course in that direction. On the road he came upon the farm of Adam Goudelock near Thicketty Creek, and having lost the Tory Alexander Chesney as his guide, Tarleton immediately impressed Goudelock into the service of delivering him to Hamilton Ford on Broad River. Shortly thereafter, when Washington and his dragoons thundered up to the front door of the same farmhouse in search of Tarleton's trail, Mrs. Goudelock, fearful for her husband's safety, sent the Americans off on a wild goose chase.

Washington and his cavalry then renewed the pursuit down the road to Grindal Shoals, all, of course, to no effect. By the time Washington realized his error, it was already too late, for darkness was closing, and he was forced to return to the Cowpens, herding almost a hundred British fugitives he had collected en-route, but Tarleton and his party had escaped his clutches.[6] Kirkwood and the valiant Delaware Line had also been ordered forward by Morgan to serve as an infantry reserve should Washington require reinforcement. Kirkwood marched a considerable distance, secured the British supply train that had been left abandoned, but saw no further action. Late that evening Washington and Kirkwood returned to the Cowpens, bringing an end to a long but wildly successful day for the Flying Army.

Thomas Young, meanwhile, still remained a British prisoner while Tarleton flew into a rage and demanded his weary men cross over Broad River, but the intrepid youngster had no intention of remaining captive for long. With the Americans falling back toward Cowpens, Young plotted his escape. "During the confusion," he later wrote, "a young Virginian by the name of Deshaser (also a prisoner) and myself, managed to get into the woods. In truth a British soldier had agreed to let us escape, and to desert if we would assist him in securing the plunder he had taken. We slipped away one at a time up the river, Deshaser first, then myself. I waited what I thought a very long time for the British soldier, and he came not. At last I began to think the British were across, and I gave a low whistle – Deshaser answered me, and we met. It was now very dark and raining when we came to the Pacolet. I could not find the ford, and it was well, for the river was swimming. We therefore made our way up the river, and had not gone far before we approached a barn. It had a light in it, and I heard a cough. We halted and reconnoitered, and finding it occupied by some British soldiers, we pressed on and soon arrived at Old Captain Grant's where I was glad to stop. The old man and his lovely daughter washed and dressed my wounds, and in looking over the bag of plunder which the soldier had given us, they found a fine ruffled shirt, which I put on and went to bed. I shall never forget that girl or the old man for their kindness!"

But Young's adventure remained far from complete, and would not be until he recovered from his wounds, and located a substitute for the fine gray stallion he had been forced to hand over to the British. "On the next day I left with Deshaser, and arrived at home that evening, where I was confined by a violent fever for eight or ten days; but thanks to the kind nursing and attention of old Mrs. Brandon, I recovered. I now slept in the woods for about three weeks, waiting for some of the Whigs to come in and commence operations. I was concerned about a horse. The British soldiers, when they took me, dismounted me form the fine charger I captured at the Cowpens and put me on a pacing pony. One day I met old Molly Willard riding a very fine sorrel horse, and told her we must swap. She wouldn't listen to it—but I replied that there was no used in talking, the horse I would have, and the exchange was made not much to the old woman's satisfaction, for she didn't love the Whigs; I don't believe the Willards have forgiven me for that horse swap to this day."[7]

Thomas Young would rise to the rank of major in the service of his country, and would fight till the end of the war. Wounded but alive, his time and service with Daniel Morgan's Flying Army had ended fortunately, leaving him with the respect of his peers, Molly Willard's fine sorrel, and many exciting tales with which he could thrill strangers, friends, and family alike for the remainder of his life.

CHAPTER TWENTY TWO

POST MORTEM

Both Kirkwood and Washington returned to the Cowpens on the evening of the 17th, only to find the Flying Army long gone. Morgan, no fool, realized only too well that Cornwallis was on the other side of Broad River still in excellent position to cut off any American retreat if he dallied, so dally he would not. He quickly packed up the Flying Army and had it in motion by noon, leaving behind as he did the melancholy scene of one of the most important and dramatic American victories of the Revolution. Morgan may not have had time to remain behind and celebrate his win, but an accounting was soon to be tabulated, thus an examination of the facts surrounding Tarleton's defeat certainly in order at this juncture of our story. So we will convene a drum-head inquiry of our own, a post mortem trial of sorts in which the evidence will be fairly presented in the hope that justice might speak for itself.

The American victory proved entirely lopsided. Two days after the engagement, Morgan wrote his official report and sent it off to Nathanael Greene. "The troops I have the honor to command," he penned, "have gained a complete victory over a detachment from the British Army commanded by Lieut.-Col. Tarleton." The final tally was breathtaking. Said Morgan, "The enemy were entirely routed, and the pursuit continued upwards of twenty miles. Our loss was inconsiderable, not having more than twelve killed and sixty wounded. The enemy's loss was 10 commissioned officers and over 100 rank and file killed and 200 wounded, 29 commissioned officers and about 500 privates prisoners which fell into our hands with two pieces of artillery, two standards, 800 muskets, one travelling forge, thirty-five baggage wagons, seventy negroes and upwards of 100 dragoon horses, with all their musick."[1]

Tarleton, recoiling from criticism, would later fudge those numbers considerably: "The number of the killed and wounded," he later asserted, "in the action at the Cowpens, amounted to near three hundred on both sides, officers and men inclusive: This loss was almost equally shared, but the American took two pieces of cannon, the colours of the 7th regiment, and near four hundred prisoners."[2] Thus began Tarleton's campaign of damage control through which he attempted to shift the blame for his own failures onto the shoulders of Lord Cornwallis and also what he later insisted to be the inexplicable failure of his own officers and men. He had, he claimed, made good decisions; others had failed *him*.

"A diffuse comment upon this affair would be equally useless and tiresome:" Tarleton opined in his "history" only then to go off for several pages offering just such a tiresome and useless self-absolution. "Two observations will be sufficient:" he suggested, "One will contain the general circumstances which affected the plan of the campaign, and the other the particular incidents of action." Tarleton then went on to review the general string of events that had brought both he and Morgan to blows at the Cowpens before finally lowering the boom on Cornwallis. Here he notes that he received a message from Cornwallis on the 14th of January indicating that Leslie had "surmounted his difficulties" [the high water] and that, based upon that information, Tarleton responded that he would move forward and force the action with Morgan, assuming that Cornwallis would march to his aid and assume a position on the Broad in "as high a station as possible, in order to stop their retreat." But Cornwallis failed to make that march or assume that position, and this failure, according to Tarleton's analysis, was the primary reason for his inglorious misfortune at Cowpens. "It would be mortifying to describe the advantages that might have resulted," he insisted, "from his lordship's arrival at the concerted point, or to expatiate upon the calamities which were produced by this event."

It was therefore, at least according to Tarleton's self-serving logic, Cornwallis' failure to properly support and coordinate his efforts that led directly to the disaster at Cowpens, and this was not, Tarleton pointed out, the first time that Cornwallis had failed in that regard. "Many instances of this nature occurred during the war," he insisted. "The fall of Ferguson was a recent and melancholy example: that catastrophe put a period to the first expedition into North Carolina; and the affair of the Cowpens overshadowed the commencement of the second."[3]

Omitted entirely from Tarleton's line of reasoning is the simple but obvious fact that he had raced into battle at

Cowpens entirely on his own, without even a cursory reconnaissance of the American position, and without taking the time to properly deploy his infantry. Indeed, had Cornwallis marched to the proper "concerted point" Tarleton refers to he would have in no way been able to prevent the disaster at Cowpens or to have marched to Tarleton's support in time to make the slightest difference. Indeed, blaming Cornwallis for Tarleton's laundry list of failures seems little more than a transparent attempt at shifting the blame; a sleight of hand and nothing more. For his readership in far off Britain long after the fight, this may have sounded reasonable, but for anyone familiar with the facts, Tarleton's rationale appears transparently deficient, indeed little more than an intentional deception.

Few who witnessed the battle at the Cowpens that January morning, for instance, would agree with any of Tarleton's deflections or accusations. The Tory guide, Alexander Chesney, for instance, minced no words when he later wrote that he was "near the Cow-pens on Thickety Creek where we suffered a total defeat by some dreadful bad management. ... I was with Tarleton in the charge who behaved bravely but imprudently the consequence was his force disperced in all directions the guns and many prisoners fell into the hands of the Americans."[4]

Chesney, you may recall, had been a prominent landowner in the area, but found himself in utter ruin after returning home from the action, no small part of which can be laid directly at Tarleton's feet. "I proceeded towards home to bring off my wife and child on the 17 Jan and found there was nothing left not even a blanket to keep off the inclement weather; or a change of garments; then leaving a pleasant situation in a lamentable state without a shilling in my pocket; proceeded for General Cunningham's, sleeping encamped that night; As we could not prevail on General Cunningham to use any exertions to embody his brigade of Militia we went to Edisto river in order to settle there having nothing but two horses and our clothes left, everything else being in the hands of the Americans and by them confiscated."[4]

Roderick MacKenzie, who it can be recalled, was marching with the 71st Highlanders at Cowpens, later offered a thoughtful and thorough deconstruction of Tarleton's arguments along with a very critical review of his commander's actions that fateful morning. In this he was not kind. "The first error in judgment," MacKenzie insisted, "is not halting his [Tarleton's] troops before he engaged the enemy. Had he done so, it was evident that the following advantages would have been the result of his conduct. General Morgan's force and situation might have been distinctly viewed, under cover of a very superior cavalry; the British infantry, fatigued with rapid marches, day and night, for some time past, as has been already observed, might have had rest and refreshment; a detachment from the several corps left with the baggage, together with batt-men, and officers servants, would have had time to come up, and join in the action. The artillery all this time might have been playing on the enemy's front, or either flank, without risque of insult; the commandants of regiments, Majors M'Arthur and Newmarsh, officers who held commissions long before our author [Tarleton] was born, and who had reputations to this day unimpeached, might have been consulted, and,...

time would have been given for the approach of Earl Cornwallis to the preconcerted point, for the unattainment of which he has been so much and so unjustly censured."[5]

Mackenzie then went on to enumerate what he believed to be four other critical failures on Tarleton's part, the first being: "the un-officer-like impetuosity of directing the line to advance before it was properly formed, and before the reserve had taken its ground; in consequence of which, as might have been expected, the attack was premature, confused, and irregular." He then noted that Tarleton failed to provide discretionary authority to his unit commanders to respond to the situation as they saw fit. Third, he should never have ordered the cavalry charge on the Continental left without having first reconnoitered Morgan's position and determined the strength of Washington's cavalry, and the final failure "was in not bringing up a column of cavalry, and completing the rout, which, by his own acknowledgement, had commenced through the whole American infantry."[6]

Unfortunately Mackenzie, like virtually all British analysis of the engagement at the time, either never understood or would never admit that the American infantry had not been routed, but was, in fact, at all times and at several locations, performing controlled withdrawals in accordance with Morgan's plans, the last of which, although initiated in error, was still perfectly executed under his guidance and command. The American withdrawals were not a rout in process, but a trap being sprung, and a trap that had worked almost flawlessly, ultimately luring Tarleton to his doom.

Having sullied Cornwallis' reputation as best he could, Tarleton then turned on the remainder of his infantry and officers in an attempt to throw the lot of them under the bus by suggesting that "The defeat of the British must be ascribed either to the bravery and good conduct of the Americans, to the loose manner of forming which had always been practiced by the King's troops in America; or to some unforeseen event, which may throw terror into the most disciplined soldiers, or counteract the best-concerted designs," and Tarleton, dismissing American fighting capabilities, naturally chose to blame the "misbehavior" of his own men.[7]

A number of days after his defeat at Cowpens Tarleton asked Cornwallis to call an inquiry into his handling of the battle (Tarleton must have been feeling an enormous amount of animosity from his fellow officers to traffic in such a potentially dangerous strategy), but Cornwallis, no doubt grasping the bigger picture and realizing he would need Tarleton for future operations, demurred, writing that "You have forfeited no part of my esteem as an officer by the unfortunate event of the action of the 17th: The means you used to bring the enemy to action were able and masterly, and must ever do you honor. Your disposition was unexceptionable; the total misbehavior of the troops could alone have deprived you of the glory which was so justly your due."[8]

Publicly Cornwallis had little choice: He needed Tarleton for future cavalry operations, and he had praised the young cavalryman in the past to such a flattering extent that a highly critical reevaluation would surely have called his own judgment into question in the eyes of his own superiors;

hardly a course of action senior military officers tend to cherish, in any century or on any continent. So Tarleton would get off essentially scot-free, but his reputation had taken an enormous hit, and we will allow Roderick Mackenzie the final, bitter, and emotional word on Tarleton's self-serving analysis. "I believe it will be found that it fell to Lieutenant Colonel Tarleton alone to lead the troops of Britain into a situation, from which they could be driven by an equal, or even by double or treble their number....I have now done with the action at Cowpens and on this occasion confess that I am not without my feelings as an individual for so wanton an attack on characters and entire corps, whose conduct had been, till then, unsullied. There is not an officer who survived that disastrous day who is not far beyond the reach of slander and detraction; and with respect to the dead, I leave to Lieutenant colonel Tarleton all the satisfaction which he can enjoy, from reflecting that he led a number of brave men to destruction, and then used every effort in his power to damn their fame and posterity."[9]

Any reasonable evaluation of the Battle of Cowpens would of necessity have to relieve, I believe, the other British officers and men of any negligence or misbehavior. They had for days covered in pursuit a considerable territory at a tremendous clip through frigid weather and wet conditions and deserve every respect for their extraordinary efforts. They had, for the past few days at least, not eaten well, slept little, and yet they performed and executed Tarleton's orders without question or delay after an early morning march of twelve exhausting miles across difficult terrain. No, the entire fault for the debacle at Cowpens lay with Banastre

Tarleton alone while, conversely, the credit for this remarkable American success belongs to Daniel Morgan and his officers who handled his creative deployment with coolness and skill. Tarleton was an excellent cavalryman, hard driving and relentless, but chasing down small bands of American militia or retreating Continentals proved a far different business than confronting a capable field commander on ground of his own choosing, not to mention one of the finest field commanders the United States military would ever produce. Tarleton had not simply met his match in Morgan, he had, in fact, stumbled headfirst into a situation *far* beyond his depth that frigid January morning, and his command paid a terrible price for his inexperience and arrogance.

The American response to the victory at Cowpens, on the other hand, was nothing less than euphoric. As historian John Buchanan notes, Morgan detailed Major Edward Giles along with his aide, the Baron de Glabuck to deliver his formal report to Nathanael Greene, then still in camp on the Pee Dee. We can justly presume that Greene was at the time overwrought with worry over Morgan's situation, and Giles' message not only relieved that worry, but sent Greene's entire camp into a state of instant jubilation. Bottles were uncorked, guns fired, backs slapped in utter glee. "On 23 January Morgan's aide, Major Edward Giles, rode his mud-splattered horse into Nathanael Greene's camp carrying the news of the great victory. The camp went wild. The rum was broken out. They had a *feu de joie* or musket fire; one man after another firing a round into the air in a continual toast."[10] Giles then continued riding north, spreading the joyful news as he went, town-to-town, state-to-state. And that was just the beginning.

Upon receiving the wondrous news, North Carolina General William Davidson declared Morgan the savior of the young nation. "You'l please to accept my warmest congratulations on your late glorious victory," he wrote. "You have in my opinion paved the way for the Salvation of this Country."[11] Otho Williams, then also at the Continental camp with Greene, grabbed his pen and wrote that "I rejoice exceedingly at your success. The advantages you have gained are important and do great Honor to your little Corps... Next to the happiness which a man feels at his own good fortune is that which attends his Friend. I am much better pleased that you have plucked the laurels from the brow of the hitherto fortunate Tarleton than if he had fallen by the hands of Lucifer."[12] Morgan would not publicly boast of his success, of course, but in a private letter to his friend William Snickers Morgan summed up the scope of his victory. "When you Left me you remember I was desirous to have a Stroke at Tarleton —my wishes are Gratified, & I have Given him a devil of a whipping, a more compleat victory never was obtained."[13] But perhaps it was a weary Robert Kirkwood who best described the American victory late that January 17 when, after returning from his duties in support of Washington's dragoons, he jotted down this simple journal entry: "Defeated Tarleton."[14] That said just about everything anyone really had to know, and there we will let the matter rest.

But one important fact would not rest. Regardless of fault, at Cowpens Cornwallis had lost a full quarter of his effective strength; the cream of his light infantry. It was a loss that could not be made good, and a blow that would negatively affect the remainder of his campaigning throughout the American South. That fact would very soon alter history, and bring Cornwallis to ruin.

CHAPTER TWENTY THREE

CORNWALLIS

While the battle at Cowpens was over, and the American victory soon to be hailed all across the land, Daniel Morgan realized at once that all of his success might be instantly squandered should the Flying Army fall prey to Cornwallis and the main body of the British Army that was then lurking, just the other side of Broad River. The British plan, after all, had been to crush Morgan between the pincer-like columns of Tarleton and Cornwallis, thus if Cornwallis were to succeed where Tarleton had failed, the Redcoats could still claim success – albeit at a significant cost – and Morgan's "victory" reduced to little more than an historical footnote.

In that sense the battle was over but the campaign was not, for soon Cornwallis was sure to have Morgan square in his sights. While Cornwallis did not pose an immediate threat to Morgan at Cowpens, the British command, situated on the other side of the Broad, with some hard marching, was certainly in a position to block Morgan should he delay in any move north to rejoin Nathanael Greene and the rest of the Southern Army. Morgan knew that the Flying Army had to survive for American hopes in the South to remain viable. And since Cornwallis' army significantly outmanned Morgan's, battle outright was unthinkable, thus a rapid movement north towards Greene the only true option left open. In this Daniel Morgan lost no time.

Morgan had the Flying Army in motion by noon on the 17th (just hours after the last shots had been fired at Cowpens), but before leaving there were, of course, the dead and wounded to be cared for. Robert Jackson, a British surgeon's assistant (whom Morgan treated, not as a captured foe, but almost as a heroic compatriot) had bravely remained behind with the wounded to provide whatever assistance he could manage, but conditions afterward were, to say the least, primitive. While the numbers are imprecise, it appears that there were less than 100 wounded Americans while the wounded British left behind numbered somewhere around 200.[1] The battle had taken place on what was then the fringe of the American frontier, and there were no hospitals nearby, few doctors, or any organized means of caring for so many wounded and disabled men. Several locals flocked to help, but by and large the situation was far beyond anyone's capacity to handle.

Those wounded Americans who might be quickly patched together enough to hobble along, headed off with Morgan while nearby homes and farmhouses – unfortunately the area surrounding the Cowpens was sparsely populated – were sought out where the wounded might be removed to rest, convalesce, or die in peace. To say the least, it was a grim and difficult business. To Morgan's credit, the British wounded were cared for just as professionally and compassionately as were the Americans, and every attempt was made to make them comfortable. The British prisoners – some 600 all told – were then separated into small, more manageable contingents, and started off ahead of the Flying Army under a guard of militia. Morgan realized that Cornwallis would march furiously to get these men back, and do virtually anything within his means to regain them.

Surgeon Jackson, desperate for medical support, felt comfortable enough in his relationship with Daniel Morgan to write directly to him on the 18th requesting permission to pursue assistance. "As the wounded must suffer much from want of necessaries," he explained, "and even medical assistance, with your permission I should wish to inform Lord Cornwallis of their situation, that if he thinks proper he may order something for their relief, some Surgeons of the General Hospital and Hospital appointments. From your very great politeness to me I am confident that you will grant everything that is reasonable or proper."[2]

One day after that, on 19 January, Tarleton wrote Morgan from Cornwallis' camp near Turkey Creek inquiring as to the condition of the British wounded, and if the tone of his correspondence provides a clue to his state of mind, it appears the arrogant Banastre Tarleton might have felt at least a little chastened as a result of his recent run in with Morgan. "Sir—The action of the 17th instant having thrown into your hands a number of British Officers and Soldiers I primarily request of you that Attention and Humanity may be exhibited towards the Wounded Officers and Men, for whose assistance I now send a Flag, Doctor Steward and the Surgeon's Mate of the Seventh Regt. I secondly desire you to inform me the Number and Inability of the Prisoners, which the Fortune of War has placed in your possession. I have the Honour to be Sir, your most obedient and most humble servant,... [3]

A few days later Doctor Pindell, the American surgeon on the scene, sent off a dispatch to Morgan as well, and his correspondence provides some insight as to the dire conditions under which the wounded were laboring. “Enclosed I send a Flagg which arrived yesterday from Colo. Tarleton. You will see his own requisitions, in addition to which Doct’r Jackson, in communication with the Gentlemen who came with the Flagg, (finding it impossible to have the wounded properly provided for in this country) are desirous of having the men paroled and to have permission to take them within the British lines. ... I am of opinion also that they cannot be provided for here, and think their proposals of equal advantage to us....If it is not agreeable to you to have the men paroled the surgeons will give a receipt for the men and be accountable for them. Some of them are still in the field and have no salt. You will please to dispatch an answer as soon as possible, that we may know in what manner to act, there is no Regular Supply established yet....I wish some mode could be established to remove our wounded to Salisbury. I am entirely out of Brandy and Lint and shall soon need a supply of medicines.”[4]

It can be recalled that, after the battle on the 17th Tarleton had splashed across Broad River during the cover of night, and he soon made his way back to Cornwallis’ camp early the next morning. Other British fugitives had already stumbled into camp with word of the Cowpens debacle, but it is reasonable to assume that Cornwallis would not necessarily have credited those reports (Tarleton destroyed?

Impossible!), and awaited, rather, the first-hand report form his favorite young officer.

Fortunately, some American prisoners were nearby to overhear and record what transpired when Tarleton did finally arrive and offer his version of the facts to his troubled commander. In what can be considered one of the more famous and intense scenes of the American Revolution, Cornwallis was said to have listened silently but intently, leaning stiffly on his sword, as Tarleton explained the loss of virtually his entire corps. As Tarleton continued, Cornwallis was seen to lean harder and harder upon his sword, slowly digesting the scope of the disaster, until his sword finally snapped in two from the pressure exerted. Cornwallis was not one to lose his composure, but he was hardly inhuman, and Tarleton's shocking rout at the Cowpens must surely have unnerved him. A quarter of his army's strength had simply evaporated, and now Morgan was making off with perhaps as many as six or even seven hundred of the cream of his infantry as prisoners of war. For the British general this news must have seemed not only stunning, but virtually inexplicable.

But Cornwallis was not one to brood over spilt milk. He would move at once to cut Morgan off, bring him to battle, and gain the release of his imprisoned infantrymen. Of that he was certain. Orders were promptly issued, and this new movement to find and ensnare Morgan initiated in earnest the following day. "The 19th, the army with the cavalry on their left flank," Tarleton tells us, "moved towards King's creek." Both Tarleton and Cornwallis presumed – incorrectly, as time would soon demonstrate – that Morgan had remained near the Cowpens in order to maintain the separation of commands that Greene had previously ordered, and which appeared to be the fundamental strategy of the Americans at the time. Thus Tarleton was ordered out to find the location of his nemesis. "The 20th, Lieutenant-colonel Tarleton was directed to pass Broad river with the dragoons and the yagers, to obtain intelligence of General Morgan, and to give protection to the fugitives who might yet have escaped the power of the victorious Americans."[5]

As Tarleton hurried off on his mission to locate Morgan, Cornwallis put the finishing touches on a report to Sir Henry Clinton in New York, a copy of which he also forwarded to Lord George Germain in London. This, surely, had to have been a truly distasteful piece of business. How to explain such a disaster as Cowpens? Tarleton, not just beaten, but routed, his corps not just defeated, but annihilated. Cornwallis did his best, issuing a somewhat polished and sanitized version of events. "The enemy [the Americans] were drawn up in an open wood," he explained, "and, having been lately joined by some militia, were more numerous; but the different quality of the corps under Lieutenant-colonel Tarleton's command, and his great superiority in cavalry, left him no room to doubt of the most brilliant of success."

The British general then went on to explain Tarleton's assault and ultimately what was presumed to be the rout of both the American militia and Continental lines. "The enemy's line soon gave way, and their militia quitted the field; but our troops having been thrown into some disorder by the pursuit, General Morgan's corps faced about, and gave them a heavy fire: This unexpected event occasioned the utmost confusion in the first line: The 1st battalion of the 71st, and the cavalry, were successively ordered up; but neither the exertions, entreaties, or example of Lieutenant-colonel Tarleton, could prevent the panic from becoming general." Cornwallis then went on to laud Tarleton and the heroic efforts of the artillerymen to man their guns to the bitter end, before assuring Clinton of his intent to carry on his planned campaign into North Carolina. "It is impossible to foresee all the consequences that this unexpected and extraordinary event may produce; but your excellency may be assured that nothing but the most absolute necessity shall induce me to give up the important object of the winter's campaign."[6]

Yet we must remember that Morgan suffered no illusions when it came to the strength of his corps, his own abilities, or the strategic situation he was facing, and by the evening of the 17th he had already reached the banks of Broad River where he encamped for the night at Island Ford. As historian Lawrence Babits points out, "The Broad River bivouac was tactically sound and necessary. Morgan's men needed rest and the river would interrupt a sudden British move. The halt gave the wounded a chance to recover before moving again. Some wounded could hardly go much further."[7] Very few other officers would have moved so rapidly after fighting and winning a major action, and while Morgan has over the years received plaudits as an inventive tactical fighter, his grasp of the overall situation and his willingness to drive his men when necessary are often overlooked. By January 1781 his instincts for command appeared to have been finely honed.

By morning of the 18th Washington's cavalry and many of the militia units that had taken part in the pursuit had caught back up with the Flying Army. Here Morgan made another simple but efficient decision. Rather than traveling en masse, he would ultimately divide his command, sending the prisoners off with Washington and the Virginia and North Carolina militias, while heading off with the regulars himself. This maneuver accomplished a number of important things. First, by sending the British prisoners on a more northerly route under the command of Pickens he insured greater speed for both parties than had they all been traveling on the same mud-filled road. Secondly, by taking a more southerly route, the Flying Army effectively screened Pickens' column from the main body of the British Army, thus protecting the prisoners from Cornwallis, who, Morgan knew, was soon to be out after them. And finally, by using the various militias as guards, who were soon to be mustered out of service anyway, he effectively protected the prisoners without needlessly occupying any of the Continental regulars with that bothersome duty.

On the morning of the 18th Morgan broke the Island Ford camp and had his corps back on the road, marching for Gilbert Town, which was hailed by nightfall; a hard march of almost twenty-five miles for weary and wounded men. The following morning Washington headed northeast with the prisoners, while Morgan set his course for the more southerly fords on the Catawba River. The plan was for Washington and Pickens to cross the Catawba further north and then rejoin Morgan and the Flying Army at Sherrald's Ford on the North Fork of the river after both columns had made the crossing. Morgan marched for Ramseur's Mill, some forty miles east of Gilbert Town, with Sherrald's Ford still another twenty miles distant from there. The next day

Morgan once again pushed his men forward, and while it would be a hard and demanding march over miserable roads, within days they had finally managed to ford the Catawba and there the Flying Army finally went into camp on the eastern bank. For an exhausted army, the rapid withdrawal from the Cowpens to the relative safety of the Catawba, proved a remarkable achievement.

And Cornwallis? The British commander had the best of intentions, but due to Tarleton's rout at Cowpens, he now had no idea where Morgan really was. "Two days after he started Cornwallis finally picked up Morgan's trail. Tarleton, ranging west of the Broad with the Legion horse and Jagers, had discovered that Morgan was nowhere near Cowpens, and Cornwallis, who camped on the 21st at Buffalo Creek, just north of Cherokee Ford, and a few miles south of the North Carolina line, learned that Morgan had set out for Gilbert Town."[8] It seems that on the 20th Tarleton had "recrossed the river in the evening, having received information that Morgan, soon after the action, had quitted the field of battle, to pass his corps and the prisoners at the high fords on Broad river, leaving the wounded under the protection of a flag of truce. This news induced Earl Cornwallis to cross Buffaloe creek and Little Broad river, in hopes of intercepting General Morgan."[9] In other words, after days of stumbling about almost blindly, Cornwallis finally set his sights on Ramseur's Mill, hoping to put the British Army in a position to cut Morgan off on his northward march. It was at Ramseur's Mill, we can therefore presume, that Cornwallis intended to bring Morgan to battle and dispatch the Flying Army for good, regaining the British prisoners in the process.

Once more General Cornwallis led his forces into North Carolina, and on the 25th they finally marched into Ramseur's Mill, located on the south fork of the Catawba. He was spoiling for a fight at the time, but there was no fight to be had, for Tarleton tells us that "the celerity made use of by the Americans, after their unexpected advantage at the Cowpens, enabled them to evade his lordship's army, and reach the Catawba."[10] Morgan was long gone, now safely encamped on the eastern bank of the Catawba's north fork, a good twenty miles from Ramseur's Mill.

One can easily imagine Cornwallis' frustration upon receiving this news, and it is not difficult to envision him standing on the muddy road at Ramseur's Mill, staring vacantly east in the direction Morgan and his entire corps had apparently vanished. After all, this was not supposed to have happened. Cornwallis was a first-rate soldier and he had had every intention of trapping Morgan on the road leading north, but now Morgan's corps was long gone while Cornwallis had not even come close to bagging him. It may well have been at that moment that the British general finally realized that Morgan was not Sumter or Lincoln or Gates or Buford, and that the American victory at Cowpens – seemingly so bizarre and inexplicable to the British mind – had been no fluke after all, but rather the handiwork of a highly skilled opponent. Morgan had destroyed Tarleton, and now he had both outwitted and out-marched Cornwallis, and if an extraordinary soldier of that caliber was to be caught – Cornwallis surely had to have reasoned – extraordinary means would be required to catch him.

Perhaps then Cornwallis recalled that day in early January, 1777 when he'd led his command down the road from Princeton, N.J. bound for the hamlet of Trenton. There in the afternoon he found Washington's army in line of battle not far from the Delaware River, and Cornwallis immediately went over to the attack. Washington had his back against the river that day, and after a hard afternoon of fighting, as darkness closed on the field of battle, Cornwallis knew he had the Americans trapped. At that moment the American cause appeared utterly doomed. Confident of victory, confident he would destroy Washington and end the rebellion the following morning, Cornwallis eschewed a night attack – always risky and dangerous to pull off – and waited instead for dawn. But when his infantry swept forward at first light the following day they found only empty fields and smoldering campfires. Washington was gone, slipped away by back roads to attack the British garrison at Princeton, only then to march off unmolested to winter quarters in the New Jersey mountains overlooking New York. Washington seemed then to have simply vanished, and after that remarkable bit of maneuvering the British began referring to him as "The Fox," a flattering sobriquet he had earned on more than one occasion. But even The Fox had never inflicted a defeat upon British arms as overwhelming as Morgan had done to Tarleton at Cowpens, so exactly what was Cornwallis to make of Daniel Morgan?

No doubt Cornwallis had heard all the reports and hearsay of Daniel Morgan's physical stature and ferocity at Quebec, his riflemen's lethal fire at Freeman's Farm, the speed and resilience of his corps outside of New York, but no doubt he had also heard many rumors and reports that in the end had proven untrue. After all, hadn't Horatio Gates arrived in the South as the Hero of Saratoga, only then to be run from the field at Camden? Yet if Cowpens had not been a fortunate accident for the Americans, but rather the deliberate work of a skilled battle captain, then in terms of its utterly lopsided outcome, Cowpens might actually be compared favorably to the incomparable Cannae, Hannibal's great victory over the Roman commander Varro.

There, near the small Apulian town of Cannae in 216 BC, Hannibal, reversing the standard battle tactics of the day, weakened his center, thus luring the Romans into a frontal assault which the great Carthaginian general promptly enveloped from his wings, consuming sixteen Roman legions as he did. It was one of the worst defeats in Roman history, and Hannibal's greatest victory.[11] From that day forward Cannae had become the Holy Grail, so to speak, of field commanders everywhere, Hannibal's brilliant double envelopment the very symbol of martial excellence, and the one victory every knowledgeable military commander strove to emulate. Yet disturbing reports – which the British naturally refused to credit – that Morgan might have lured Tarleton into a similar trap at Cowpens surely must have reached Cornwallis' ear. So just who was Cornwallis facing in Daniel Morgan, a backwoods brawler who had blindly stumbled into good fortune at Cowpens, or a crafty American with the battlefield instincts of the great Carthaginian general himself – an American Hannibal?

It was at this point, then – perhaps as he stared down the long road that led east from Ramseur's Mill toward the distant Catawba fords – that Lord Cornwallis made one of the most fateful and fatal decisions of the American Revolution, and in a letter to Lord Germain he later explained his thinking: "The unfortunate affair of the 17th of January," he confided, "was a very unexpected blow; for besides reputation, our loss did not fall short of six hundred men: However, being thoroughly sensible that defensive measures would be certain ruin to the affairs of Britain in the southern colonies, this event did not deter me from prosecuting the original plan." The British had headed off to locate and trap Morgan on the morning of the 18th of January, Cornwallis explained, and "great exertions were made by part of the army, to intercept General Morgan's corps on its retreat to the Catawba; but the celerity of their movements, and the swelling of numberless creeks in our way, rendered all our efforts fruitless."

Morgan was gone. What to do? Cornwallis decided he would ignore Henry Clinton's insistence that he hold South Carolina at all cost, and instead he would pursue Morgan into North Carolina, and to do this Cornwallis decided he had to strip his force down to the bare bones if he were ever to catch up with the quick-moving Americans. Once that had been accomplished, once he had thrown away or burned everything unnecessary, he would chase Morgan to the ends of the earth, if that's what it would take to recapture his prisoners and claim victory for British arms in the South. "I therefore assembled the army on the 25th at Ramsoure's mill," he continued in his letter to Germain "on the south fork of the Catawba; and as the loss of my light troops could only be remedied by the activity of the whole corps, I employed a halt of two days in collecting flour, and in destroying superfluous baggage, and all my wagons, except those loaded with hospital stores, salt, and ammunition, and four reserved empty in readiness for sick and wounded."[12]

It was at Ramseur's Mill, somewhere near the 25th of January, 1781, that Cornwallis' thinking seems to have slipped over that thin line that separates campaign from compulsion; military operation from martial obsession. He would chase Morgan to the gates of hell, if that's what it took, and there would be no looking back. It was a decision that would send his army on a desperate, obsessive, reckless, and exhausting march through North Carolina; to battle at Guilford Court House, and ultimately on to its fatal defeat on a spit of land on the Chesapeake Bay named Yorktown.

CHAPTER TWENTY FOUR

MORGAN

At his camp near Sherrald's Ford on the Catawba River, Daniel Morgan had every reason to rejoice, but that pleasure had been unfortunately denied him. For while he had applied "a devil of a whipping" to Tarleton's Legion, then out-marched and outwitted Cornwallis himself, the scope of his recent success could not mollify the pain and discomfort he was now experiencing. Morgan's body had betrayed him once more. His sciatica had returned and along with it weakness and almost unbearable pain. As his biographer Don Higginbotham notes, the condition Morgan called sciatica had flared ominously, "mild at first, but now considerably worse, probably because of his strenuous activity."[1] Long days on the march and nights sleeping on the ground in the cold of winter, not to mention the sheer stress of battle, had all conjoined to do to Daniel Morgan what the British had not been able to achieve.

But at least one factor had turned in his favor. The rains had fallen hard, the Catawba had risen noticeably as a result, and the river could not be forded by the trailing British – for the time being at least. So there would be time to rest and hopefully regain his stamina while reorganizing his corps. Upon arriving at the ford Morgan quickly dashed off a report to Nathanael Greene notifying him of his location, circumstance, and the fact that the British prisoners had come through the long march essentially intact and would be sent on to Salisbury come morning. This initial report, written on January 23, if not brimming with Morgan's usual self-confidence, was at least concise and straight to the point.

The following day, however, after what appears to have been a bad night in cold weather, Morgan wrote again, and this report had the ring of despondency. It seems the Old Wagoner's condition had taken a decided turn for the worse, and he had no illusions as to what it meant. He had difficulty moving, and he knew now from long experience that he had not the physical capacity to remain in field command. For a man of Daniel Morgan's fighting reputation and physical renown, it must have been an exceedingly discouraging admission. "I grow worse every hour," he confided to Greene." I cant ride out of a walk. I am exceedingly sorry to leave the field at such a time as this, but it must be the case. Pickens is an enterprising man and a very judicious one: perhaps he might answer the purpose. With regard to Gen. Sumter, I think I know the man so well that I shall take no notis of what he has done, but follow your advice in every particular."[2]

With no help on the immediate horizon, and no word from Nathanael Greene, Morgan had little choice but to plot his options. He suggested to Greene a potential move to the west toward the mountains, for he realized that Cornwallis was now at Ramseur's Mill, and feared he could not stop the

British with his limited corps if Cornwallis attempted to cross the Catawba at any number of the local fords. Then he received a letter from William Davidson, who was at the moment gathering militia at Charlotte with the intention of marching to Morgan's assistance. "The enclosed dispatches from head Quarters came to my hand to-day enclosed in a letter from General Greene. The Gen'l mentions to me the plan you suggested of making a diversion to the Westward, and seems to depend much on your judgment respecting that matter. In the meantime I am directed to make you acquainted with my numbers and situation and hold myself in readiness to execute any order you may think proper to give. As the troops are now collecting, returns cannot be made for some time. Seventeen British Soldiers taken on the retreat the 17th inst. were brought in here to-day. Your victory over Tarleton has gladdened every countenance in this part. We had a Feu de Joy to-day in consequence of it."[3]

A few days later Davidson, riding at the head of 800 militiamen, marched into Morgan's camp at Sherrald's Ford. They were a sight for sore eyes, and Davidson's arrival gave Daniel Morgan a burst of energy and hope. Now he believed he had enough men to offer a stern resistance at the fords should Cornwallis attempt to force the issue. "I am Trying to Collect the militia, to Make a stand at this place," he wrote. "Genl Davidson, with five hundred militia two hundred and fifty of which are without flints, I have ordered to Beaties Ford. We are filling all the Private fords to Make them impasseable. The one that I Lie at I intend to Leave Open. On Lord Cornwallis' approach, I thought it advisable to Order all the Prisoners and Stores from Salisbury towards the Moravian town [today's Winston Salem]. I am told they are gone under a Weak guard; I wish some of them don't get away."[4] Here now Morgan at least had a plan and the men to execute it. If his scouts kept him well-informed of Cornwallis' movements, he felt comfortable that the fords could be defended, and the British, if not stopped, at least delayed before crossing the river.

Meanwhile at Ramseur's Mill, Cornwallis had ordered virtually every extraneous piece of equipment and personal baggage destroyed to lighten the load and speed his march. Tarleton, a witness to all of this, tells us that "The King's troops, after their ineffectual pursuit [of Morgan] pointed their course towards the Catawba: The train of wagons that now attended them met with great obstacles on the march, which considerably impeded the progress of the army. On the 25th, a halt was made at Ramsoure's mills, for the purpose of destroying all the baggage and carriages, except such as were absolutely necessary. Earl Cornwallis reduced the size and quantity of his own baggage, and this laudable example was followed by the generals and other officers under his command."[5] All went up in a great fireball of smoke and flames – china, books, extra clothing, tents, wines, etc., etc., and for the weary infantrymen, even their barrels of rum. Cornwallis intended to beat the Americans at their own game and had decided that drastic measures were called for to do so.

Light Horse Harry Lee, soon to receive orders to rejoin the main body of Continental troops farther north himself, accurately characterized Cornwallis' motives at the moment: "This arrangement being finished, Lord Cornwallis moved from Fisher's Creek, determined on unceasing efforts to destroy Morgan, and recover his captured troops; to keep separate the two divisions of Greene's army; and, should he fail in these attempts, to bring Greene to action before he could reach Virginia."[6] Charles O'Hara, an officer under Cornwallis describes the extraordinary scene as the British column marched off from Ramseur's Mill on January 28, stripped of their wagons and minus virtually all extraneous supplies. "In this situation, without Baggage, necessaries, or Provisions of any sort for Officer or Soldier, in the most barren inhospitable unhealthy part of North America, opposed to the most savage, inveterate perfidious cruel Enemy, with zeal and with Bayonets only, it was resolved to follow Green's Army to the end of the World."[7] To the end of the world! – surely O'Hara grasped at the moment the sheer obsession to which Cornwallis had fallen prey, for the British Army, although highly motivated and professional to the core, was hardly trained or prepared to weather such an expedition in the wilds of the American frontier while deliberately abandoning its line of supply. What would become of it will soon be told.

At any rate, scouts were thrown out ahead of the main body to locate the Americans, for Tarleton tells us that "Patroles were dispatched to reconnoiter the neighboring fords: parties of continentals and militia were discovered on the opposite banks:"[8] As the British approached, Morgan, watching from the opposite river bank at Beattie's Ford, and spotting the approaching Redcoats, dashed off this dispatch to Nathanael Greene. "I have just arrived at this place to view the situation. Gen Davidson is here with Eight hundred men. The enemy is within ten miles of this place in force, their advance is in sight."[9] It was then that Morgan received information that Cornwallis had burned his wagons and stripped his army to the bone, and Morgan grasped instantly what it meant – Cornwallis was coming after him as hard and as fast as he could possibly manage. What Morgan did not know, however, was that Nathanael Greene had made the decision to consolidate his army, and that he had left the Pedee on the 28th accompanied by only a small detachment of dragoons to make the trip from his camp to join Morgan. "Foreseeing the enemy's object," Light Horse Harry explains, "he [Greene] hastened his march in conformity with his previous disposition, and dispatched a courier to Marion and Lee, apprising them of his decampment, and ordering the latter to rejoin with all celerity. Escorted by a few dragoons, General Greene hastened to reach Morgan, which he happily accomplished on the last day of January."[10]

Mud-splattered and exhausted, Greene and his small contingent galloped into Morgan's camp, and the general had a quick look about. Greene apparently liked what he saw, for he soon dashed off a note to General Huger whom he had left in charge of the main body of Continentals with orders to march to Salisbury as soon as time would permit. "It is necessary we should take every possible precaution. But I am not without hopes of ruining Lord Cornwallis, if he persist in his mad scheme of pushing through the Country and it is my earnest desire to form a junction as soon as possible for this purpose. Desire Lt. Col Lee to force a march to join us. Here is a fine field and great glory ahead."[11]

Sadly, just as Davidson's militia arrived, the Virginia militias turned and marched off for home, their enlistments having expired. The lack of commitment on the part of the people often infuriated Daniel Morgan, and as to this most recent example, he dashed off a bitter letter to Thomas Jefferson, then governor of Virginia. "The British army are on the [far] ....side of the River and I with my Little Detachment on the other. I think they will attempt to cross this morning. Never the less, we have filled up all the fords and thrown every obstruction imaginable in their way, they are in force and I have about two hundred and thirty Regular infantry, and about sixty horse. General Davidson near five hundred Malitia. The inhabitentes seem to make a stir, what they will do is unceartain, but I fear not much. Genl. Green arrived yesterday, he has ordered his little army to join us, they are not more than seventeen or eighteen hundred. This number and my detachment when join'd will be much inferior to the enemy, who must be Near three thousand, well supplyd and provided for, and our men almost Naked."

Angry, sore, and weary, Morgan then unburdened himself to Jefferson. "Great God," he exclaimed, "what is the reason we cant Have more men in the field—so many men in the country Nearby idle for want of employment. How distressing it must be to an anxious mind to see the country over Run and destroyed for want of assistance which I am realy afraid will be the case if proper exertion are not made... I have been so harassed and exposed this winter that I am entirely emaciated. An old pain in my breast and Hip aceazed me so that shant be much use in the field this winter—if ver I am, but as I have been broke down in the services of my country shall bear the infirmitys of old age with more satisfaction."[12]

Upon Greene's arrival a rare scene took place. While usually making military decisions entirely on his own, Greene decided for once to consider other views. And why not, Morgan had just routed the British at Cowpens, and Washington had been there to help. Thus a council of war was called in which Greene, Morgan, Davidson, and William Washington took part. Some distance from Morgan's tent, on a fallen log by the river, all four sat to discuss strategy, while directly across the swollen stream British officers were spotted, actively surveying the American positions. Options, it was admitted, were few. At the moment the Catawba was running high, fueled by recent rains, but the rains had stopped and everyone knew that as soon as the river began to fall the British would attempt a fording. The numbers weren't encouraging. The Redcoats numbered perhaps 2,500 regular troops, while the Americans could field barely 1,000; 800 of whom were Davidson's militia. Moreover, there were many fords along the river where the British might choose to cross and Greene and Morgan both realized that they had not the manpower to guard them all.

A prudent decision was quickly agreed to. The Americans had no real hope of stopping the Redcoats from fording the river, only slowing them, thus the crossing would be disputed by Davidson's militia while all American units would fall back upon Salisbury where the army would be reunited. As Light Horse Harry tells us, Nathanael Greene decided that "his light troops, joined by some of the neighboring militia, were disposed... to dispute the passage of the river. This was attempted with the hope of retarding the British general in his advance so long as to allow time for Brigadier Huger, of

South Carolina,... to reach Salisbury, the first point assigned for the junction of the two divisions of the American army."[13]

This course of action was agreed upon none too soon. The very next day, February 1, morning dawned cold and foggy along the length of the Catawba. Cornwallis had decided overnight that the river had fallen enough for his troops to effectively force a crossing, and his plan to do so had been put into motion long before first light. Lt. Colonel Webster was detailed to lead a diversionary attack at Beattie's Ford, where Morgan was encamped, holding the American defenders in place at that point, while General Charles O'Hara would direct the main assault across a smaller, private ford named Cowan's, some four to five miles downriver from Beattie's. Once the British were across, Tarleton was to dash ahead with his dragoons and attack the retreating column of Americans, securing the main road north to Salisbury as he did. It was a sound plan.

Cornwallis hoped that Cowan's would be undefended, but his hopes went unfulfilled. It was defended, but only lightly. Davidson himself was there with about 250 militia infantry and a meager contingent of cavalry. The main British assault, approximately 1,200 regulars, moved out at about 1:00 A.M toward Cowan's Ford. "At the time appointed," Tarleton recalled, "Earl Cornwallis commanded the guides to conduct him, with the principal part of the army and two three pounders, to M'Cowan's, six miles to the southward of the public ford. Owing to the intricacy of the roads, and the darkness of the morning, one of the three pounders was overset, and for some time caused a separation of the 23rd regiment, the cavalry, and the artillery men, from the main body." As the British scouts reached the bank of the river opposite Cowan's Ford, it became evident that the Americans were there in a defensive posture – smoldering campfires could be seen flickering on the opposite bank.

The British decided to attempt the crossing with extreme stealth, in the hopes of catching the American napping. "Brigadier-general O'Hara formed the guards into column," Tarleton explains, "and directed them to move forwards, and approach the Americans without firing. As soon as the light company entered the water, supported by the grenadiers and the two battalions, the enemy commenced a galling and constant fire, which was steadily received by the guards, without being returned. The column advanced without the smallest halt, though the soldiers were frequently above their middle in water, and a rapid stream, upwards of five hundred yards wide, was passed in the face of an enemy with great gallantry and resolution."

The ford, in mid-stream, split into two distinct passages, a wagon crossing that ran more or less straight across, and another shallower crossing that ran off a good quarter mile to the south. Davidson, sensibly believing the British would use the shallower of the two fords, had deployed his 250 militia at that point. Davidson's men were sleeping lightly at the shallow ford when the British silently entered the river. But rather than shifting south toward the lower ford as anticipated, when the Tory guide noticed the fires on the opposite bank, he subsequently led the British into the deep water of the wagon crossing, where they headed straight across. The British were soon heard splashing and struggling in the water, but they were well north of Davidson's militia at that moment, and had virtually flanked the American position, purely as a product of luck.

The Americans awoke to the sound of the struggling Redcoats in the water and began firing at shadows and phantoms and ghosts in the night while the British continued struggling through the current. Before long the redcoats finally emerged on the opposite bank then climbed a small bluff that overlooked the ford. Men screamed, muskets flashed in the darkness, and the militia made a short but valiant stand before realizing that the British were in position above them, and would soon be capable of cutting off their retreat. British bayonets quickly convinced the militia that it was time to leave, and leave they did with all dispatch.

In all the confusion Davidson – an accomplished and respected officer – was shot from his horse and killed. "The attack," Tarleton observed, "of the light and grenadier companies, as soon as they reached the land, dispersed the Americans, who left their leader, General Davidson, dead upon the spot, and about forty men killed and wounded. Lieutenant-colonel Hall [who led the British advance], of the light infantry, fell as he quitted the stream. The guards had very few men killed, and only thirty-six wounded, on this trying occasion."[14] While Tarleton's casualty report may be true in a sense, John Buchanan points out that numerous British soldiers were found drowned in the river the following day, having succumbed to the Catawba as they crossed that night, and that the British dead could not have been less than 100, most swept away by the powerful current and drowned as a result.[15]

But the Redcoats were across the Catawba and now the Americans were running as fast as their legs could carry them. This was what Cornwallis had dreamed of. Now speed was of the essence to run the Americans down and crush them in detail on the road to Salisbury. "Lord Cornwallis followed the guards; and, as soon as his division had passed, detached Lieutenant-Colonel Tarleton with the cavalry, supported by the twenty-third regiment, in pursuit of the militia."[16] Fortunately for the American cause, both Morgan and Greene were already on the road toward Salisbury with the rest of the army, but each realized that Cornwallis would spare no effort to chase them down. Twelve miles behind Cowan's Ford sat Tarrants's Tavern, the location designated for the various militia units to rendezvous after delaying the British. The road to Salisbury was then choked with Morgan's Corps, scattered militia units, and hundreds of panicked civilian refugees seeking safety from the storm. Many had congregated at Tarrant's.

Into this chaotic mix rode Banastre Tarleton and his dragoons, on the hunt for American militia and surely anxious to even the score for what had happened at Cowpens. Heavy rain began to fall. Tarleton had been "instructed to make a partole into the country, to gain intelligence of the enemy," and he was pushing forward with his usual vigor. At the time it was not clear to the British what, if any, Americans still remained in their defensive positions at the other fords along the Catawba, but, "The advanced dragoons soon brought some prisoners to Tarleton, who informed him, that the different guards upon the fords had quitted the river, and were making a precipitate retreat." This intelligence must have been music to Tarleton's ears. Fighting an opponent like Morgan on even terms was one thing, while chasing down dispirited and retreating militia quite another. Tarleton – due to the heavy rains and bad roads – left his infantry behind then turned and galloped up the road toward Salisbury in hot pursuit with his cavalry.

Banastre Tarleton had not traveled too far when he "gained intelligence, that the fugitives from the fords, and other parties of militia from the counties of Rohan and Mecklenburgh, were to assemble at two o'clock in the afternoon at Tarrant's tavern." In his *history* Tarleton writes that he agonized over the decision to push on and attack the militias – the distance was considerable and, at least according to Tarleton, the number of militia reported to be consolidating at Tarrant's far greater than his own force – but, he decided, nevertheless, to press on. The heavy rain favored cavalry over infantry (the saber over the musket, cold steel over wet powder) and if radically outnumbered he reasoned he might always beat a quick retreat.

Colonel Tarleton then goes on in his *history* to provide a rather stirring and obviously embellished version of this clash at Tarrant's Tavern. Others, it should be pointed out, passing by shortly thereafter noted little in the way of human carnage.[17] Indeed, Light Horse Harry's characterization of the action and subsequent casualties reflects little more than a minor altercation on the road to Salisbury. "Tarleton, approaching this place [the tavern], discovered a body of troops in his front, and fell upon them with vigor. The militia made little or no resistance and fled. A few of them were killed, but none taken."[18]

Tarleton, on the other hand, describes a brave, spirited, magnificent charge. The dragoons approached the tavern, formed for attack, when Tarleton, turning in his saddle cried out "Remember the Cowpens!" This bracing encouragement, Tarleton insists, was all the dragoons really needed, and promptly dashed forward like madmen. The cavalry, "animated by this reproach, a furious onset ensued: They broke through the center with irresistible velocity," he tells us, "killed near fifty on the spot, wounded many in pursuit, and dispersed above five hundred of the enemy. Small parties of dragoons were detached in every direction, to continue their confusion, and prevent their assembling. The remainder of the cavalry halted at Tarrant's."[19] This recollection appears questionable at best, and it seems far more likely that many years after the fact Tarleton simply claimed with his pen the satisfaction his sword had failed to deliver.

At any rate, the British breakthrough at Cowan's Ford had surely created a sudden and dramatic problem for the Americans. Cornwallis was now hot on Morgan's trail, and a rapid retreat northward the only true option. Harry Lee tells us that Greene immediately grasped the implications of the crossing and "dispatched orders to Brigadier Huger to relinquish the route to Salisbury, and to take the direct course to Guilford Court House, to which point he pressed forward with the light corps under Morgan. Passing through Salisbury, he proceeded to trading ford on the Yadkin [River] where he arrived on the night of the second of February."[20] The Americans were now sprinting to cross over the Yadkin River and unite the two wings of their army at Guilford Court House while the British nipped at their heels. Greene had to get away and put a river or two between his force and the approaching Redcoats in order to avoid disaster. What would be called the "Race to the Dan"— that river just across the North Carolina state line in Virginia that was Nathanael Greene's ultimate goal – had begun.

The rains continued to fall, flooding the roads and turning them into little more than muddy pools. Through these cold, miserable, inhospitable conditions both armies pressed on; the Americans racing ahead, the British trying desperately to catch-up. Morgan was in terrific pain the entire way, but carried on nevertheless, through the sheer force of willpower alone. Greene left for Salisbury in order to take care of supplies left stored there, while the Old Wagoner marched his corps straight for the Yadkin River. Morgan and Greene finally rendezvoused at Trading Ford where the Yadkin was tumbling high and almost out of its banks due to incessant rains. Fortunately, Greene had had the foresight to have his officers gather all the boats in the area long before, and it can be recalled that he also had previously ordered the construction of flat boats for just such an occasion. It was a logistical conception and implementation of the highest order. But at the moment the river looked forbidding and impassable, boats or no boats, and Nathanael Greene naturally hesitated – he might well lose his army, or much of it, in the river if he attempted a fording with the water so high. But with Charles O'Hara leading the British van coming up rapidly behind, Greene soon realized he had little choice, and changed his mind. The Yadkin had to be crossed, and crossed quickly, to boot.

"General Greene passed the Yadkin during the night of, and the following day, his arrival at the river," Light Horse Harry tells us. "The horse forded the stream, the infantry and most of the baggage were transported in flats. A few wagons fell into the hands of the enemy; for notwithstanding the unfavorable condition of the roads and weather, O'Hara pressed forward with the British van, and overtook our rear guard. The retreating corps was again placed in a critical situation, and heaven was again propitious. The rain continued during the night; the Yadkin became unfordable; and Greene had secured all the flats on its northern bank."[21]

Tarleton, riding with the British van, recalled the scene as the Redcoat advance approached Trading Ford in the dead of night, hoping to make short work of whatever Americans they managed to catch on the southern bank. "Owing to the rain, darkness, and bad roads, the troops did not arrive at the Yadkin till near midnight. After a skirmish it was discovered that Morgan's corps had crossed in the evening, leaving a detachment of riflemen to protect some wagons and stores belonging to country people, who were flying with their effects to avoid the British army. General O'Hara, having made a fruitless effort to get possession of the flats and large boats upon the river, took post with the infantry on the ground which commanded the ford and the ferry, and sent back the cavalry to Salisbury."[22] O'Hara could do nothing but wait and watch as the river rose higher and higher; there were no boats to shuttle his troops across, for all were now beached high upon the opposite bank. Weather or Providence or good fortune (or perhaps all three in combination) had again thwarted the British pursuit, while smiling warmly upon the American withdrawal.

The next morning Morgan's Corps marched off, bound for Guilford Court House, some forty-plus miles distant. The rains continued to fall, and Morgan's condition worsened. The march was nevertheless completed in two days, and Morgan's Corps went promptly into bivouac as the Old Wagoner sent out foraging parties far and wide to try and scare up some food for his famished and exhausted men. They were drenched, in some cases shoeless, and nearly naked from their efforts, but the long march from the Cowpens to Guilford Court House had been accomplished with rare skill and determination. Within days Huger's column also marched into the Court House, thus reuniting Greene's army again. Accompanying Huger was Light Horse Harry Lee, recently detached from his mission with Francis Marion, riding at the head of his Legion consisting of "two hundred and eighty in horse and foot."[23]

Light Horse Harry Lee (Lt. Colonel Henry Lee, Jr.), whose "Memoirs" we have quoted on numerous occasions, was then a twenty-five year old cavalry officer of high reputation. One of his sons, Robert E. Lee, would eventually edit those "Memoirs" after becoming far more famous as the great captain of the Southern Confederacy some eighty years later, but by 1781 Henry had already achieved a considerable degree of fame on his own. The Lees were an old line Virginia family. We are told by Robert that "Richard Lee, a younger son of the house of Litchfield, emigrated to America [from England] in the year 1600." Light Horse Harry was thus born in comparative luxury into a planter family of wealth and substance. "Henry Lee, the subject of this memoir, was born on the 29th of January, 1756, at Leesylvania, which is situated on a point of land jutting into the Potomac, three miles above Dumfries, then the county town of Prince William." Henry proved a bright and energetic student, graduated from Princeton, and was preparing to study law when the clashes at Lexington and Concord hurled the colonies into war with Great Britain. Bypassing a career in law, Henry entered the army as a captain in the cavalry at the age of only nineteen, and soon won George Washington's admiration and trust as a bright and gifted leader of cavalry in the Northern Department. After the fall of Charleston in 1780, Washington sent Lee's Legion south in order to bolster the American presence in the Southern colonies, and while cooperating with Francis Marion, Light Horse Harry had done little to tarnish either his dashing image or reputation for competence in the saddle.[24]

Leading his Legion into Guilford Court House in early February, then, Light Horse Harry commanded one of the truly well-trained and elite forces in the Continental service, and his arrival was much valued by Morgan and Greene alike. United at last, the Americans now numbered around 2,000 while Cornwallis, despite his losses at Cowan's Ford maintained a regular force of about 2,400. The great difference between the two, of course, was in the quality of the troops along with their provisioning. The Americans were hungry and ill-supplied, while the British, despite being stripped to the bone by Cornwallis, still marched with reasonable supplies of food and ammunition.

But regardless of the relative strengths of the competing armies, Daniel Morgan, as a field officer, was finished. Enfeebled, in almost unbearable pain, he could go on no longer, and at Guilford Court House, having seen to the uniting of the army, Morgan officially asked Nathanael Greene to be relieved of his command. Greene, Otho Holland Williams, and Harry Lee all tried desperately to dissuade Morgan from leaving, but his condition was such that he could stay on no more. Greene offered the Old Wagoner command of a light force intended to cover the army's rear as it marched northward (something Morgan surely would have relished a year or two earlier), but Morgan turned him down, and recommended instead Otho Williams for the position. Reluctantly then, Greene issued this order on February 10 relieving Dan Morgan of command: "General Morgan, of the Virginia line, has leave of absence until he recovers his health so as to take the field again."[25]

Morgan's heart, no doubt, was broken; no one wanted to see the war through to its conclusion more than he, but his body was now just as broken as his heart. He then took part in a last council of war, urging Greene not to attempt battle with Cornwallis, but rather continue his retreat across the Dan River into Virginia, where he might locate more recruits willing to join the cause while re-provisioning the army. The council unanimously agreed, and the following morning, February 10, Greene headed north with the army while Morgan, dragging himself into a carriage, started for home. More than once he was forced to stop due to pain and exhaustion, on one occasion sending Greene a letter explaining his tactical thoughts should the American commander ever decide to take Cornwallis on in pitched a battle.

Few if any would grasp it at the time, but Daniel Morgan had in four short months altered the course of the American

Revolution. By thrashing Tarleton at Cowpens, he had greatly reduced British strength in the South, given American morale an enormous boost, while putting Cornwallis on an obsessive course that would ultimately lead to doom and surrender. Morgan's track record in the Carolinas was one of remarkable success, and success for which the Old Wagoner would rarely receive his fair due.

Still weary and in pain, Morgan finally arrived home in late February 1781, promptly hugged his wife, and fell away into bed for a convalescence that was hard-earned and well-deserved. Morgan's Flying Army had by then been reabsorbed into Greene's Southern command, and the Old Wagoner would never lead troops into battle again, but there is little question that their short alliance had left a profound and positive mark on the course of American history.

EPILOGUE

With Morgan's departure, the race to the Dan moved into its most intense and therefore most critical phase. Cornwallis, thinking well ahead and leaning on Tory informants, sent Tarleton on a mission north and west to try and locate more accessible fords across the Yadkin River. His thinking was simple: The British commander felt that Greene would eventually have to move both north and west to cross the Dan River at the higher, shallower fords, thus if Cornwallis could get to that area before the Americans, he would as a consequence already be in position to cut Greene off as he marched toward the Dan. This sort of thinking – punch and counter punch, move and counter move – would continue unabated for the better part of a week. Tarleton recounts that "Earl Cornwallis finding that he could not attempt the Trading ford, on account of the advantageous position of the enemy and depth of the river, detached the cavalry, supported by the 23rd regiment, on the afternoon of the 6th, to reconnoiter Grant's creek, and the country beyond it." Tarleton then undertook a long, sweeping reconnaissance throughout the region, located the necessary fords, and found the territory agreeable. "Lieutenant-colonel Tarleton made a long patrole with the cavalry, and finding no obstacles to impede the course of the main army to the upper fords, and no probability of opposition in crossing the Yadkin above the forks, he returned towards his infantry, and sent a written report of his discoveries to Salisbury."[1]

Cornwallis responded immediately. With O'Hara once again leading the way, the British swept north and west and arrived at the Moravian town of Salem (modern Winston-Salem) on the 9th of February.[2] According to Banastre Tarleton, the king's troops were well-received in this area, and as a consequence able to resupply their small train of wagons with "abundant and seasonable supplies."[3] But there would be no time for rest. Cornwallis allowed his men to eat but not to dally, and the Redcoats were promptly back on the road, hard marching for the upper fords of the Dan River (which becomes the Roanoke River further south).

Meanwhile, back at Guilford Court House, Nathanael Greene renewed his movement north while carefully cobbling together an elite unit of light infantry and cavalry to cover the army's rear as it moved. For this important duty he selected his finest officers and men. The light force consisted of, among others, William Washington's cavalry, John Eager Howard's Continentals, and Light Horse Harry Lee's Legion. The entire corps numbered about seven hundred, and would have to contend with the van of Cornwallis' army. The goal was to harass and confound Cornwallis, at once slowing his advance while at the same time beclouding the actual direction in which the main American columns were moving. Otho Holland Williams was in command, and Williams realized that the slightest miscalculation on his part might spell disaster for the American cause. He had to stay close to the fire, so to speak, yet without getting burned.

On February 10, Williams set off on a northwest course, separating from Greene and the main body as it marched due north, hoping to deceive Cornwallis into thinking he was in fact the van of the retreating American Army. His ploy worked. "The greater the distance between the main body and the light troops, the surer would be Greene's retreat," noted Light Horse Harry. "This movement was judicious, and had an immediate effect. His lordship, finding a corps of horse and foot close in front, whose strength and object were not immediately ascertainable, checked the rapidity of his march to give time for his long extended line to condense."[4] Cornwallis had been told by Tory agents that the lower fords on the Dan River were impassable during the winter, and he was thus confident that his strategy was working to perfection. "I concluded he [Greene] would do every thing in his power to avoid an action on the south side of the Dan;" wrote Cornwallis, "and it being my interest to force him to fight, I made great expedition, and got between him and the upper fords; and being assured that the lower fords are seldom practicable in winter, and that he could not collect many flats at any of the ferries, I was in great hopes that he would not escape me without receiving a blow."[5]

Once again Cornwallis had been outwitted. O'Hara took the bait and began chasing the American light force, while at the same time not getting too far ahead of Cornwallis and the main body of British troops. It proved a dangerous game of cat-and-mouse, the British maneuvering in the attempt to get around Williams and find Greene, Williams always trying to keep his light force between the two. In the long run it was a game played almost perfectly by Williams as he continually maneuvered to keep the British to his southwest while Greene marched off to the northeast. As Light Horse Harry later put it, "This was exactly the proper position for the light corps, and Williams judiciously retained it." But this required an enormous effort of both man and beast. Skirmishing and maneuver between the two opposing forces was almost constant, and soon took a physical toll on the troops. "The duty, severe in the day, became more so at night; for numerous patrols and strong pickets were necessarily furnished by the light troops, not only for their own safety, but to prevent the enemy from placing himself, by a circuitous march, between Williams and Greene."[6]

As this was playing out, at Boyd's and Dix's Ferries on the Dan, Greene had left his quartermaster, the masterful Edward Carrington, with instructions to make all necessary arrangements for the army's immediate passage. Carrington proved fully up to the task, having arranged for flat boats to be present in numbers sufficient to ferry the infantry across, and early on February 14 the army began crossing. Williams and his light corps were still some twenty miles away from the ferries when the infantry began to cross over, however, and in danger of being gobbled-up by the advancing British, when Williams got word from Greene that the army was crossing and to begin maneuvering back toward the fords. It was a message that was received with great relief. Then, at long last, in the late afternoon another mud-splattered courier galloped up to Williams with this note from Greene: "I am ready to receive you and give you a hearty welcome."[7]

With that Williams assigned Lee's cavalry to screen the rear of the light force as it withdrew, while his infantry began a hurried and harried march to the fords. Greene was waiting for them on the river bank along with Edward Carrington as they arrived, both officers supervising every detail to the last. The infantry piled into the boats and promptly made the crossing, and Lee's cavalry soon galloped up to the ford just as the boats were returning. Lee's troops crossed in the boats as the cavalry horses swam the river. It had been a marvelous plan masterfully executed, and once on the northern bank of the river the American Army was finally out of harm's wary. The race to the Dan was over, won breathlessly and skillfully by the Americans.

But that victory, Greene knew, was also hollow. Crossing the Dan might have saved the Southern Army from immediate harm, but it would do little to drive Cornwallis from North Carolina, raise more militia for the American cause, or wrest the South from British control. Indeed, for most watching from afar, the race to the Dan appeared a sad and pathetic retreat and nothing more. To win back the Southern states Nathanael Greene knew that at some point he would have to reenter North Carolina and beat Cornwallis on the field of battle, and the time for that movement came far sooner than most would have expected.

In Virginia the Southern Army was for a short while able to rest and recruit; two key components that quickly rejuvenated the cause. The natives were more than accommodating, bringing food and other needed material into camp, and after the long and difficult march from Cowpens to the Dan River the Americans relaxed "safely enjoying wholesome and abundant supplies of food in the rich and friendly county of Halifax." Light Horse Harry recalled those days with great fondness, when "joy beamed in every face; and as if every man was conscious of having done his duty, the subsequent days to the reunion of the army on the north of the Dan were spent in mutual gratulations; with rehearsal of the hopes and fears which agitated every breast during the retreat; interspersed with the many simple but interesting anecdotes with which every tongue was strung."[8]

While the Americans were resting and replenishing their stores in Halifax County, Virginia, Lord Cornwallis moved his army south some sixty miles to Hillsborough, North Carolina. Tarleton explains the reasoning: "The continentals being chased out of North Carolina, and the militia being awed and impeded from collecting, Earl Cornwallis thought the opportunity favourable for assembling the King's friends. With this intention he retired from the Dan, and proceeded by easy marches towards Hillsborough, the capital of the province. On this movement the King's troops gradually recovered from the fatigue they had undergone on the late march, which they had borne with exemplary patience and fortitude."[9] Heavily reinforced, Nathanael Greene decided his army had now strength enough to confront Cornwallis directly, and on 18 February advanced elements of the American Army under Lee and Pickens re-crossed the Dan, in search of Cornwallis. Their goal was to harass the British while discouraging loyalists from moving to assist the king's cause.

At Hillsborough, Lord Cornwallis explained his developing strategic outlook: "My force being ill suited to enter by that quarter so powerful a province as Virginia, and North Carolina being in the utmost confusion, after giving the troops a halt of a day, I proceeded by easy marches to Hillsborough, where I erected the King's standards, and invited, by proclamation, all loyal subjects to repair to it, and to stand forth and take an active part in assisting me to restore order and constitutional government."[10] But, by and large, the loyalists stayed home, and within days Lee had confronted a party of some 400 Tory militiamen on their way to meet Tarleton. The precise sequence of events remains clouded, but it appears the loyalists presumed Lee's Legion to actually be Tarleton's horse on the way to escort them, and as Lee was passing a fight broke out and many loyalists were killed, some slaughtered. This occurrence, while rightly questioned at the time in terms of its brutality, nevertheless had the effect of completely discouraging Tory sympathy in the area. Despite his best efforts, Cornwallis would be on his own.

On February 22 Greene re-crossed the Dan with the main body of the American Army, some 4,600 effective troops, swelled by recent arrivals. Realizing that the British Army had dwindled down to an effective strength of approximately 2,000 due to casualties, illness, and desertion, the American commander was spoiling for a fight, and after weeks of maneuver, Greene finally took up a defensive position near Guilford Courthouse. "On the 14th I received information," Cornwallis wrote, "that General Butler, with a body of North-Carolina militia and the expected reinforcements from Virginia, said to consist of a Virginia state regiment, a corps of Virginia eighteen-months men, three thousand Virginia militia and recruits from the Maryland line, had joined General Greene, and that the whole army, which was reported to amount to nine or ten thousand men, was marching to attack the British troops. During the afternoon intelligence was brought, which was confirmed in the night, that he had advanced that day to Guilford, about twelve miles from our camp. Being now persuaded that he had resolved to hazard an engagement,... I marched with the rest of the corps at daybreak on the morning of the 15th, to meet the enemy, or attack them in their encampment."[11] A fighting showdown with Greene was precisely what Cornwallis had marched and hoped and prayed for since leaving South Carolina, and he was not about to let the opportunity slip away.

As for the American deployment that morning, the Old Wagoner might have been absent, but his tactical brilliance was not. Following Morgan's written suggestions, Greene deployed his army in the three line arrangement Morgan had utilized at the Cowpens, intent on forcing the British to fight through a defense in depth. The terrain selected was favorable, being similar in nature to that which Morgan had fought upon at Cowpens. Light Horse Harry Lee, leading his legion cavalry, describes the country as he viewed it early that morning. "Guilford Court-House, erected near the great State road, is situated on the brow of a declivity, which descends gradually with an undulating slope for about a half mile. It terminates in a small vale, intersected by a rivulet. On the right of the road is open ground with some few copses of wood until you gain the last step of the descent where you see thick glades of brushy wood reaching across the rivulet; on the left of the road from the court-house a deep forest of lofty trees, which terminates nearly in a line with the termination of the field on the opposite side of the road. Below this forest is a small piece of open ground, which appeared to have been cultivated in corn the preceding summer."[12]

Greene posted his infantry in three lines, 300 yards separating each. In the front line were the North Carolina militia, with Kirkwood's Continentals, Lee's cavalry, and

Washington's dragoons manning the flanks. The second line was comprised of Virginia militia, many of whom had panicked and run the preceding summer at Camden. Their commander, Edward Stevens, had been living with the nightmare of that memory for seven months, and was determined it would not happen again. Behind that line – and at Morgan's suggestion – Stevens posted veteran riflemen with orders to shoot any man who dared desert his post. Finally, in the last line Greene deployed his Virginia and Maryland Continentals, the sturdiest troops at his disposal.

Around dawn Tarleton led his dragoons forward and promptly ran into Lee's cavalry. "The British had proceeded seven miles," Tarleton recalled, "on the great Salisbury road to Guilford, when the light troops drove in a picket of the enemy. A sharp conflict ensued between the advanced parties of the two armies."[13]

Heavy fighting continued for over two hours as Cornwallis poured into the contest virtually everything he had. The first American militia line proved inconsequential at best and quickly gave way. Some fire was delivered at long range, but soon – with the sight of British bayonets once again gleaming in the morning sun – the line collapsed in near panic. Nathanael Greene, furious, later wrote: "The whole [all of the British attacking units] moved through the old fields to attack the North Carolina brigades, who waited the attack until the enemy got within one hundred and forty yards, when part of them began to fire, but a considerable part left the ground without firing at all." Fortunately, the second militia line acquitted itself far better than the first, putting up a very stiff resistance before finally being overrun. "The Virginia militia," said Greene approvingly, "gave the enemy a warm fire for a long time; but being beat back, the action became general almost everywhere."[14] The line of Continentals then engaged the charging British, and the fight became furious indeed before a newly arrived Maryland regiment of green troops fled the field, causing a disastrous break in the line. The intrepid John Eager Howard quickly responded with his Maryland veterans and succeeded in stemming the tide, but Greene, fearing that the issue was then far too close for comfort, ordered an orderly withdrawal.

Cornwallis was thus left in command of the field and could technically claim a complete British victory on that basis alone, which presently he would do. But it had been a furious, deadly, and ghastly affair for the British, a Pyrrhic victory at best, for no true advantage had been gained; the Americans were now redeployed just down the road, prepared to fight yet another day. Meanwhile the cost, for Cornwallis, had been staggering. General O'Hara was down, badly wounded. O'Hara's lieutenant son had also been killed, Lt. Col. Webster was dying, Lt. Col. Stewart already dead. Tarleton had been wounded, Captain Swanton wounded, Captains Schutz, Maynard, and Goodricke all dead. And so it went, on and on, the list of dead, wounded, and missing far surpassing anything the British could afford.[15] "They had taken over twenty-seven percent casualties: ninety-three killed in action, 413 wounded of whom fifty died during the night, twenty-six missing. The casualty rate of the Guards alone was fifty percent. Cornwallis had set out in January with between 3,200 and 3,300 men. Despite Tarleton's disaster at Cowpens he had pushed on with some 2,550 men. Now his force was reduced to slightly over 1,400 effectives, and they were no longer fit to campaign. Charles, 2nd Earl of Cornwallis, had ruined his army."[16]

And he had ruined it in pursuit of a multifaceted chimera; the self-delusion of the British Model, to begin with, that whimsical belief that the king's friends would rise in numbers sufficient to win the campaign if the British flag were simply displayed along the line of march, and this despite months of evidence to the contrary. Coupled with that delusion was the fanciful notion that he could strip his army to the bone, abandon his line of supply, and live off the land while in pursuit of a mercurial foe that could come and go, intermittently inflate and deflate like a bagpipe, and fight only at a time and place of its own choosing. Finally, Cornwallis appears to have been suffering from the misbegotten belief that Camden was the norm for American fighting abilities; that his foe would turn and run in every instance, and thus the sight alone of British bayonets would carry the day. Thus had the action at Cowpens been grasped all along by high ranking British officers, not as a defeat, but rather as an inexplicable curiosity.

A hard, cold rain began to fall, pelting the wounded that still lay unattended across the open fields surrounding Guilford Court House. General Charles O'Hara, wounded and suffering greatly himself, later summed up the desolate mood in the British camp that prevailed after the battle. "I never did, and hope I never shall, experience two such days and Nights as those immediately after the Battle, we remained on the very ground on which it had been fought cover'd with Dead, Dying and with hundreds of wounded, Rebels as well as our own—a violent and constant Rain that lasted above Forty hours made it equally impracticable to remove or administer the smallest comfort to many of the Wounded."[17]

As an effective fighting force, Cornwallis' army was finished, and he knew it. Tarleton tells us, therefore, that "The position and strength of General Greene, at the iron works on Troublesome creek, about twelve miles distant from Guilford, did not invite the approach of the British army; Earl Cornwallis, therefore, commenced his march on the 18th for Deep river, in his way to Cross creek."[18] At Cross creek on the Cape Fear River, Cornwallis expected to find provisions and a viable water route to Wilmington, the destination he had selected for his army to rest and recuperate. But he found neither. So off again the exhausted troops marched, hobbling finally into Wilmington, North Carolina during the first week of April. With the British Army removed to the coast Nathanael Greene now had an open route south to return to South Carolina and play havoc upon the remaining British forces stationed there under Lord Francis Rawdon, which he promptly took, initiating a campaign that would continue until war's end.

At Wilmington Lord Cornwallis, meanwhile, had time to reflect upon the course of his campaign, and finally came to admit that the "King's friends" were neither as numerous nor as motivated as had previously presumed they would be. Moreover, he also came to the stark conclusion that the desolate, frontier country of North America itself – into which he had sallied forth without reconnaissance, information, knowledge of, or prior experience – simply defied subjugation in any European sense, for "the immense extent of this country, cut with numberless rivers and creeks, and the total want of internal navigation, which renders it impossible for our army to remain long in the heart of the country, will make it very difficult to reduce this province to obedience by a direct attack upon it."

Those consequential factors now readily acknowledged, nevertheless, Cornwallis went on to make one of the most illogical decisions of the war, a decision in all likelihood born far more of ego and wounded pride than any rational strategic conception. In order to secure both South and North Carolina for the crown, the general now somehow reasoned an invasion of Virginia the wisest alternative, where he might cooperate with British forces already on the ground. "I take the liberty of giving it as my opinion," he wrote to Lord Germain in London, "that a serious attempt upon Virginia would be the most solid plan, because successful operations might not only be attended with important consequences there, but would tend to the security of South Carolina, and ultimately to the submission of North Carolina."[19]

Despite some grave reservations – Cornwallis soon got word of Nathanael Greene's movement south, and despaired for the British defenses in South Carolina – Cornwallis had his army in motion by late April, and the lead elements marched into Petersburg, Virginia on May 20, 1781.[20] There he joined with the British forces already on the ground under Generals Phillips and Arnold (the American turncoat), bolstering his strength to over 7,000 effective troops, and began operations in the areas around Richmond. Military stores were burned, militias put to the run as the British began to pacify the area. Tarleton, on a dashing mission to Charlottesville, captured a few members of the Virginia Assembly, and came very near capturing governor Thomas Jefferson to boot, but strategically speaking, little of consequence was accomplished by these efforts. By June Cornwallis had marched to Williamsburg, the old colonial capital of the commonwealth – trailed all the way by an American force under the Marquis de la Fayette – where he received a new set of worried orders from Henry Clinton.

In New York City Clinton had become distressed over the build up of Continental and French forces in his vicinity, and he wanted Cornwallis to return a portion of the army that he had originally detailed for activity in the South. In July Cornwallis was instructed to move to the Chesapeake Bay, take up a defensive position, and prepare to receive the Royal Navy, Clinton writing that "we both seemed to agree in our opinion of the propriety of taking a healthy station on the Neck, between York and James rivers, for the purpose of covering a proper harbor for our line-of-battle ships."[21]

As Cornwallis moved toward Yorktown in compliance with this fresh set of orders, Lafayette sent word quickly back to George Washington of the British movement, a movement that suggested Cornwallis might be pinned at Yorktown with his back against the Chesapeake Bay. Alerted to this potential, in mid-August Washington began a carefully disguised shift of his army from New York to Virginia, the lead elements arriving at Yorktown by late September. This American force contained a substantial number of French regulars under the Comte de Rochambeau, forces sent by the French through a negotiated agreement after the British defeat at Saratoga. Additionally, the French Fleet under the Comte de Grasse was by good fortune returning from the Caribbean at this time, and met the British Fleet in the Battle of the Chesapeake. The British were routed and their fleet forced to return to New York, while the commanding French Fleet took up a position blocking entry into to the Bay. Presto, Cornwallis was suddenly trapped between the Americans on land and the French at sea.

Washington and Rochambeau began siege operations at Yorktown in early October and for a brief period the British resisted. But, faced with a virtually hopeless situation, on October 17 Cornwallis requested terms, and on October 19, 1781 he surrendered. Lord Cornwallis, pleading illness, could not face the humiliation of surrender, and sent out poor Charles O'Hara to act in his stead. By day's end some 8,000 British troops had surrendered to the Americans along with all their wagons, ordnance, and supplies, and with that, for all intents and purposes, the American Revolution came to an end.

In only nine months of fruitless, irrational maneuver and battle, Lord Cornwallis had managed to accomplish what even George Washington had been unable to achieve in almost seven years of conflict: the defeat of the most powerful military force in the world, and, as a consequence, the birth of a new nation. That extraordinary nine-month period ended for the Americans at Yorktown, but it had been put in motion by Daniel Morgan's stunning victory at Cowpens, and thus it would hardly be exaggeration to suggest that, had there been no Cowpens, there would have been no Yorktown. After all, no less than Sir Henry Clinton himself wrote that the British defeat at Cowpens was "the first link of a chain of events that followed each other in regular succession until they at last ended in the total loss of America."[22] The Old Wagoner may have been absent the final surrender, but the fruits of his remarkable victory at Cowpens were not.

THE END

AFTERWORD

The British

Charles O'Hara In early 1782 General Charles O'Hara was exchanged and immediately took command of a detachment of troops in the Caribbean. He was then promoted to major general and returned to Britain after the Treaty of Paris was signed. Living well beyond his means in England, in 1784 O'Hara was forced to flee to Italy in order to escape his creditors, and there he fell in with the lovely Mary Berry. In 1792 the crown appointed him lieutenant governor of Gibraltar, and while leading a mission against Napoleonic forces in 1793, he was captured and imprisoned in Paris for two years. After his release, O'Hara was promoted to full general and appointed governor of Gibraltar. Known for his many mistresses and affairs as well as his military prowess, O'Hara finally succumbed to his wartime wounds on February 25, 1802.

Lord Charles Cornwallis Cornwallis returned to England in January, 1782, only months after his surrender at Yorktown. His folly during the Southern Campaign was either largely forgotten or misunderstood, for Cornwallis returned a hero. In 1786 he received the appointment of Governor General of India, and served with both competence and grace. He returned to England in1793, handled a number of governmental posts, and was then reappointed

Governor of India in 1805. He died there of a lingering illness that year and was buried in Ghazipore, India.

Alexander Chesney After the Cowpens campaign, loyalist Alexander Chesney moved his family to a farm on the Ponpon River in South Carolina. He continued, however, to serve the British military in the South, and was wounded in action near Dorchester, S.C. in May of that year. He also accompanied Lord Rawdon in lifting the siege of Ninety Six. By war's end Chesney's health had deteriorated, he'd lost his wife to illness, and in April, 1782 – after sending his child off to relatives – sailed for Ireland. There, while seeking redress for the losses he suffered while in the service of the king, Chesney took a position in the Customs House in Dublin. He later remarried and spent years in pursuit of his claim for losses in America, for which he eventually was paid a greatly reduced sum in 1786. He was later appointed to a customs post in Annalong, County Down. There he raised a new family and remained in Ireland until his death. Chesney, although a minor character in the Southern drama, is included in this Afterword not only for the contributions he made, but as an example of the thousands of loyal citizens who lost everything they owned and were virtually forced to flee the United States as a result of the American victory, in most cases due to little more than their political sympathies.

Banastre Tarleton Tarleton had received such good press during the course of the Southern Campaign, that, like Cornwallis, he returned to England in 1782 to national acclaim. He was mobbed, honored, and feted far beyond his true accomplishments and, initially at least, Cowpens seemed not to be a weight around his neck. But the middle-aged Tarleton turned out to be just as arrogant and self-centered as the youthful one, and over time his star began to fade. His self-serving account of the Southern Campaign – *A history of the campaigns...* – earned him few friends, while his slandering of Lord Cornwallis aroused many enemies. He was elected to the House of Commons as a strong Whig politician, most notably for his advocacy of the slave trade and verbal abuse of abolitionists. He married in 1798, but the marriage produced no children. Tarleton was ultimately promoted to the rank of general, was awarded the Knight Grand Cross in 1820, but his post-revolutionary military career proved unexceptional. Sir Banastre Tarleton died in 1833 at Leintwardine, Herefordshire at the age of seventy-eight.

The Americans

John Eager Howard Served with Nathanael Greene until the end of the war and was wounded at the battle of Eutaw Springs in South Carolina. After the war, Howard returned to his ancestral home named Belvedere in Maryland which he later inherited. He was elected Governor of Maryland in 1789 and served three one-year terms. Howard also was elected to Congress and later the United States Senate, while turning down an offer from George Washington to serve as Secretary of War. He was eventually awarded a silver medal by Congress for his actions at the Cowpens. In 1789 Howard married "Peggy" Chew of the prominent Chews of Pennsylvania, and they had two sons,

George and Benjamin. Howard became a political force in Maryland, and his sons followed in his footsteps. He died on October 12, 1827 and was buried in Baltimore, Maryland.

Horatio Gates After being removed from command of the Southern Army, Gates remained in military limbo until 1782 when Congress repealed a resolution calling for a court of inquiry into his conduct at Camden. Washington then assigned Gates to duty at his headquarters at Newburg, New York, where Gates once again fell into intrigue. He, among others, was rumored to have been involved in the infamous Newburg Conspiracy, by which Congress was anonymously threatened via unsigned resolutions circulated in Newburg, purportedly issued by Continental officers disgruntled with their lack of pay. Washington, upon getting wind of the resolutions, promptly put an end to any threat, real or imagined, and the plot's true dimensions have never been clarified. After the war Gates returned to Traveler's Rest for a period, but in 1783 his wife died. He later remarried, moved to New York City, and lived out his remaining years as a member of New York society. He died in 1806 and was buried in the city of New York.

Robert Kirkwood Fought with Greene and Howard until the end of the revolutionary conflict. Kirkwood was considered by many one of the finest officers in the Continental Line, but due to strict promotional procedures in each state, he was never able to rise above the rank of captain. In all, Robert Kirkwood fought in thirty-two Revolutionary War battles without ever suffering a serious wound. At war's end in 1783 Kirkwood returned to his home in Newark, Delaware. He married one Sarah England, and they had a son, Joseph, and a daughter, Mary. The family moved to St. George Station (present day Kirkwood, Delaware), but Mary passed away in 1787. That year Kirkwood purchased a sizeable plot of land in the Northwest Territory, in what is today Ohio. He moved there and served as Justice of Peace until 1791 when he accepted an officer's commission in an expedition led by Arthur St. Clair, then Governor of the Norwest Territory to put down numerous Indian raids that were devastating the region. Robert Kirkwood, along with a substantial number of the militia was killed in 1791 in a battle outside of present day Fort Wayne, Indiana by Native Americans of the Miami tribe. He was thirty-five years old at the time of his death. Kirkwood was a graduate of the Newark Academy (present day University of Delaware) and the university later adopted as its mascot the name by which Kirkwood's Delaware Line regiment had come to be known – the fighting blue hens.

Francis Marion The Swamp Fox continued his guerrilla operations against the British until the end of hostilities, at times cooperating with Nathanael Greene. At Eutaw Springs, for instance, Marion handled the right wing of the American force with skill. After the war he returned to his old plantation home, which he found burned to the ground by the British. Rebuilding, he later married a cousin, Mary Esther Videau, and served for years in the South Carolina Senate. Marion, a quiet and self-effacing soul, was content to remain a farmer for most of his post-war years. He is credited by many with the creation of American guerrilla or ranger tactics, and was a highly respected man throughout the South. Light Horse Harry Lee had this to say about the legendary Swamp Fox: "Beloved by his friends, respected by his enemies, he exhibited a luminous example of the beneficial effects to be produced by an individual, who, with only a small means at his command, possesses a virtuous heart, a strong head, and a mind devoted to the common good." Francis Marion died in 1795.

William Richardson Davie The North Carolina militia commander had been born in England in 1756 then brought to South Carolina after the French and Indian War by his father. There he was raised by his uncle, William Richardson, graduated from Princeton in 1776, and became a lieutenant of dragoons in North Carolina soon thereafter. After the revolution, Davie practiced law, was elected to the North Carolina House of Commons, and was a member of the Constitutional Convention. He later became governor of North Carolina, and was a founding force in the creation of the University of North Carolina at Chapel Hill. Davie married in 1782, and died in November, 1820.

Otho Holland Williams Williams skillfully handled his duties in the Southern Army until the end of the war. At Guilford Court House he again commanded the army's rear guard, allowing Nathanael Greene to withdraw from the action unmolested. Greene later promoted Williams to Adjutant General of the army for his invaluable service. After the revolution, he returned to Maryland, married Miss Mary Smith of Baltimore, with whom he had four sons. The governor then appointed him Commissioner of the Port of

Baltimore, a lucrative position from which he lived well. Later Williams moved to Frederick County and began laying out the dimensions of what is today Williamsport, Maryland on the Potomac River; the town he hoped would be chosen as the eventual capital of the United States. Unfortunately, Williams was slender and frail, and his wartime activities had taken a toll on his health. He died in July 1794 at the age of 46 while seeking medical treatments in Virginia.

Andrew Pickens After the battle at the Cowpens, Andrew Pickens was promoted to brigadier general by the Governor of South Carolina. He returned to that state to organize militia units, and later took part in the siege of Augusta, Georgia, the siege of Ninety Six, and the battle of Eutaw Springs. Prior to the war Pickens had married Rebecca Floride Calhoun, with whom he had twelve children. After the revolution Pickens served in the South Carolina legislature and was later elected to Congress. He died on August 11, 1817 in Tamassee, South Carolina and was buried in Clemson, S.C.

Henry Lee III After Guilford Court House, Light Horse Harry Lee continued on with the Southern Army, and fought at the siege of Ninety Six, Eutaw Springs, and Yorktown. Lee then left the army, complaining of fatigue and symptoms of depression, and he may well have been suffering from what today would be diagnosed as post traumatic stress disorder, but of course went unrecognized and undiagnosed at the time. Lee then went on to have one of the more dramatic and chaotic careers after the war of any revolutionary hero, experiencing many highs and painful lows. He was a delegate to the Continental Congress, the Governor of Virginia from 1791 – 1794, and a member of the House of Representatives from 1799 – 1801. In 1794 Washington selected Lee to command the United States force sent to quell the Whiskey Rebellion in Western Pennsylvania, which he accomplished superbly without firing a shot. At George Washington's funeral he offered the famous phrase "first in war, first in peace, first in the hearts of his countrymen" in honor of Washington, and for which Lee is probably best remembered. But Lee seemed also to have a naïve and almost unbounded confidence that American independence would automatically translate into financial prosperity for the ruling class, and he unwisely speculated in many land deals that ultimately brought him ruin. As a result of indebtedness, Lee lost his family home, Stratford, and he was eventually imprisoned as a debtor for a year. It was while in prison that he took the time to pen his autobiography, which was later edited by his youngest son, Robert Edward. He was a firm Federalist in terms of his political orientation, and while helping defend a Federalist printer in Baltimore in 1812 Lee was brutally attacked by a crowd of Democrats and beaten savagely, incurring injuries from which he would never truly recover. Bankrupt, his reputation in tatters, and in ill-health, Lee left for the West Indies in hopes that a better climate might restore his health, but he continued instead to deteriorate. One last, desperate attempt to return home to see his loved ones failed. Arriving off the Georgia coast in early March, 1818, Light Horse Harry Lee was brought to Dungeness, the plantation home Nathanael Greene had planned, but never lived to see, that was located on Cumberland Island. There Henry Lee III died on March 25, 1818. His remains were later removed to a family tomb at Washington & Lee College, Lexington, Virginia.

Nathanael Greene After breaking off the fight at Guilford Court House, Nathanael Greene marched his army back to South Carolina. North of Camden, he engaged Lord Rawdon at Hobkirk's Hill, and was once again defeated. But Rawdon's force, bloodied by the contest, had to withdraw from the area, thus Greene, while losing the battle, still won the campaign, a technique he was soon to master. The same could be said for Greene's failed siege of Ninety Six, and again the Battle of Eutaw Springs. "We fight, get beaten, rise, and fight again," said Greene. Indeed, while losing all of these contests on the field, the British were consistently battered to the point of withdrawal, thus Nathanael Greene, while never winning a battle against his British foe, effectively won the war in the South, ultimately limiting the British to the occupation of Charleston and a few other minor towns. By war's end Nathanael Greene had demonstrated a strategic, logistical, and tactical ability rarely exceeded, and his reputation as a soldier was second only to George Washington. During the course of war Greene had personally paid for many supplies required by his army, but these expenses were never made good by Congress, and after the war Greene suffered financial problems as a result. He was granted lands and money by Georgia, North and South Carolina, but his finances were always short of his debts. In 1785 Greene moved into his Georgia estate named Mulberry Hill with his beautiful wife Caty, but in June of 1786, after a lengthy inspection of another estate in the heat of the sun, Greene succumbed to sunstroke and died within days. He was forty-three years old at the time.

Daniel Morgan Morgan was in many ways a perfect representation of the coming meritocracy that would replace in the United States old world ideas of aristocracy and royalty with status based instead upon excellence, merit, and accomplishment.

In Europe Morgan would never have risen above the grade of wagon driver or perhaps noncommissioned officer had he joined the service; in the infant United States he became a brigadier general, a congressman, and a legend on two continents. Rough and tumble, but intelligent, gifted, and driven, Daniel Morgan became a living embodiment of the rags-to-riches story that would be duplicated – in many ways and in many variations – with increasing frequency on the North American Continent. Morgan survived his sciatica – although the condition would never truly resolve – and even returned to the service briefly to help Lafayette as he trailed Cornwallis toward Yorktown. After the war he returned to the Shenandoah Valley, farmed, invested in land, joined the Presbyterian Church, and built an estate he named Saratoga not terribly far from Berry's Tavern where he had met Horatio Gates so many Junes before. Sitting on a bluff overlooking the Blue Ridge, Saratoga is today listed as a National Historic Landmark. Congress awarded Morgan a gold medal for his victory at Cowpens in 1790. His politics, like many of the revolutionary generation, were strongly Federalist. In 1794 Morgan returned to the army to help Light Horse Harry Lee in the suppression of the Whiskey

Rebellion in Western Pennsylvania, and in 1797 he was elected to Congress. For most of his remaining years Daniel Morgan enjoyed his family, his grand children, and meeting with his old compatriots to reminisce about their revolutionary adventures. In the spring of 1802 his health took a dramatic turn for the worse, however, and when it became clear that death was rapidly approaching a doctor was summoned to his bedside. One of the last conversations the old general ever had was faithfully recorded by a neighbor. When advised that death was near Morgan responded: "Doctor, if I could be the man I was when I was twenty-one years of age, I would be willing to be stripped stark naked on the top of the Allegheny Mountain to run for my life with the hounds of death at my heels." But youth had deserted Daniel Morgan just as it ultimately deserts us all, and Morgan passed away on July 6, 1802 at his daughter's home in Winchester, his life's story serving as a powerful example of the enormous and vibrant potential beating in every human heart. He was sixty-six years old at the time of his passing. The Old Wagoner was buried in Mt. Hebron Cemetery, Winchester, Virginia.

Notes – Prologue

1. Don Higginbotham, *Daniel Morgan: Revolutionary Rifleman* (Chapel Hill, University of North Carolina Press, 1961) 103.
2. Ibid., 49.
3. Theodore P. Savas and J. David Dameron, *A Guide to the Battles of the American Revolution* (New York, Savas Beatie, 2006) 237.
4. Higginbotham, as quoted 102.
5. Ibid., 62.
6. Ibid., 64.
7. Savas and Dameron, xxxv.
8. Jim Piecuch and John Beakes, *John Eager Howard in The American Revolution* (Charleston, S.C., The Nautical and Aviation Publishing Co. of America, 2009) 22.
9. Higginbotham, as quoted 61.
10. Robert Lagemann and Albert C. Manuey, *The Long Rifle* (Eastern Acorn Press, 1993) as quoted 26.
11. Higginbotham, 103.
12. John Buchanan, *The Road To Guilford Courthouse* (New York, John Wiley & Sons, Inc., 1997) 161, 316.

Notes – One

1. Otho H. Williams, "A Narrative of the Campaign of 1780" In *Sketches of the Life and Correspondence of Nathanael Greene,* Edited by William Johnson, Charleston, S.C., 486-487.
2. Jim Piecuch and John Beakes, *John Eager Howard in The American Revolution* (Charleston, S.C., The Nautical and Aviation Publishing Co. of America, 2009) 12.
3. Williams, 495.
4. Ibid., 495.
5. Henry Lee, *The Revolutionary War Memoirs of General Henry Lee,* Edited by Robert E. Lee (New York, Da Capo Press, 1998) 182.
6. Williams, 495.
7. Ibid., 495.
8. Ibid., 496.
9. Lee, as quoted, 182.
10. Ibid., 179.
11. Theodore P. Savas and J. David Dameron, *A Guide to the Battles of the American Revolution* (New York, Savas Beatie, 2006) 250.
12. Piecuch and Beakes, 39.
13. Williams, 496.
14. Savas and Dameron, 250.
15. Piecuch and Beakes, 8.
16. Williams, 496.
17. Ibid., 496.
18. Lee, 183.
19. Williams, 496.
20. Ibid., 497.

21. Ray Raphael, *A People's History Of The American Revolution* (New York, New Press, 2001) as quoted, 69.
22. Savas and Dameron, 252.
23. Williams, 497.
24. Ibid., 498.

Notes – Two

1. Banastre Tarleton, Lieutenant-General, *A history of the campaigns of 1780 and 1781, in the southern provinces of North America* (Manchester, England, A Reproduction, John Rylands University) 109.
2. Ibid., 109.
3. John Buchanan, *The Road To Guilford Courthouse* (New York, John Wiley & Sons, Inc., 1997) as quoted, 60.
4. Anthony J. Scotti, Jr., *Brutal Virtue; The Myth and Reality of Banastre Tarleton* (Westminster, Md., Heritage Books, 2007 14.
5. Ibid., 15.
6. Buchanan, 60.
7. Ibid., 62.
8. Ibid., 62.
9. Tarleton, 16.
10. Ibid., 17.
11. Buchanan, 63.
12. Ibid., 63.
13. Martha McHutchison Dimock, *A Chronicle Of The American Revolution 1763—1783* (New York, Perennial Library, 1976) 161.
14. Tarleton, 30.
15. Buchanan, 82.
16. Tarleton, 30.
17. Ibid., 31.
18. Buchanan, as quoted, 84.
19. Tarleton, 32.

20. Henry Lee, *The Revolutionary War Memoirs of General Henry Lee,* Edited by Robert E. Lee (New York, Da Capo Press, 1998) 165.
21. Otho Williams, "A Narrative of the Campaigns of 1780," in *Sketches of the Life and Correspondence of Nathanael Greene,* Edited by William Johnson, 497.
22. Tarleton, 110—111.

Notes – Three

1. Robert Kirkwood, *The Journal and Order Book Of Captain Robert Kirkwood Of The Delaware Regiment Of The Continental Line* (Dover, Delaware, Press of the Delawarean, 1910) 11.
2. Henry Lee, *The Revolutionary Memoirs of General Henry Lee,* Edited by Robert E. Lee (New York, Da Capo Press, 1998) 184.
3. Russ Pickett, *Delawarean's That Gave Their All During the Revolutionary War,* 21 Mar. 2010. Web. 9 Feb. 2016 http://www.russpickett.com/history/revolw.htm.
4. David McCullough, *1776* (New York, Simon & Schuster, 2005) as quoted, 176.
5. Kirkwood, 9.
6. Ibid., 9.
7. Jim Piecuch and John Beakes, *John Eager Howard in The American Revolution* (Charleston, S.C., The Nautical and Aviation Publishing Co. of America, 2009) 32.
8. John Buchanan, *The Road To Guilford Court House* (New York, John Wiley & Son Inc., 1997) 127.
9. Otho Williams, "A Narrative of the Campaign of 1780" in *Sketches Of The Life And Correspondence Of Nathanael Greene*, edited by William Johnson, 486.
10. Kirkwood, 10.
11. Ibid., 10.
12. Williams, 486.
13. Kirkwood, 108 – 109.
14. Williams, 487.
15. Ibid., 487.

16. Kirkwood, 10.
17. Williams, 487.
18. Ibid., 487.
19. Ibid., 494.
20. Ibid., 494.
21. Ibid., 492.
22. Pickett
23. Kirkwood, 113.
24. Lee, 184.
25. Williams, 497.
26. Pickett
27. Lee, 185.
28. Banastre Tarleton, *A history of the campaigns of 1780 and 1781, in the southern provinces of North America* (Manchester, England, A Reproduction, John Rylands University) 111.
29. Lee, 186.
30. Williams, 498.

Notes – Four

1. John Buchanan, *The Road To Guilford Courthouse* (New York, John Wiley & Sons, Inc., 1997) 171.
2. Mark M. Boatner III, *Encyclopedia of the American Revolution,* Alexander Hamilton to James Duane, September 6, 1780, as quoted (Mechanicsburg, Pa., Stackpole Books, 1994) 415.
3. Jim Piecuch and John Beakes, *John Eager Howard in The American Revolution* (Charleston, S.C., The Nautical and Aviation Publishing Co. of America, 2009) 43.
4. Henry Lee, *The Revolutionary War Memoirs of General Henry Lee,* Edited by Robert E. Lee (New York, Da Capo Press, 1998) 186.
5. Piecuch and Beakes, 43.
6. Ibid., 43.
7. Robert Kirkwood, *The Journal And Order Book Of Captain Robert Kirkwood Of The Delaware Regiment Of The Continental Line* (Dover, Delaware, Press of the Delawarean, 1910) 11.
8. Banastre Tarleton, *A history of the campaigns of 1780 and 1781, in the southern provinces of North America* (Manchester, England, A Reproduction, John Rylands University) 111-112.
9. Charles Steadman, *The History of the Origin, Progress, and Termination of the American War,* 2 Volumes (London, 1794) Vol. 2, 183.
10. Otho Williams, "A Narrative of the Campaign of 1780" in *Sketches Of The Life And Correspondence Of Nathanael Greene,* Edited by William Johnson, 499.
11. Ibid., 499.

12. Ibid., 498-499.
13. Ibid., 500.
14. Ibid., 501.
15. Ibid., 500.
16. Ibid., 501.
17. Ibid., 501.

Notes – Five

1. Banastre Tarleton, *A history of the campaigns of 1780 and 1781, in the southern provinces of North America* (Manchester, England, A Reproduction, John Rylands University) 114.
2. John Buchanan, *The Road To Guilford Courthouse* (New York, John Wiley & Sons, Inc., 1997) 155.
3. Tarleton, 114.
4. Ibid., 114.
5. Henry Lee, *The Revolutionary War Memoirs of General Henry Lee,* Edited by Robert E. Lee (New York, Da Capo, 1998) 188.
6. Tarleton, 115.
7. Lee, 189.
8. Tarleton, 115.
9. Lee, 189.
10. Buchanan, 115.
11. Tarleton, 116.
12. Ibid., 112.
13. Ibid., 117.
14. Ibid., 117.
15. Ibid., 117.
16. Lee, 189.
17. Buchanan, 175.
18. Don Higginbotham, *Daniel Morgan, Revolutionary Rifleman* (Chapel Hill, University of North Carolina Press, 1961) 105.

Notes – Six

1. Otho Williams, "A Narrative of the Campaign of 1780" in *Sketches Of The Life And Correspondence Of Nathanael Greene,* Edited by William Johnson, 501.
2. Ibid., 501 – 502.
3. Ibid., 502.
4. Ibid., 502.
5. Ray Raphael, *A People's History Of The American Revolution* (New York, The New Press, 2001) 231.
6. Edwin G. Burrows, *Forgotten Patriots* (New York, Basic Books, 2008) 21-22, xi.
7. Henry Lee, *The Revolutionary War Memoirs of General Henry Lee,* Edited by Robert E. Lee (New York, Da Capo Press, 1998) 592 – 594.
8. Williams, 502.
9. Jim Piecuch and John Beakes, *John Eager Howard in The American Revolution* (Charleston, S.C., The Nautical and Aviation Publishing Company of America, Inc., 2009) 43.
10. Robert Kirkwood, *The Journal And Order Book Of Captain Robert Kirkwood Of The Delaware Regiment Of The Continental Line* (Dover, Delaware, Press Of The Delawarean, 1910) 11.
11. Williams, 503 – 504.
12. Ibid., 504.
13. Ray Raphael, *A People's History Of The American Revolution* (New York, The New Press, 2001) as quoted, 90.
14. Williams, 505.
15. Ibid., 505.

16. John Buchanan, *The Road To Guilford Court House* (New York, John Wiley & Sons, Inc., 1997) 170.
17. Banastre Tarleton, *A history of the campaigns of 1780 and 1781, in the southern provinces of North America* (Manchester, England, A Reproduction, John Rylands University) 158 – 159.
18. Lyman Draper, *King's Mountain and its Heroes: History of the Battle of King's Mountain, October 7th, 1780, and the Events which led to it* (Cincinnati, 1881: 1992 reprint, 73.
19. Lee, 193.
20. Tarleton, 138, Note F.
21. Piecuch and Beakes, 44.
22. Williams, 507.
23. Ibid., 508.

Notes – Seven

1. Otho Williams, "A Narrative of the Campaign of 1780" in *Sketches Of The Life And Correspondence Of Nathanael Greene,* edited by William Johnson, 505 – 506.
2. Ibid., 506.
3. Ibid., 507.
4. Ibid., 508.
5. Martha McHutchinson Dimock, *A Chronicle Of The American Revolution* (New York, Perennial Library, 1976) 164.
6. Don Higginbotham, *Daniel Morgan, Revolutionary Rifleman* (Chapel Hill, N.C., University of North Carolina Press, 1961) 107.
7. Ibid., 108.
8. Ibid., 109.
9. Ibid., 109.
10. John Buchanan, *The Road To Guilford Court House* (New York, John Wiley & Sons, Inc., 1997) 279.
11. Higginbotham, 109.
12. Williams, 509.
13. Jim Piecuch and John Beakes, *John Eager Howard in The American Revolution* (Charleston, S.C., The Nautical and Aviation Publishing Co. of America, 2009) 49.
14. Higginbotham, 110.
15. Robert Kirkwood, *The Journal And Order Book Of Captain Robert Kirkwood Of The Delaware Regiment Of The Continental Line* (Dover, Delaware, Press of the Delawarean, 1910) 12.
16. Williams, 509.

Notes – Eight

1. Banastre Tarleton, *A history of the campaigns of 1780 and 1781, in the southern provinces of North America* (Manchester, England, A Reproduction, John Rylands University) 82, as quoted from note M.
2. Ibid., 138 note F.
3. Ibid., 204 note H.
4. John Buchanan, *The Road To Guilford Court House* (New York, John Wiley & Sons, Inc., 1997) 76.
5. Tarleton, 159.
6. Henry Lee, *The Revolutionary War Memoirs of General Henry Lee*, Edited by Robert E. Lee (New York, Da Capa Press, 1998) 196 – 197.
7. Tarleton, 163.
8. Ibid., 163.
9. Ibid., 167.
10. Buchanan, 230.
11. Lee, 202.
12. Tarleton, 172.

Notes – Nine

1. Henry Lee, *The Revolutionary War Memoirs of General Henry Lee,* Edited by Robert E. Lee (New York, Da Capo Press, 1998) 208 – 209.
2. Don Higginbotham, *Daniel Morgan, Revolutionary Rifleman* (Chapel Hill, North Carolina, University of North Carolina Press, 1961) 116.
3. Otho Williams, "A Narrative of the Campaign of 1780," in *Sketches Of The Life And Correspondence Of Nathanael Greene,* Edited by William Johnson, 509.
4. Ibid., 510.
5. Lee, 209.
6. Williams, 510.
7. Robert Kirkwood, *The Journal And Order Book Of Captain Robert Kirkwood Of The Delaware Regiment Of The Continental Line* (Dover, Delaware, Press Of The Delawarean, 1910) 12 – 13.
8. Williams, 510.
9. Higginbotham, as quoted, 114.
10. Banastre Tarleton, *A history of the campaigns of 1780 and 1781, in the southern provinces of North America* (Manchester, England, A Reproduction, John Rylands University) 211.
11. Ibid., 174.
12. Ibid., 211.
13. Ibid., 211.
14. Higginbotham, 119.
15. John Buchanan, *The Road To Guilford Courthouse* (New York, John Wiley & Sons, Inc., 1987) 276.
16. Ibid., 276.
17. Ibid., 276

18. Lee, 221.
19. Williams, 511.
20. Higginbotham, as quoted, 120.
21. Buchanan, 288.
22. Jim Piecuch and John Beakes, *John Eager Howard in The American Revolution* (Charleston, S.C., The Nautical and Aviation Publishing Co. of America, 2009) as quoted, 52.
23. Theodorus Bailey Myers, *Cowpens Papers: Being Correspondence Of General Morgan And The Prominent Actors* (Charleston, S.C., The News and Courier, 1881) 9.
24. Higginbotham, 121.

Notes – Ten

1. Henry Lee, *The Revolutionary War Memoirs of General Henry Lee,* Edited by Robert E. Lee (New York, Da Capo Press, 1998) 203.
2. Ibid., 203.
3. Banastre Tarleton, *A history of the campaigns of 1780 and 1781, in the southern provinces of North America* (Manchester, England, A Reproduction, John Rylands University) 203, note G.
4. Lee, 584 – 585.
5. John Buchanan, *The Road To Guilford Court House* (New York, John Wiley & Sons, Inc., 1997) 183.
6. Ibid., 184.
7. Tarleton, 174.
8. Lee, 203.
9. Tarleton, 175.
10. Ibid., 175.
11. Buchanan, 247.
12. Tarleton, 175 – 176.
13. Buchanan, as quoted, 247.
14. Tarleton, 176.
15. Lee, 204.
16. Buchanan, 247.
17. Tarleton, 205.
18. Ibid., 207.
19. Ibid., 177.
20. Ibid., 206.
21. Ibid., 177.
22. Ibid., 178 – 179.
23. Buchanan, 253.
24. Tarleton, 179 – 180.

25. Ibid., 180.
26. Ibid., 181.
27. Ibid., 182.
28. Ibid., 182.
29. Lee, 206.
30. Buchanan, as quoted, 256.
31. Tarleton, 183.
32. Ibid., 207.
33. Ibid., 210.
34. Buchanan, 257.
35. Tarleton, 249.

Notes – Eleven

1. Don Higginbotham, *Daniel Morgan, Revolutionary Rifleman* (Chapel Hill, University of North Carolina Press, 1961) 122.
2. Robert Kirkwood, *The Journal And Order Book Of Captain Robert Kirkwood Of The Delaware Regiment Of The Continental Line* (Dover, Delaware, Press Of The Delawarean, 1910) 13.
3. Ibid., 13.
4. Lawrence E. Babits, *A Devil of a Whipping: The Battle of Cowpens* (Chapel Hill, University of North Carolina Press, 1998) 48.
5. Higginbotham, 122.
6. Henry Lee, *The Revolutionary War Memoirs of General Henry Lee,* Edited by Robert E. Lee (New York, Da Capo, 1998) 594-595.
7. Higginbotham, as quoted, 125-126.
8. Theodorus Bailey Myers, *The Cowpens Papers* (Charleston, S.C., The News and Courier, 1881) 10-11.
9. Ibid., 11-12.
10. Banastre Tarleton, *A history of the campaigns of 1780 and 1781, in the southern provinces of North America* (Manchester, England, A Reproduction, John Rylands University) 250.
11. Ibid., 213-214.
12. John Buchanan, *The Road To Guilford Courthouse* (New York, John Wiley & Sons, Inc., 1997) 302.
13. Higginbotham, 124.
14. Ibid., 124.
15. Tarleton, 250-251.
16. Ibid., 217.

17. Ibid., 249-250.
18. Ibid., 252-253.
19. Myers, 16.
20. Ibid., 17.
21. Babits, 49.

Notes – Twelve

1. Banastre Tarleton, *A history of the campaigns of 1780 and 1781, in the southern provinces of North America* (Manchester, England, A Reproduction, John Rylands University) 215.
2. Ibid., 253.
3. Lawrence E. Babits, *A Devil of a Whipping: The Battle of Cowpens* (Chapel Hill, University of North Carolina Press, 1998) 45.
4. Jim Piecuch and John Beakes, *John Eager Howard in The American Revolution* (Charleston, South Carolina, The Nautical and Aviation Publishing Co. of America, 2009) 53; Don Higginbotham, *Daniel Morgan, Revolutionary Rifleman* (Chapel Hill, University of North Carolina Press, 1961) 130; Babits, 9.
5. Theodorus Bailey Myers, *Cowpens Papers: Being Correspondence Of General Morgan And The Prominent Actors* (Charleston, S.C., The News And Courier, 1881) 19.
6. Ibid., 21 – 22.
7. Babits, 49.
8. John Buchanan, *The Road To Guilford Court House* (New York, John Wiley & Sons, Inc., 1997) as quoted, 311.

Notes – Thirteen

1. Lawrence E. Babits, *A Devil of a Whipping: The Battle of Cowpens* (Chapel Hill, University of North Carolina Press, 1998) 51.
2. John Buchanan, *The Road To Guilford Court House* (New York, John Wiley & Sons, Inc., 1997) 312.
3. Don Higginbotham, *Daniel Morgan: Revolutionary Rifleman* (Chapel Hill, University of North Carolina Press, 1961) as quoted, 132.
4. Banastre Tarleton, *A history of the campaigns of 1789 and 1781, in the southern provinces of North America* (Manchester, England, A Reproduction, John Reynolds University) 218-219.
5. Theodorus Bailey Myers, *Cowpens Papers: Being Correspondence Of General Morgan And the Prominent Actors* (Charleston, S.C., The News and Courier, 1881) 24.
6. Babits, 52.
7. Tarleton, 219.
8. Ibid., 254-255.
9. Ibid., 219.
10. Ibid., 219.
11. Ibid., 219.
12. Babits, 53.
13. Higginbotham, 130.

Notes – Fourteen

1. Banastre Tarleton, *A history of the campaigns of 1780 and 1781, in the southern provinces of North America* (Manchester, England, A reproduction, John Rylands University, 1787) 220.
2. Lawrence E. Babits, *A Devil of a Whipping: The Battle of Cowpens* (Chapel Hill, University of North Carolina Press, 1998) 53.
3. Tarleton, 220.
4. John Buchanan, *The Road To Guilford Courthouse* (New York, John Wiley & Sons, Inc., 1997) as quoted, 311.
5. Tarleton, 220.
6. Ibid., 220.
7. Babits, 53.
8. Jim Piecuch and John Beakes, *John Eager Howard in The American Revolution* (Charleston, S.C., The Nautical and Aviation Publishing Co. of America, 2009) as quoted, 58-59.
9. Don Higginbotham, *Daniel Morgan: Revolutionary Rifleman* (Chapel Hill, University of North Carolina Press, 1961) 131.
10. Thomas Young, *Memoirs of Major Thomas Young; a Revolutionary Patriot of South Carolina,* Orion Magazine, October, 1843.
11. Robert Kirkwood, *The Journal And Order Book Of Captain Robert Kirkwood Of The Delaware Regiment of the Delaware Line* (Dover, Delaware, Press of The Delawarean, 1910) 13.
12. Theodorus Bailey Myers, *Cowpens Papers: Being Correspondence Of General Morgan And The Prominent Actors* (Charleston, S.C., The News and Courier, 1881) 24.
13. Buchanan, as quoted, 284

Notes – Fifteen

1. Thomas Young, *Memoirs of Major Thomas Young; a Revolutionary Patriot of South Carolina,* Orion Magazine, October, 1843.
2. James Collins, *Autobiography of a Revolutionary Soldier, Sixty Years in the Nueces Valley*: 1870 – 1930 (San Antonio: Naylor Printing Co., 1930)
3. Young.
4. William Richardson Davie, *The Revolutionary War Sketches of William R. Davie,* Blackwell P. Robinson, ed. (Raleigh, North Carolina Division of Archives & History, 1976) 12.
5. Young.
6. Lawrence E. Babits, *A Devil of a Whipping: The Battle of Cowpens* (Chapel Hill, University of North Carolina Press, 1998) 55.
7. Young.
8. Don Higginbotham, *Daniel Morgan: Revolutionary Rifleman* (Chapel Hill, N.C., University of North Carolina Press, 1961) 4 – 5.
9. Young.

Notes – Sixteen

1. Jim Piecuch and John Beakes, *John Eager Howard in The American Revolution* (Charleston, S.C., The Nautical and Aviation Publishing Co. of America, 2009) 60.
2. Banastre Tarleton, *A history of the campaigns of 1780 and 1781, in the southern provinces of North America* (Manchester, England, A Reproduction, John Rylands University, 1787) 221.
3. Ibid., 221.
4. Lawrence Babits, *A Devil of a Whipping: The Battle of Cowpens* (Chapel Hill, University of North Carolina Press, 1998) 58.
5. Tarleton, 221.
6. Thomas Young, *Memoirs of Major Thomas Young; a Revolutionary Patriot of South Carolina,* Orion Magazine, October, 1834.
7. Tarleton, 221.
8. Lawrence Everhart, Pension Application S25068, 1834, Transcribed and annotated by C. Leon Harris.
9. Tarleton, 221.
10. Babits, 58.
11. Tarleton, 221.
12. Ibid., 221-222.

Notes – Seventeen

1. Joseph McJunkin, *Memoirs of Major Joseph McJunkin – Revolutionary Patriot,* By Reverend James Hodge Saye, originally appearing as a series of articles in the *Watchman and Observer,* Richmond, Virginia, 1847-48. All quotations from McJunkin are from pages 76–79.
2. Don Higginbotham, *Daniel Morgan: Revolutionary Rifleman* (Chapel Hill, University of North Carolina Press, 1961) as quoted, 136.
3. Theodorus Bailey Myers, *Cowpens Papers: Being Correspondence Of General Morgan And The Prominent Actors* (Charleston, S.C., News and Courier, 1881) 24.
4. James Collins, *Autobiography of a Revolutionary Soldier, Sixty Years in the Nueces Valley: 1870 – 1930* (San Antonio: Naylor Printing Co., 1930)
5. Thomas Young, *Memoirs of Major Thomas Young; A Revolutionary Patriot of South Carolina,* Orion Magazine, October, 1834.
6. McJunkin
7. John Buchanan, *The Road to Guilford Courthouse* (New York, John Wiley & Sons, Inc., 1997) 319.
8. Higginbotham, as quoted, 136.
9. Ibid., as quoted, 136.
10. Henry Lee, *The Revolutionary War Memoirs of General Henry Lee,* ed., Robert E. Lee (New York, Da Capo Press, 1998) 227.
11. Jim Piecuch and John Beakes, *John Eager Howard in The American Revolution* (Charleston, S.C., The Nautical and Aviation Publishing Co. of America, 2009) as quoted, 60.

12. Higginbotham, as quoted, 136.
13. McJunkin
14. Collins
15. Myers, 24 – 25.

Notes – Eighteen

1. Banastre Tarleton, *A history of the campaigns of 1780 and 1781, in the southern provinces of North America* (Manchester, England, A Reproduction, John Rylands University, 1787) 222.
2. Roderick Mackenzie, *Strictures on Lt. Col. Tarleton's History of the campaigns of 1780 and 1781, in the southern provinces of North America* (London, printed for the author and sold by R. Faulder, New Bond's Street; T. And J. Egerton, Charing-Cross, R. Jameson, Strand; and T. Swell, Cornhill, 1787) 97.
3. Henry Lee, *The Revolutionary War Memoirs of General Henry Lee,* ed. By Robert E. Lee (New York, Da Capo Press, 1998) 222.
4. Thomas Young, *Memoirs of Major Thomas Young; A Revolutionary Patriot of South Carolina,* Orion Magazine, October, 1834.
5. Tarleton, 222.
6. Ibid., 222.
7. Thomas Young.
8. Ibid.
9. Joseph McJunkin, *Memoirs of Major Joseph McJunkin – Revolutionary Patriot,* By Reverend James Hodge Saye, originally appearing as a series of articles in the *Watchman and Observer,* Richmond, Virginia, 1847-48. All quotations are from pages 78 – 79.
10. Thomas Young.
11. Lawrence Babits, *A Devil of a Whipping; The Battle of Cowpens* (Chapel Hill, University of North Carolina Press, 1998) 86.

12. Richard C. Swearingen, Pension Application S31402, 1832, Transcribed by Will Graves.
13. Thomas Young.
14. Mackenzie, 99.
15. John Buchanan, *The Road To Guilford Courthouse* (New York, John Wiley & Sons, Inc., 1997) 322.
16. Thomas Young.
17. Babits, 94.
18. Ibid., 95.
19. Mackenzie, 99.

Notes – Nineteen

1. Jim Piecuch and John Beakes, *John Eager Howard in The American Revolution* (Charleston, S.C., The Nautical and Aviation Publication Company of America, 2009) as quoted, 61 – 62.
2. James Collins, *Autobiography of a Revolutionary Soldier, Sixty Years in the Nueces Valley: 1870 – 1930* (San Antonio: Naylor Printing Co., 1930)
3. Collins.
4. Banastre Tarleton, *A history of the campaigns of 1780 and 1781, in the southern provinces of North America* (Manchester, England, A Reproduction, John Rylands University, 1787) 223.
5. Joseph McJunkin, *Memoirs of Major Joseph McJunkin – Revolutionary Patriot* By Reverend James Hodge Saye, originally appearing as a series of articles in the *Watchman and Observer,* Richmond, Virginia, 1847 – 49. All quotations are from pages 78 – 79.
6. Lawrence Babits, *A Devil of a Whipping: The Battle of Cowpens* (Chapel Hill, University of North Carolina Press, 1998) as quoted, 98.
7. Collins.
8. Ibid.
9. Ibid.
10. Jim Piecuch and John Beakes, 62.
11. Ibid., as quoted, 62.
12. Thomas Young, *Memoirs of Major Thomas Young; A Revolutionary Patriot of South Carolina,* Orion Magazine, October, 1834.
13. Tarleton, 223.
14. McJunkin.

15. Theodore Bailey Myers, *Cowpens Papers: Being Correspondence Of General Morgan And The Prominent Actors* (Charleston, S.C., News and Courier, 1881) 24.
16. Babits, as quoted, 104.
17. Robert Lagemann and Albert C. Manucy, *The Long Rifle* (New York, Eastern Acorn Press, 1993) 21 – 22.
18. Henry Lee, *The Revolutionary War Memoirs of General Henry Lee,* ed., Robert E. Lee, (New York, Da Capo Press, 1998) 228.
19. Tarleton, 223.
20. Ibid., 223.
21. Babits, 104.
22. Tarleton, 223.
23. Babits, as quoted, 109.
24. Jim Piecuch and John Beakes, 62 – 63.
25. John Buchanan, *The Road to Guilford Courthouse* (New York, John Wiley & Sons, Inc., 1997) as quoted, 324.
26. Ibid., as quoted, 324.
27. Tarleton, 223.
28. Jim Piecuch and John Beakes, as quoted, 63.
29. Myers, 25.

Notes – Twenty

1. Roderick Mackenzie, *Strictures On Lt. Col. Tarleton's History Of The Campaigns of 1780 And 1781, In The Southern Provinces Of North America* (London, R. Faulder, New Bond-Street; T. And J. Egerton, Charing-Cross, R. Jameson, Strand; And T. Sewell, Cornhill, 1787) 99 – 100.
2. Theodore Bailey Myers, *Cowpens Papers: Being Correspondence Of General Morgan And The Prominent Actors* (Charleston, S.C., News and Courier, 1881) 25.
3. Henry Lee, *The Revolutionary War Memoirs of General Henry Lee,* ed., Robert E. Lee (New York, Da Capo Press, 1998) 228 – 229.
4. Banastre Tarleton, *A history of the campaigns of 1780 and 1781, in the southern provinces of North America* (Manchester, England, A Reproduction, John Rylands University, 1787) 223.
5. Lawrence Babits, *A Devil of a Whipping: The Battle of Cowpens* (Chapel Hill, University of North Carolina Press, 1998) as quoted, 117.
6. Thomas Young, *Memoirs of Major Thomas Young; A Revolutionary Patriot of South Carolina,* Orion Magazine, October, 1834.
7. Jim Piecuch and John Beakes, *John Eager Howard in the American Revolution* (Charleston, S.C., The Nautical and Aviation Publication Company of America, 2009) as quoted, 63.
8. John Buchanan, *The Road to Guilford Courthouse* (New York, John Wiley & Sons, Inc., 1997) as quoted, 325.
9. Babits, as quoted, 122.

10. Ibid., as quoted, 120.
11. Joseph McJunkin, *Memoirs of Major Joseph McJunkin – Revolutionary Patriot,* By Reverend James Hodge Saye, originally appearing as a series of articles in the *Watchman and Observer,* Richmond, Virginia, 1847– 49. All quotations are from pages 78 – 79.
12. Tarleton, 222.
13. Ibid., 224.
14. Mackenzie, 100.
15. Ibid., 100 – 101.
16. Tarleton, 224.
17. Daniel Higginbotham, *Daniel Morgan: Revolutionary Rifleman* (Chapel Hill, University of North Carolina Press, 1961) as quoted, 141.
18. Mackenzie, 101.
19. Lee, as quoted, 229.
20. McJunkin.

Notes – Twenty One

1. Lawrence Everhart, Pension Application, attached letter from James Simmons to William Washington, November 3, 1803.
2. Ibid., Simmons to Washington.
3. James Collins, *Autobiography of a Revolutionary Soldier, Sixty years in the Nueces Valley: 1870 – 1930* (San Antonio: Naylor Printing Co., 1930)
4. Banastre Tarleton, *A history of the campaigns of 1780 and 1781, in the southern provinces of North America* (Manchester, England, A Reproduction, John Rylands University, 1787) 224.
5. Thomas Young, *Memoirs of Major Thomas Young; A Revolutionary Patriot of South Carolina,* Orion Magazine, October, 1834.
6. Lawrence Babits, *A Devil of a Whipping: The Battle of Cowpens* (Chapel Hill, University of North Carolina Press, 1998) 134.
7. Young.

Notes – Twenty Two

1. Theodore Bailey Myers, *Cowpens papers: Being Correspondence Of General Morgan And The Prominent Actors* (Charleston, S.C., News and Courier, 1881) 26.
2. Banastre Tarleton, *A history of the campaigns of 1780 and 1781, in the southern provinces of North America* (Manchester, England, A Reproduction, John Rylands University, 1787) 224.
3. Ibid., 226 – 227.
4. Alexander Chesney, *The Journal of Alexander Chesney, a South Carolina Loyalist in the Revolution and After,* ed., by E. Alfred Jones (London, The Ohio State University, 1921) 22.
5. Roderick Mackenzie, *Strictures On Lt. Col. Tarleton's History Of The Campaigns of 1780 And 1781, In The Southern Provinces Of North America* (London, R. Faulder, New Bond-Street; T. And J. Egerton, Charing-Cross, R. Jameson, Strand; and T. Sewell, Cornhill, 1787) 108.
6. Ibid., 109 – 110.
7. Tarleton, 227 – 228.
8. Ibid., 258.
9. Mackenzie, 115 – 118.
10. John Buchanan, *The Road To Guilford Court House* (New York, John Wiley & Sons, Inc., 1997) 329.
11. Myers, 31.
12. Ibid., 33.
13. Buchanan, as quoted, 329.
14. Robert Kirkwood, *The Journal And Order Book Of Captain Robert Kirkwood Of The Delaware Regiment Of The Continental Line* (Dover, Delaware, Press of the Delawarean, 1910)

Notes – Twenty Three

1. Lawrence Babits, *A Devil of a Whipping: The Battle of Cowpens* (Chapel Hill, University of North Carolina Press, 1998) 143.
2. Theodore Bailey Myers, *Cowpens Papers: Being Correspondence Of General Morgan And The Prominent Actors* (Charleston, S.C., News and Courier, 1881) 28.
3. Ibid., 29.
4. Ibid., 30.
5. Banastre Tarleton, *A history of the campaigns of 1780 and 1781, in the southern provinces of North America* (Manchester, England, A Reproduction, John Rylands University, 1787) 229.
6. Ibid., 257 -258.
7. Babits, 143.
8. John Buchanan, *The Road to Guilford Court House* (New York, John Wiley & Sons, Inc., 1997) 338.
9. Tarleton, 229.
10. Ibid., 229.
11. John Keegan, *A History of Warfare* (New York, Alfred A. Knopf, 1994) 271.
12. Tarleton, 267 – 268.

Notes – Twenty Four

1. Don Higginbotham, *Daniel Morgan: Revolutionary Rifleman* (Chapel Hill, University of North Carolina Press, 1961) 145.
2. John Buchanan, *The Road to Guilford Court House* (New York, John Wiley & Sons, Inc., 1997) as quoted, 339.
3. Theodore Bailey Myers, *Cowpens Papers: Being Correspondence Of General Morgan And The Prominent Actors* (Charleston, S.C., News and Courier, 1881) 32.
4. Buchanan, as quoted, 339.
5. Banastre Tarleton, *A history of the campaigns of 1780 and 1781, in the southern provinces of North America* (Manchester, England, A Reproduction, John Rylands University, 1787) 220 – 230.
6. Henry Lee, *The Revolutionary War Memoirs of General Henry Lee,* ed., Robert E. Lee (New York, Da Capo Press, 1998) 232.
7. Buchanan, as quoted, 341
8. Tarleton, 230.
9. Buchanan, as quoted, 340.
10. Lee, 232 – 233.
11. Buchanan, as quoted, 342.
12. Higginbotham, as quoted, 150 – 151.
13. Lee, 233.
14. Tarleton, 232.
15. Buchanan, 348.
16. Lee, 234.
17. Buchanan, 349.
18. Lee, 234.
19. Tarleton, 232 – 233.

20. Lee, 235.
21. Ibid., 235.
22. Tarleton, 233 – 234.
23. Lee, 223.
24. Ibid., 12 – 25.
25. Myers, 36.

Notes – Epilogue

1. Banastre Tarleton, *A history of the campaigns of 1780 and 1781, in the southern provinces of North America* (Manchester, England, A Reproduction, John Rylands University, 1787) 234.
2. Jim Piecuch and John Beakes, *John Eager Howard in The American Revolution* (Charleston, S.C., The Nautical and Aviation publication Company of America, 2009) 75.
3. Tarleton, 235.
4. Henry Lee, *The Revolutionary War Memoirs of General Henry Lee,* ed., Robert E. Lee (New York, Da Capo Press, 1998) 237 – 238.
5. Tarleton, 271.
6. Lee, 238.
7. Piecuch and Beakes, as quoted, 77.
8. Lee, 249 – 251.
9. Tarleton, 236.
10. Ibid., 272.
11. Ibid., 312.
12. Lee, 275.
13. Tarleton, 278.
14. Ibid., 324.
15. Ibid., 319.
16. John Buchanan, *The Road to Guilford Court House* (New York, John Wiley & Sons, Inc., 1997) 378.
17. Ibid., as quoted, 381.
18. Tarleton, 286.
19. Ibid., 333.
20. Ibid., 358.
21. Ibid., 417.
22. Ron Chernow, *Washington; A Life* (New York, Penguin Books, 2011) 391.

Bibliography

Babits, Lawrence E., *A Devil of a Whipping: The Battle of Cowpens*. Chapel Hill, University of North Carolina Press, 1998.

Bass, Robert, D., *The Life and Campaigns of General Thomas Sumter*. New York, Henry Holt, 1961.

Billias, George, *George Washington's Opponents*. New York, Morrow, 1969.

Black, Jeremy, *War For America: The Fight For Independence, 1775 – 1783*. New York, St. Martin's Press, 1991.

Boatner, Mark Mayo III, *Encyclopedia of the American Revolution*. Mechanicsburg, Pa., Stackpole Books, 1994.

Buchanan, John, *The Road To Guilford Court House*. New York, John Wiley & Sons, Inc., 1997.

Burrows, Edwin G., *Forgotten Patriots*. New York, Basic Books, 2008.

Calhoon, Robert M., *The Loyalists in Revolutionary America: 1760 – 1781*. New York, Harcourt Brace Jovanovich, 1965.

Carrington, Henry B., *Battles of the American Revolution, 1775 – 1781*. New York, Barnes, 1876.

Chernow, Ron, *Washington; A Life*. New York, Penguin Books, 2011.

Chesney, Alexander, *The Journal of Alexander Chesney, a South Carolina Loyalist in the Revolution and After*. ed. by E. Alfred Jones, The Ohio State University, 1921.

Coggins, Jack, ed., *Boys in the Revolution, Young Americans Tell Their Stories in the War for Independence*. Harrisburg, Pa., Stackpole Books, 1967.

Cohen, Lester H., *The Revolutionary Histories: Contemporary Narratives of the American Revolution*. Ithaca, N.Y., Cornell University Press, 1980.

Collins, James, *Autobiography of a Revolutionary Soldier, Sixty Years in the Nueces Valley: 1870 -1930*. San Antonio: Naylor Printing Co., 1930.

Constable, George, ed., *Winds of Revolution*. Alexandria, Va., Time-Life Books, 1990.

Cummings, William P. and Rankin, Hugh, eds, *The Fate of a Nation: The American Revolution Through Contemporary Eyes*. London, Phaidon Press, 1975.

Dann, John, *The Revolution Remembered*. Chicago: University of Chicago Press, 1980.

Davie, William Richardson, *The Revolutionary War Sketches of William R. Davie, ed.,* Blackwell P. Robinson. Raleigh, N.C., North Carolina Division of Archives & History, 1976.

De Tocqueville, Alexis, *Democracy In America*. New York, Mentor Books, 1984.

Dimock, Martha McHutchison, *A Chronicle Of The American Revolution*. New York, Harper & Row, 1976.

Draper,Lyman, *King's Mountain and its Heroes: History of the Battle of King's Mountain, October 7th,1780, and the events which led to it (Cincinnati, 1811: 1992, report, 73.*

Edgar, Walter B., *Partisans and Redcoats: The Southern Conflict That Turned the Tide of the American Revolution*. New York, William Morrow, 2001.

Ellis, Joseph J., *His Excellency George Washington*. New York: Vintage, 1984. *American Creation*. New York, Vintage Books, 2006.

Everhart, Lawrence, Pension Application S25068, 1834, Transcribed and annotated by C. Leon Harris.

Ewald, Johann, *Diary of the American War: A Hessian Journal,* ed., Joseph P. Trustin. New Haven, Yale University Press, 1979.

Ferling, John, *Almost a Miracle; The American Victory in the War of Independence*. New York: Oxford University Press, 2007.

Freeman, Douglas Southall, *R.E. Lee*. New York, Touchstone,1997.

Gaines, James R., *For Liberty And Glory: Washington, Lafayette, And Their Revolutions*. New York, W.W. Norton & Co., 2007.

Gallagher, Gary W., *Lee & His Army in Confederate History*. Chapel Hill, University of North Carolina Press, 2001.

Gavin, John R., *The Minute Men, the First Fight: Myths and Realities of The American Revolution*. Washington, D.C., Brassey's, 1996.

Graham, James, *The Life of General Daniel Morgan of the Virginia Line of the Army of the United States*. New York, Derby & Jackson, 1856.

Green, Charles E., *The Story of Delaware in the Revolution*. Wilmington, Press of William N. Cann, 1975.

Hammond, Samuel, Pension Application S21807,1832, Transcribed by Will Graves.

Hibbert, Christopher, *Redcoats and Rebels: The American Revolution Through British Eyes*. New York, Avon Books, 1991.

Higginbotham, Don, *Daniel Morgan: Revolutionary Rifleman*. Chapel Hill, University of North Carolina Press, 1961. *The War of American Independence: Military Attitudes, Polices, and Practice, 1763 – 1789. New York, Macmillan Company, 1971.*

Keegan, John, *A History of Warfare*. New York, Alfred A. Knopf, 1994.

Ketcham, Richard M., *Victory At Yorktown; The Campaign That Won The Revolution*. New York, Henry Holt & Co., 2004.

Kirkwood, Robert, *The Journal And Order Book Of Captain Robert Kirkwood Of The Delaware Regiment Of The Continental Line. Dover, Delaware, Press of the Delawarean, 1910.*

Kwasny, Mark V., *Washington's Partisan War, 1775 – 1783*. Kent, Ohio, Kent State University Press, 1996.

Larrabee, Harold, *Decision at the Chesapeake*. New York, Clarkson Porter, 1964.

Lee, Henry, *The Revolutionary War Memoirs of General Henry Lee*. New York, Da Capo Press, 1998.

Lagemann, Robert and Mauncy, Albert, *The Long Rifle*. Eastern Acorn Press, 1993.

Mackenzie, Roderick, *Strictures On Lt. Col. Tarleton's History "Of The Campaigns Of 1780 And 1781, In The Southern Provinces of North America*. London, R. Raulder, New Bond-Street; T. and J. Egerton, Charing-Cross, R. Jameson, Strand; and T. Swell, Cornhill, 1787.

Mahan, Alfred Thayer, *The Major Operations of the Navies in the War of American Independence*. Boston, Little Brown, 1913.

Martin, Joseph Plumb, *Private Yankee Doodle: Being a Narrative of Some of the Adventures, Dangers & Sufferings of a Revolutionary Soldier*. George F. Scheer, ed., Boston, Little Brown, 1981.

May, Robin, *The British Army in North America; 1775 – 1783*. London, Osprey, 1997.

McCullough, David, *1776*. New York, Simon & Schuster, 2005.

McJunkin, Joseph, *Memoirs of Major Joseph McJunkin – Revolutionary Patriot,* Reverend James Dodge Saye, originally appearing as a series of articles in *Watchman and Observer,* Richmond, Virginia, 1847 – 49.

Mintz, Max, *The Generals of Saratoga: John Burgoyne and Horatio Gates*. New Haven, Yale University Press, 1990.

Morrisey, Brendan, *Yorktown 1781; The World Turned Upside Down*. London, Osprey, 1997.

Myers, Theodorus Bailey, *Cowpens Papers*. Charleston, S.C., The News and Courier, 1881.

Nelson, Paul David, *General Horatio Gates: A Biography*. Baton Rouge, LSU Press, 1976.

Palmer, Dave A., *George Washington's Military Genius*. Washington, D.C., Regnery History, 2012.

Pancake, John, S., *The Destructive War: The British Campaign in the Carolinas, 1780 – 1782*. Tuscaloosa, University of Alabama Press, 2003.

Pickett, Russ, *Delawarean's That Gave Their All During the Revolutionary War,* 21 Mar. 2010. Web. 9 Feb. 2016.

Piecuch, Jim and Beakes, John, *John Eager Howard in The American Revolution*. Charleston, S.C., The Nautical and Aviation Publishing Co. of America,2009.

Rankin, Hugh, *Francis Marion: the Swamp Fox*. New York, Crowell, 1973. *The North Carolina Continentals*. Chapel Hill, University of North Carolina Press, 1971.

Raphael, Ray, *A People's History of The American Revolution*. New York, The New Press, 2001.

Robinson, Blackwell P., *William R. Davie*. Chapel Hill, University of North Carolina Press, 1957.

Rossie, Jonathan Gregory, *The Politics of Command in the American Revolution*. Syracuse, N.Y., Syracuse University Press, 1975.

Royster, Charles, *Light-Horse Harry Lee, and the Legacy of the American Revolution*. Baton Rouge, LSU Press, 1981.

Scotti, Anthony J. Jr., *Brutal Virtue; The Myth and Reality of Banastre Tarelton*. Westminster, Md., Heritage Books, 2007.

Stempel, Jim, *The Nature of War; Origins and Evolution of Violent Conflict*. Jefferson, N.C., McFarland & Co., Inc., Publishers, 2012.

Steadman, Charles, *The History of the Origin, Progress, and Termination of the American War,* 2 Volumes (London, 1794) Vol. 2.

Stephenson, Michael. *Patriot Battles; How the War of Independence Was Fought*. New York: Harper Collins, 2007.

Swearinger, Richard, *Pension Application S31402,1832,* Transcribed by Will Graves.

Tarleton, Banastre, *A history of the campaigns of 1780 and 1781, in the southern provinces of North America.* Manchester, U.K., A Reproduction, John Rylands University, 1787.

Treacy, M. F., *Prelude to Yorktown: The Southern Campaign of Nathanael Greene, 1780 – 1781.* Chapel Hill, University of North Carolina Press, 1962.

Von Steuben, Frederick William, *Baron von Steuben's Revolutionary War Drill Manual.* New York, Dover Publications, Inc., 1985.

Volo, Dorothy Denneen and James M., *Daily Life During The American Revolution.* Westport, Ct., Greenwood Press, 2003.

Weigley, Russell, F., *The Partisan War: The South Carolina Campaign of 1780 – 1782.* Columbia, University of South Carolina Press, 1970.

Wickshire, Franklin & Mary, *Cornwallis: The American Adventure.* New York, Houghton Mifflin, 1970.

Williams, Otho Holland, "A Narrative of the Campaign of 1780, in *Sketches Of The Life And Correspondence Of Nathanael Greene,* Edited by William Johnson.

Young, Thomas, *Memoirs of Major Thomas Young; a Revolutionary Patriot of South Carolina.* Orion Magazine, October, 1834.

ABOUT THE AUTHOR

JIM STEMPEL

Jim Stempel lives with his family in Western Maryland overlooking the Blue Ridge. His wife, Sandie, is on staff at nearby McDaniel College where she teaches astronomy and physics. His three children—a daughter and two sons—have moved on to professional careers. An avid athlete for most of his life, Jim is also the author of seven books ranging from satire, psychology, spirituality, to scholarly works of historical nonfiction. He is a graduate of the Citadel, Charleston, S.C.

Jim is considered an authority on the Eastern campaigns of the American Civil War. His recent book, *The Nature of War: Origins and Evolution of Violent Conflict* has been well received by an international audience for its willingness to delve into the basic motivations of human warfare and the true prospects for peace those motivations suggest. His novel *Albemarle* was nominated for the James Fenimore Cooper Prize in Historical Fiction.

IF YOU ENJOYED THIS BOOK

Visit

WINDMILL POINT

BY

JIM STEMPEL

Gripping historical fiction vividly brings to life two desperate weeks during the spring of 1864, when the resolution of the American Civil War was balanced on a razor's edge.

At the time, both North and South had legitimate reasons to conclude they were very near victory. Ulysses S. Grant firmly believed that Lee's Army of Northern Virginia was only one great assault away from implosion; Lee knew that the political will in the North to prosecute the war was on the verge of collapse.

Jim Stempel masterfully sets the stage for one of the most horrific battles of the Civil War, contrasting the conversations of decision-making generals with chilling accounts of how ordinary soldiers of both armies fared in the mud, the thunder, and the bloody fighting on the battlefield.

"We must destroy this army of Grant's before he gets to the James River. If he gets there it will become a siege, and then it will be a mere question of time." – General Lee.

PENMORE PRESS
www.penmorepress.com

BLUE WATER SCARLET TIDE

BY

JOHN DANIELSKI

It's the summer of 1814, and Captain Thomas Pennywhistle of the Royal Marines is fighting in a New World war that should never have started, a war where the old rules of engagement do not apply. Here, runaway slaves are your best source of intelligence, treachery is commonplace, and rough justice is the best one can hope to meet—or mete out. The Americans are fiercely determined to defend their new nation and the Great Experiment of the Republic; British Admiral George Cockburn is resolved to exact revenge for the burning of York, and so the war drags on. Thanks to Pennywhistle's ingenuity, observant mind, and military discipline, a British strike force penetrates the critically strategic region of the Chesapeake Bay. But this fight isn't just being waged by soldiers, and the collateral damage to innocents tears at Pennywhistle's heart.

As his past catches up with him, Pennywhistle must decide what is worth fighting for, and what is worth refusing to kill for —especially when he meets his opposite number on the wrong side of a pistol.

Benjmain Franklin
and The Quaker Murders

by

John Harmon McElroy

Everyone in Philadelphia thinks Jacob Maul, the Quaker stonecutter, is a murderer. How could there be any doubt? In September of 1785, two women were found dead on his property—one of them in his bed—with bruise marks on their throats. The only person who comes to a different conclusion is the city's most famous citizen, Benjamin Franklin.

But at seventy-nine years of age, Franklin doesn't want to acquire a reputation for solving his neighbors' problems. Instead, he recruits a younger man, Revolutionary War veteran James Jamison, to make inquiries under his direction and collect information that could prove the Quaker's innocence. Franklin's considerable intelligence guides Jamison, but as the investigation unfolds, details emerge that threaten to dismantle the great man's assumptions.

The Quaker Murders contains rich details about both Benjamin Franklin and life in eighteenth-century Philadelphia, a large, bustling city that was still recovering from the rigors of the war for independence.

The Lockwoods

of Clonakilty

by

Mark Bois

Lieutenant James Lockwood of the Inniskilling Regiment has returned to family, home and hearth after being wounded, almost fatally, at the Battle of Waterloo, where his regiment was decisive in securing Wellington's victory and bringing the Napoleonic Wars to an end. But home is not the refuge and haven he hoped to find. Irish uprisings polarize the citizens, and violence against English landholders – including James' father and brother – is bringing down wrath and retribution from England. More than one member of the household sympathizes with the desire for Irish independence, and Cassie, the Lockwood's spirited daughter, plays an active part in the rebellion.

Estranged from his English family for the "crime" of marrying a Irish Catholic woman, James Lockwood must take difficult and desperate steps to preserve his family. If his injuries don't kill him, or his addiction to laudanum, he just might live long enough to confront his nemesis. For Captain Charles Barr, maddened by syphilis and no longer restrained by the bounds of honor, sets out to utterly destroy the Lockwood family, from James' patriarchal father to the youngest child, and nothing but death with stop him – his own, or James Lockwood's.

The Chosen Man

by

J. G Harlond

From the bulb of a rare flower bloom ambition and scandal

Rome, 1635: As Flanders braces for another long year of war, a Spanish count presents the Vatican with a means of disrupting the Dutch rebels' booming economy. His plan is brilliant. They just need the right man to implement it.

They choose Ludovico da Portovenere, a charismatic spice and silk merchant. Intrigued by the Vatican's proposal—and hungry for profit—Ludo sets off for Amsterdam to sow greed and venture capitalism for a disastrous harvest, hampered by a timid English priest sent from Rome, accompanied by a quick-witted young admirer he will use as a spy, and bothered by the memory of the beautiful young lady he refused to take with him.

Set in a world of international politics and domestic intrigue, *The Chosen Man* spins an engrossing tale about the Dutch financial scandal known as tulip mania—and how decisions made in high places can have terrible repercussions on innocent lives.

CPSIA information can be obtained
at www.ICGtesting.com
Printed in the USA
LVHW020753020820
662080LV00001B/26